A Moment
towards the
End of the Play . . .

By the same author

I'm Here I Think, Where Are You?
Letters from a touring actor

TIMOTHY WEST

A Moment towards the End of the Play . . .

London
NICK HERN BOOKS
www.nickhernbooks.co.uk

A Nick Hern Book

A Moment towards the End of the Play . . .
first published in Great Britain in 2001
by Nick Hern Books Limited,
14 Larden Road, London W3 7ST

A CIP catalogue record for this book is available
from the British Library

ISBN 1 85459 619 5

Typeset by
Country Setting, Kingsdown, Kent CT14 8ES

Printed by Biddles, Guildford

Illustrations

My first stage appearance (*Bristol Evening Post*)
My mother, Olive Carleton-Crowe
My father, Lockwood West

Shanklin, Isle of Wight, 1939
South Ruislip, Middx., 1947
Redland Hill, Bristol, 1940 (*Peter Davey Collection*)

The Polytechnic Student Players in *Harlequinade*
    by Terence Rattigan
Jacqueline
The Box Office Manager, Frinton
Lionel Hampton (*Bryan Douglas*)
Reginald Salberg
The Summer Season at Newquay, 1956 (*Paul Drake*)

John Barton (*Donald Cooper, RSC*)
Clifford Williams (*Nevis Cameron, RSC*)
'Dirty Plays' Christmas card

Toby Robertson
Richard Cottrell
The Tempest, 1967

Front cover of *Marketing Weekly*

Melbourne, 1972

California, 1992

Mikhail Gorbachev (*Radio Times*)
Josef Stalin (*Old Vic Theatre*)
Winston Churchill (*ABC-TV, Australia*)
King Edward VII (*ATV*)
Horatio Bottomley (*Radio Times*)
Sir Thomas Beecham (*John Selkirk, Dominion and NZ Times*)
Dr John Bodkin Adams (*BBC-TV*)
Lord Reith

Hard Times, 1976 (*Granada TV*)
Brass, 1982-3 (*Granada TV*)

With Joe and Pru
Joe: Zongoro, Zimbabwe

Filming the Talyllyn Railway, 1989 (*HTV*)
Taking on water (*Ed Castellan*)
The *Waverley*, Brodick, Arran, 1997

Sam and Joe sailing, Isle of Wight, 1978
Aboard our Narrow Boat

With Sam in *Henry IV, Parts 1 & 2*, 1997
    (*Stephen Vaughan, English Touring Theatre*)
Sir John Falstaff in conversation with his grandson

Most of the unattributed photos are owned by the author. Should the publishers have failed to make acknowledgment where it is due, they would be glad to hear from the respective owners in order to make amends.

*T*here used to be a magazine called *Theatre World* – a precursor of *Plays and Players* – which treated each current production in the West End to a six-page spread of captioned photographs depicting key moments in the story.

The final picture always provided us with a full view of the stage, on which, in a handsome set by Reece Pemberton or Hutchinson Scott, the drama reached its dénouement. Usually there would be a Detective-Inspector, glaring balefully at a sensitive looking middle-aged man in a dinner jacket. Phyllis Calvert or somebody would be standing nearby, looking concerned, and there might also be a sympathetic family doctor, and a smartly-dressed older woman weeping in an armchair. Stage left, there was usually a juvenile couple, holding hands.

Beneath this last photograph would be the words:

A moment towards the end of the play . . .

Chapter One

My father carefully slid the new wireless from its corrugated-cardboard packing, and setting it on the table, tentatively twirled the needle through the display of exotic names on the panel – Hilversum, Droitwich, Schenectady. As the valves began to glow and the faint odour of warm bakelite invaded the room, my father drew out the instruction manual and settled down for a good read.

I believe the greatest pleasure he derived from any new acquisition was to be able to muse at length over the Directions for Use. Faced with even a relatively simple artefact like a tin of sardines, he would switch on the standard lamp, take the tin to his favourite armchair, put on his glasses – perhaps light up a pipe – and devote himself to a careful study of what was printed on the side of the tin. Whereas my mother, dismissive of conventional guidance, would attack the article with kitchen scissors or a screwdriver, or simply hurl the tin round the room until olive oil and small particles of sardine began to leak out over the floor.

I therefore inherited on the one hand a fear of doing something the wrong way; and on the other, an unwillingness to be told how to do it right.

We listened to that wireless set every evening, sitting together, Ovaltineys in the firelight, letting our imagination wander across the boundless geography of radio drama. A rare period of family stability, after a hitherto nomadic and rackety childhood.

My parents, the actors (Harry) Lockwood West and Olive Carleton-Crowe, met in 1927 on a tour of *The Ghost Train*. Theirs was a theatrical existence that was shared by many at the time, but would be quite impossible today. They were not West End actors – my father was not to begin appearing in Central London for another twenty years – but they were constantly in work, together or separately, on tour or in regional repertory; appreciated by their audiences and respected by their colleagues, working sometimes for very reputable and sometimes less than reputable managements. They lived in theatrical digs when on tour, and in rented accommodation during a repertory season. Financially they just about kept their heads above water, but even had it been practicable to put down roots in any one place, they would have found it impossible to advance money on somewhere permanent to live.

They married, and in due course I was born, whilst my father was playing in a short season at the Prince's Theatre Bradford. This has entitled me to call myself a Yorkshireman; but though for various reasons I maintain close links with the county, it should be acknowledged that had I been born three weeks later, it would have been in Eastbourne. A month after that, and the company had moved on to Blackburn.

Perhaps unsurprisingly, I have no clear memory of living anywhere until in 1939, when I was four, we alighted briefly on a small house in Argyle Road, Ealing, round the corner from (and I suspect financed by) my paternal grandparents.

In those days the massive Stoll Theatre chain had Hippodromes, Empires and Lyceums all over outer London, and producing managements could tour a play for a week at Shepherd's Bush, a week at Chiswick, a week at Streatham Hill and so on, knowing that audiences clung to their local theatre and there was no danger of trying to catch the same people in two different places. My father had secured a part in one such play, and had the luxury of being, for a whole six months, able to commute to every single theatre from Ealing, on his shining new Raleigh bicycle.

My sister Patricia was born in May, and amid the first rumblings of global hostilities it was decided that my mother should take the two of us down to the West Country on a short holiday, my father should negotiate for a resident job in repertory in Bristol, where he knew the management, and we should join him when he'd sorted out some accommodation. As it turned out, this took rather a long time. We had already just begun to outstay our welcome at Manor Farm, Bishopsteignton, Devon, when war was declared; and shortly afterwards, to our not altogether delighted surprise, a bus pulled up in the village and disgorged twenty of the very same children I had been with at nursery school in Ealing.

The baffled-looking evacuees, labelled and clutching their gasmasks, were moved into line and briskly led away down the road to their assigned billets. My mother, concealed behind a tree, looked on aghast. Here were we, living off the fat of the land – the farm's unlimited supply of cream, eggs, butter, fresh pork sausages – while my schoolmates would have to be content with whatever sustenance the rigours of rationing and the parsimony of their reluctant new guardians allowed. The social situation would be insupportable. Hastily we packed our bags and made the diplomatic move into a vacant set of dingy rooms in the main street of the village.

Weeks passed, and still my father had been unable to arrange for us to join him. I loathed our changed surroundings, and particularly resented being separated from our farmer's father, who owned the family transport company. This consisted a fleet of four buses that ran a service into the nearby town of Teignmouth. I was friendly with three of the four drivers, though Mr Banham, a cantankerous elderly man who drove the most decrepid of the vehicles and was consigned to the less popular service to Newton Abbot, justifiably thought me a bloody nuisance.

The bus garage was next door to the farm, and I had been able to go round there to check each arrival and departure. Our horrible new quarters were too far away to do that. I therefore got very cross, and one morning I nearly killed my baby sister.

I'm pretty sure I didn't actually *mean* to kill her. We've had our ups and downs like any brother and sister, but actually I'm very fond of her, and it was more in a melancholy spirit of scientific research that I released the brake on her perambulator while my mother was inside a shop, and sent it hurtling down a steep hill. Somebody ran across the street and stopped it just before it got to the cross-roads, but it must have been a near thing. My sister rather enjoyed it. I think.

Eventually we did get to Bristol, and the unpacking of the new wireless inaugurated an unprecedented period of six whole years under the same roof, in a semi-basement flat in Clarendon Road, Redland.

As time went on and Churchill felt unable to promise us anything other than blood, toil, tears and sweat, the Government decreed that all able-bodied men of my father's age who were not in reserved occupations must join either the armed forces, the fire service or the police. So Lockwood West, the leading man of the resident company at the Little Theatre Bristol, became PC46, 'C' Division of the Bristol Constabulary.

He adapted with ease to his new life; the comradeship of the police force was not unlike that of a theatre company, and the discipline hardly arduous to one who was used to Weekly Rep – performing eight times a week, learning an act of the next play each night when he got home, and rehearsing it the following morning. Of course there were physical dangers; it was part of a policeman's duty to stand guard over unexploded bombs, and there were plenty of those in Bristol. But quite a lot of his time was occupied in organising, scripting, directing and acting in the various morale-boosting shows which the police provided as entertainment for the war-time public.

With another constable who became his unofficial stage-manager, he would roam the streets in search of blackout infringements, and while he frightened the offending householder with a description of the dire penalties the law was bound to exact, his companion would cast an appraising eye over the house and grounds in search of possible props for their next production.

Finally, 'That's a very nice see-saw you have in your back garden, sir. If you could see your way to transporting it up to the Victoria Rooms in time for our Christmas Pantomime, we'll forget this little matter. No, sir, thank you, mustn't drink on duty – well, perhaps a cup of tea . . . '

I used to worry what would happen if on night duty he was ever called upon to engage in physical conflict with a wrong-doer. In those days, a policeman's only weapon was a wooden truncheon, kept concealed in a special long pocket in his trousers. But it was my father's habit to bring home little gifts of hard-to-come-by articles which might have been specially designed for the truncheon pocket – outsize candles, bicycle pumps, bottles of HP Sauce – so that there was no longer room for the actual truncheon, which had to be abandoned in his locker at Lower Redland Road Police Station.

His weekly salary of £3.10s. was hardly enough to support a wife and two children and pay the rent on our flat, but fortunately he was able to supplement this with the occasional Schools Broadcast – the BBC having moved that department down to Bristol soon after the outbreak of war. The WPC switchboard operator at Lower Redland Road, who had been a regular patron at the Little Theatre and to whom my father was still a romantic figure, acted as his agent (we had no telephone at home). While he was out on the beat, the light would flash on the police phone box at the corner of the street, and he would answer it:

'46 reporting.'

'Hello, Harry. Jenny here. I've got a *Senior English* for you. 2.30 tomorrow afternoon, go straight down after early turn, I managed to get them up to two guineas.'

During his rounds that morning, he might stop and buy Jenny a bunch of flowers in lieu of the conventional ten per cent, and hope they might survive in his truncheon pocket until he got back to the station.

*

I privately think this may have been the happiest period of my father's life. Not, though, of my mother's. Having finally given up the stage herself only a year or two earlier when my sister was born, and I believe missing it still; trying to fit in with her husband's eccentric work and sleep pattern – one week of duty from six in the morning to two in the afternoon, the next from two to ten at night and the third all night from ten till six in the morning – and at the same time look after two young children, cope with rationing and dodge the air-raids – it began seriously to get her down.

Of course, as children will, I felt personally responsible but at the same time too embarrassed to try and comfort her, and so while at home I kept myself very much to myself.

We should have realised the enormous amount we had to be grateful for. Many of our friends had fathers fighting abroad, some had elder brothers flying those Hurricanes and Spitfires we could see above us, sometimes engaging before our eyes in dog-fights with Heinkels and Messerschmitts. A lot of them didn't come home.

Bristol of course was terribly badly bombed; I remember waking up and finding the bedroom ceiling suffused with a bright pink glow – it looked exactly like the effect of a beautiful sunrise. It was only when I got out of bed and drew the curtains, thinking it was time to get up, that I realised it was two o'clock in the morning, and the whole of old Bristol City was on fire. The sky, though, was not like the colour of any known fire – it was an unearthly hideous pale pink, thick with choking smoke.

Marshal Goering settled into a pattern of Sunday night raids on Bristol – there were two prime targets, the aircraft factories at Filton, and Avonmouth Docks. Incendiaries, however, fell pretty well anywhere, with a few in the adjoining roads to us, and we could hear the loud explosions as we huddled in the cupboard under the stairs. *Here we sit like birds in the wilderness, birds in the wilderness, birds in the wilderness* we used to sing in our pyjamas, munching ginger biscuits and enjoying the adventure.

Of course I had friends; not many, but a few very close ones. Peter Davey and his sister Melody lived two doors away; and when I was about eight and Melody a year or so younger, she and I were taken into the underground air-raid shelter on Redland Green by a slightly older boy called Stuart Hodder, who, having lit a candle, explained to us by means of biological diagram the mysteries of procreation.

I didn't think too much about it, though I noticed Melody was a bit silent on the way home, but that evening there was a knock at the front door and I admitted a very serious-looking Mrs Davey who quietly asked to be left alone with my mother for a few minutes. She had in her hand the draft of a letter she intended to send to Stuart Hodder's parents, and such was her estimation of the gravity of her visit that she had specially donned a white hat and gloves for the thirty-yard journey from her house.

When she grew up Melody became a very good professional contralto, and then, surprisingly, a nun; but I don't think that had anything to do with Stuart Hodder. Her brother and I are still close friends after fifty-something years, and share a passionate interest in public transport.

The Headmistress of Westbury Park Primary School, where I was a pupil, was Miss Torrens, a broadly-built, tweed-clad woman with a bristling black moustache. I was terrified of her. However with her deputy, the delicate, soft-spoken Miss Heath, I was deeply in love. When she was appointed Akela to the local Wolf Cub pack, I joined like a shot, but I never made much of a success of it. New younger boys rose through the ranks of Seconds, Sixers, Senior Sixers, and passed on to the Scouts, while I remained the oldest, largest and most completely undecorated member of the pack. I could light a fire, I could read a map, but beyond that I was useless.

I was pretty useless at school, too. I went from Westbury Park to the preparatory department of Bristol Grammar School, an establishment reluctantly attended and later entertainingly chronicled by the writer Peter Nichols. Actually the main school was in the care of a very estimable man called John Garrett, but I never got that far, and my quarrel was with Mr Pitt, the head of the prep school.

Mr Pitt, I'm afraid, liked caning people; and what I, as a frequent recipient of his attentions, found peculiarly distasteful was the *time* he always took to do it. Having announced that he would deliver six strokes, and having given the first, WHACK, he would apparently lose interest for a few moments, perhaps winding his watch or changing the date on his desk calendar, before returning to the fray, WHACK.

Then he would stroll over to the window and look out over the playing fields. 'Going to be nice weather for the House Matches, I think,' he would remark pleasantly, WHACK. Conversation might then turn to the play he had seen at the Little that week (it had now been considered safe to dismiss the War Reserve Police, and father was back at the acting). 'I enjoyed *George and Margaret*', Mr Pitt would go on, a smile that he supposed to be good-natured playing for a moment on his cadaverous features, WHACK, 'and thought your father was very good. Very nice *suit* he had,' he would add thoughtfully, WHACK. Then he would prepare to light his pipe, scrabbling around in his oilskin tobacco pouch, breaking several matches and finally getting the thing lit, bup bup bup WHACK.

'Well, I think that'll do. Thank you.'

Things couldn't go on like that. I didn't complain to my parents, because it didn't occur to me that there was anything out of the ordinary in his behaviour. I had read *Tom Brown's Schooldays*, *Stalky and Co*, *Tales of a Three-Guinea Watch* and *Nicholas Nickleby*, and I suppose I just thought that was what School was supposed to be like. I had had no preparation from my parents, both of whom left school very early, and, when questioned, didn't seem to remember much about it. So I just took the law into my own hands, and played truant.

Every morning I would set off on my bicycle in the direction of school, but then turn off to spend the day pedalling through the leafy lanes of Abbot's Leigh, or, in darker mood, venture down to Christmas Steps, a narrow Dickensian alleyway that climbed steeply up from the Tramway Centre and was held to be a notorious focus for sin and depravity. I used to hang about on the steps for hours, looking very sophisticated, but, apart from seeing a copy of the

Naturist magazine *Health and Efficiency* displayed in a newsagent's window, I remained disappointingly uncorrupted.

Sometimes I would go to watch the ships unloading timber at Cumberland Basin, or peer through the handsome Georgian windows of Royal York Crescent and see delicate examples of Chinese pottery, highly coloured draperies from Jamaica, huge plaster Madonnas from Spain or Portugal; for here were to be found the remnants of a once huge cosmopolitan community, the most affluent of whom, in the great but partly disgraceful days of Bristol's maritime supremacy, would come up the hill from Hotwells to breathe the purer air of patrician Clifton.

On these illicit jaunts I used to imagine how it would feel to be in the company of the great men of Bristol's past. I rehearsed conversations with W.G.Grace as he went in to bat, with John Cabot on board the *Matthew* bound for Canada, with Isambard Kingdom Brunel standing with his hat and cigar in front of those massive chains. Turning homeward in order to arrive at a convincing time, I felt no guilt about my truancy; it seemed to me my education was better served in this way than by my regular encounters with Mr Pitt.

Of course I was expelled.

About the same time, another pupil was expelled, from the same class, and for the same offence; a flaxen-haired boy named Glover, whom I only knew by sight. Very many years later, when I was having a drink in the bar of the Arts Theatre, my eye was attracted by a tall man with very fair hair, cut in that same pudding-basin style. I had known the actor Julian Glover just well enough to say hello, but now that he had his hair bleached and cropped for his part as the Knight in John Osborne's *Luther*, things clicked into place. I went over to him.

'Glover, Lower 2B, Bristol Grammar School?'

'Good God, *yes*. Wasn't it terrible?'

We've been firm friends ever since.

Chapter Two

*T*he Rapier Players, the repertory company at the Little Theatre Bristol, was run for twenty-eight years by the indefatigable husband-and-wife team Ronald Russell and Peggy Ann Wood. As unofficial mother and father to the closely-knit community toiling away in the cramped building adjacent to the Colston Hall, Peggy Ann and Ronnie provided all the love, security and instruction that they would have lavished on the real children they never had.

I saw a play there nearly every week, and felt myself to be a part of that family – not just the actors, but the staff. The tireless business manager, Peggy Osborne, hobbling on crutches; kindly Albert Malpas, who made and painted the scenery (we didn't call them Designers in those days); the elderly stage manager Paul Smythe, whom Ronnie and Peggy Ann were too kind-hearted to sack, even when he regularly fell asleep in the prompt corner; the formidably-breasted Mrs Somers, who ran the coffee bar; Bert Hunter, who played the piano in the intervals, in heavy make-up.

The Company worked ceaselessly through the war – Ronnie, like my father, joined the Police, so that to Peggy Ann fell the main responsibility of keeping an ensemble together, with the particular problem of finding male actors who had not been called up and were neither very old, sick or seriously neurotic; while at the same time she was directing most of the plays, and acting in quite a lot of them as well.

Over the twenty-eight years of their existence they received not one penny of subsidy from the Arts Council or its predecessor CEMA, nor of revenue grant from the Corporation of Bristol. On the box-office receipts alone they managed to produce forty-five plays a year, with often eight or ten in the cast and sometimes a different set for each of the three acts. The margin between profit and loss each week was defined by Ronnie as depending on whether actors remembered to turn their dressing room lights off each time they went on stage.

Of course, the Arts Council's concern, very properly, was the major regional companies (the Bristol Old Vic, a quarter of a mile away, became one), whose policy was to present the classical repertoire, together with the work of major new writers; whereas the output at the Little concentrated largely on the plays that had just finished their West End runs, and were now licensed for Repertory use. It didn't greatly matter to the patrons that they wouldn't see Edith Evans or Diana Wynyard or Michael Redgrave in the parts they had created; what they cared about was the *play*, an evening at the theatre, a story being unfolded to them by people they recognised and loved.

Sometimes, when I have been to see a play in Rep which I first experienced in its original London production, the fact of it being stripped of either its West End glitter or its South Bank technical effects has meant that the actual writing came across to me much more strongly. Sad to admit, pressures of time and money do occasionally bring with them a refreshing simplicity.

With the outbreak of peace, my father finally closed the door on the world of Repertory. He spent the remaining forty years of his professional life playing supporting parts in the West End, mainly for the prestigious and powerful H.M.Tennent management, did a vast amount of work on radio, played numerous doctors and solicitors in low-budget British B-movies, and was one of the first actors after the war to take part in the re-emergence of television.

This last exercise involved rehearsing in a rented hall in London, and on the day of transmission (Sunday) being taken in a bus up to Alexandra Palace, where the BBC had their studios and whence the programmes were transmitted direct. The play was recorded live, and you often had to rush from set to set, changing your jacket and tie as you went, to be already in position by the time the camera got to you. The cameras themselves were enormous by today's standards; most of them were rooted to the spot and their lenses had to be changed manually, making a disruptive clicking sound, while unimaginable megawatts of lighting blazed down upon the sweltering cast and crew.

The Sunday play was the high point of the week's viewing on the single channel then operative, and for those viewers who missed it, it was repeated the following Thursday. There having been no means of recording the original transmission, on Thursday afternoon everybody had to return to Portland Place, get the bus up the hill to Alexandra Palace and do it all over again.

Father became, in other words, a *metropolitan* actor. I've always been a little wary of following in those footsteps, being by nature and inclination more of a Strolling Player. There is a vast theatre audience all over Britain, a mixed audience unified only by their geographical location, who come to their local playhouse because they like it, can afford it, and can get there easily. If they come by car, they can park, and can often eat in the building afterwards if they want to. They tend to be critical, because they see a lot of different shows, but an old play which they may be seeing for the first time will usually mean more to them than to their revival-weary London counterparts.

Of course, in many ways it's a great privilege to work in London, to live at home and make use of so much that the metropolis has to offer; nonetheless, I feel more *useful* when I'm on the road, touring this country and others, playing in different theatres, exploring different places, meeting different people. It's no way to get rich, or famous, and it drives my agent mad, but I love it.

In 1946 we moved to London. Well, when I say London, it was actually South Ruislip, an unconfident tendril sprouting in the shadow of the thrusting branches of Metroland. I went to the John Lyon School in Harrow, of which the headmaster, O.A. leBeau, was a distinct and entertaining improvement on the flagellant Mr Pitt.

Mr leBeau should never have been permitted to teach chemistry, and he should under no circumstances have been given the key to the laboratory cupboard. All his experiments ended either in a shattering explosion, showering the pupils with fragments of broken glass, or in the production of a heavy dun-coloured gas which rolled over the benches in sinister, foul-smelling clouds while we clambered on to each others' shoulders to force open the windows. The only other subject he took was Divinity, and I suppose his faith must have reconciled him to the potential consequences of those apocalyptic scenes in the chemistry lab.

The masters weren't all dotty, although there was the problem, experienced in most boys' schools immediately after the war, of staff returning from Forces life to an unfamiliar world, and taking refuge in that sort of generalised authoritarianism so uncongenial to pupils. One such was Wilmot, our Geography master, who handed out

Wednesday afternoon detentions like visiting cards. A red-haired boy in our class, named Tonge, had a strategy for dealing with this.

'Tonge,' Wilmot would call out, 'this homework is totally unsatisfactory. I'm putting you on detention.'

'Not this Wednesday, sir, I'm afraid,' Tonge would reply politely. 'I'd like to help you, but I'm already in detention for Mr Cummings.'

'Well, next Wednesday then.'

'Sorry, sir. No good. Dr Hirst.'

'Well, Tonge . . . *When* then?'

Tonge would take out a pocket diary, and start leafing through it slowly. 'Twenty-sixth of March? No, sorry, can't manage that, that's Mr Sibley. Ah. I think I can fit you in on the second of April.'

The explanation for all this was that Tonge hated football, which was what the rest of us were engaged in on Wednesday afternoons while he and his fellow detainees were sitting reading happily in the warmth of the classroom. Such was his skill in managing to engineer a full schedule of detentions, that in five years I don't remember ever seeing Tonge on the football field.

'Sammy' Cowtan, however, the senior English master, too old to have been in the war, was a man of a very different stamp. Brilliantly, he introduced me, and everyone else in that class, to the wonders of Shakespeare.

'You're never going to understand any of this,' he said to the class, 'until you feel what it's like to say those words, and to have those words said to you. Clear all the desks to the edge of the room, we're going to get up and do it.' Then he'd cast the play, and we'd start; jerkily at first, and then gradually as we used the space between each other and allowed time for our thoughts to breathe, the images would take shape in our minds and the language would begin to work its magic.

A fat, bald, bespectacled 60-year-old, Sammy nevertheless insisted on playing all the female leads himself. For a time, I wondered whether this might conceal some perhaps unfortunate psycho-biological need, but I soon realised he was simply saving the time that would be wasted in giggly embarrassment were the love scenes to be played by two fifteen-year-old boys. He was very good too – a fine Cleopatra, and a superbly lovesick Rosalind. I personally didn't feel his Juliet showed him quite at the peak of his powers, but I believe the performance had its adherents.

The main thing was, he turned that class on to the excitement of the story, and the power of the language, and I thought of him when a few years ago my son and I were playing the two parts of *Henry IV* together, and after the show one night, in Crewe it was, two boys of about fifteen came up to us and said, 'Hey! That was terrific!'

'Really? Good. Thanks,' we said.

'Yeah, terrific. Who did the translation?'

Come back, Sammy Cowtan, from those Elysian fields upon which I hope you are delicately reclining as Titania, being fed ambrosia by grateful attendant spirits. We need you, badly, here.

*

Sitting in the gallery of the Old Vic Theatre, watching Richard Burton playing Hamlet in the first production of Michael Bentall's five-year Shakespeare cycle, I thought – oh, if I could just be a spear-carrier on that stage, or even a dead body . . .

Twenty-five years later, there I was, down there on that very stage, playing Claudius, Shylock, Enobarbus, even *running* the place for a while. And when that time came, did I cast my mind back for a moment to that young man crouching, entranced, on his wooden gallery bench? No, of course I didn't. Fate always arranges for surprises to happen when they can no longer surprise; the unexpected gift arrives a few moments after you have just conditioned yourself to expect it. Admittedly by the time I got there the Old Vic was no longer quite the prestigious place it was in the fifties, but even so I should have had the grace to recognise the honour of being surrounded by so many distinguished ghosts.

I'd left school, to continue with my 'A' levels at the Polytechnic, Regent Street; and John Lyon having been a boys-only establishment, I now found myself for the first time in a working relationship with members of the opposite sex. The results were predictable. I fell in love with one girl after another, walking with them barefoot along Oxford Street in the blissfully hot summer of 1953, lying with them in Hyde Park, boating on the Serpentine, drinking Merrydown cider and dancing to George Shearing 78's in the red-shaded lamplight of someone's bed-sitter in Ladbroke Grove.

Our thoughts were not very original. We spouted about art and communism. Our heroes were Marshal Tito, Jan Sibelius and

T.S. Eliot; we liked French and Italian films, fancy waistcoats and New Orleans jazz. We drank frothy cappuccino and wrote derivative poetry. We occasionally went to lectures. I helped to set up the college newspaper, and involved myself very fully with the Student Players, both directing and acting, and had a whale of a time.

Somehow, I can't now think how, the £2 a week allowance from my parents, supplemented by a little money left over from holiday jobs, enabled me to go to the theatre, and the cinema, at least once a week. I also went to the opera – not Covent Garden, a bit expensive even in those days, but Sadler's Wells – like the Vic, one and sixpence in the gallery. Part of the enjoyment for me was getting there on the 31 tram, which rumbled along the Embankment from Westminster and then astonishingly turned left into the underneath of Waterloo Bridge to enter the Kingsway Tunnel, from which it finally emerged up a steep slope, groaning like a reluctantly awakened burrowing animal, into Southampton Row.

I loved the London trams, and was among the many thousands thronging the Embankment on their Last Night, reverently laying our pennies on the line to be squashed flat by the final tram-car on its way to Charlton Depot, there ignominiously to be burnt. Older men took off their hats as it passed by, while those who were crowded aboard the tram removed the indicator blinds, the conductor's ticket rack, and even cut buttons off his uniform as souvenirs. I was as deeply moved as anybody. I have to admit to a condition that might perhaps be termed Betjeman's Syndrome; a tendency to heave a sigh for things swept away in the march of progress – the Chelsea Arts Ball, Grape Nuts, the Authorised Version. I can't even go into Debenham's without worrying what must have happened to Freebody.

Any decision about what I was actually to do with my life when I left the Polytechnic had to be deferred until I had done my eighteen months' National Service, and while I was waiting for the summons I was offered a fill-in job as box office manager at the Frinton Summer Theatre. This theatre was, and still is I believe, a Women's Institute Hall in one of the quietest of Frinton's quiet residential roads, taken over for ten weeks in the summer as a professional repertory theatre. The young company were an interesting group – Richard Vernon and James Villiers went on to achieve great things as performers, John Osborne and Peter Nichols became distinguished dramatists, and the beautiful Pat Sandys turned into a major television producer.

My job was very simple – to man the box office, tear out the tickets, take the money, mark on the plan the seats sold, and cash up at the end of the evening. It was also my responsibility to engage two usherettes per performance, on a casual basis, for ten shillings a night. Among the young sisterhood of Frinton there was fierce competition to perform this function, so the weekly process of selection put me in a position of considerable power. There was one particularly attractive girl called Jen Stevens, who actually took me into the laurel bushes round the back of the theatre to impress me with her enthusiasm for the job. She was duly rostered for four nights a week, to the displeasure of one of the other usherettes, who lost no time in letting me know that her rival's generous nature was widely recognised as far afield as Clacton.

One day I travelled over to Ipswich to undergo medical and intelligence tests which declared me fit to join the temporary ranks of the RAF, and at the end of the Frinton season the call came to begin basic training. A few days after it started, however, I was struck down with a heavy migraine. For some years I had been suffering from occasional periods of violent vertigo, the world hurtling round and round within my brain even when I shut my eyes. Doctors could not explain it – some said I must have sustained some cranial damage falling off my bicycle a few years before (I was concussed, and lay unconscious for twenty-four hours), some thought it was stress, or a virus. Anyway, after a couple more years it stopped happening.

The corporal, however, sent me to the M.O., who was far less interested in the migraine itself than in the medication that had been prescribed to relieve it: pheno-barbitone. Now pheno-barbitone was at that time a juju word – the eight o'clock news told us nearly every morning that some doctor had left his car unlocked, with a case on the back seat containing this notorious drug. The M.O. reached for his fountain pen, and within a couple of days I found myself discharged. Of course, this was the last year of National Service and they were keen for any excuse to get rid of some of those already conscripted before they became a burden on the taxpayer.

So now, here I was, presented with an unexpected eighteen months of which I was somehow supposed to make use. I went back to living with my parents, but the domestic relationship was uneasy. Understandably, they felt I should go out and get a job, any sort of job, as soon as possible. I scanned the Situations Vacant columns, and went to interviews with various organisations like Shell, Lever Brothers and even the BBC, but my obvious lack of any real interest was detected straight away. As a surrogate for paid employment, I plunged headlong into the world of amateur dramatics, joining two or three different companies simultaneously; most notably, the Taverners, an organisation set up by the Brewers' Association to do plays in pubs, or in summer in pub gardens, all over the Home Counties. The producer/director/leading player was the professional actor Henry McCarthy, and the standard was extremely high.

About this time, I received a letter from the producer who rented the Frinton Summer Theatre, offering me an introduction to the theatre management at Leatherhead, where he believed there might be a vacancy for a student assistant stage manager. Would I be interested? I declined the offer. Why? Was it lack of confidence – my mother and father, whose opinion I trusted, had been to see nearly all my amateur performances but had never been encouraging. They had made it clear they would rather I were employed in some field quite removed from the theatre. So was I just scared of not being up to the mark? No, I'm afraid the real reason I turned it down was that I had fallen in love with the world of amateur drama, and I didn't want to *marry* my mistress.

Needing, however, actually to earn some money, I took a job with Partridge and Cooper, a charming family firm of office furniture dealers in Holborn, and helped to look after their showroom. Nearly all their business was done by mail order, so very few people ever came to the shop, which left a good deal of time for reading plays and learning the parts I had undertaken.

I am really at a loss now to explain my behaviour. Even when it occurred to me to move on to a job that held rather more of interest than could be found in tubular chairs and filing cabinets, I still didn't admit to myself that the theatre was where I essentially wanted to be. Instead, I answered an application for a quality control engineer in the new Recorded Tapes department at EMI.

This was better, because I love music; and listening to classical music was virtually what we did all day. In our tiny experimental department at Hayes, we were producing seven-and-a-half-inches-per-second tapes copied from the original LP masters, and our job was to monitor not only the general sound quality, but the stereo fidelity. Stereophonic sound was still in its infancy, and it was not unusual to find the trombone section of an orchestra apparently getting up and crossing the platform from right to left in the middle of a symphony, or the tenor who just now had been locked in an embrace with the soprano suddenly abandoning her for a surprisingly similar relationship with the baritone on the other side of the stage. Alas, the product never caught on – the quarter-inch tapes snagged, stretched or were difficult to spool, and were finally ousted by the new plastic cassettes, which were smaller and much more convenient.

However, by that time, somewhat snagged and stretched myself, I had moved on to other things.

Chapter Three

I was now twenty-one. I had become very attached to a girl called Jacqueline Boyer, whom I had known slightly at the Polytechnic when she was an art student, and had met again through mutual friends. She was an aspiring actress, having had some success as a child performer (she played Violet Elizabeth Bott in the original radio series of *Just William*), and although she had picked up some of the bad habits that sometimes go with that sort of training, she had talent – perhaps more for musicals than for the straight theatre, as she was a pretty good dancer.

She was very attractive and vivacious, but given to slightly worrying mood swings; to which there attached, I found out only later, a long history and an inauspicious prognosis. She lived in style in SW19 with her mother Leila Boyer, a wealthy widow whose late husband Jack had been Chairman of Chelsea Football Club and lessee of the Granville Theatre, Walham Green.

To be within easy reach of EMI, I was staying in lodgings in Hayes, but spending a lot of evenings, and some nights, in the Boyers' opulent thirties-style flat in Wimbledon Park, drinking endless cocktails with Leila's men friends and listening to their racing experiences. It was all very well, but it occurred to me that someone of Jacqueline's febrile nature would benefit from being removed into a more relaxed environment. I didn't quite know how to achieve this, but, seeing myself essentially as her protector, I would try.

What with Jacqueline, the Taverners and other amateur dramatic obligations, I found I had very little energy left for work in the morning. Furthermore, the Polytechnic Student Players had asked me back to direct a production of Thornton Wilder's *Our Town*, which they were to present at the first Sunday Times National Student Drama Festival, to be held that year in Bristol.

I managed to beg or steal time off from EMI to get the production on to the stage, and to our great delight, we won the Award for the year.

In the Gentlemen's lavatory at the Victoria Rooms, after the performance, I found myself standing next to Harold Hobson, the revered drama critic of the Sunday Times, who had been chairman of the judging panel. 'That was really very good,' he said. 'Tell me, are you going to take it up professionally?'

Completely nonplussed, I stared into the white porcelain, searching for guidance. ARMITAGE SHANKS, it advised me sternly. I turned back to Harold Hobson.

'Yes,' I said. 'Oh yes, certainly.'

*

On the train back to Paddington next morning, I treated myself to the old-style GWR breakfast, with porridge and kippers. I felt wonderful. That evening I told Jacqueline and her mother what I had decided. Leila's immediate and surprising response was that she knew Peter Haddon, who ran the company at the Wimbledon Theatre; that he'd mentioned he was looking for a male student assistant stage manager, and so why didn't I go along and see him?

This was almost word for word the suggestion that had been made to me about Leatherhead three years before; and I have often wondered uneasily what difference it would have made if I'd grabbed that earlier chance. Would I perhaps just have saved three years of my life? At all events, I did go to see Peter Haddon, who was quite glad to employ someone to sweep the stage, make props, help to paint the set, call the artists, give the cues, assist the electrician and go on stage as the butler, for one pound ten shillings a week. I gave in my notice at EMI, and a fortnight later began my long-delayed apprenticeship.

Peter Haddon was a tall gangly man in his sixties, who had the habit, when walking across busy Wimbledon Broadway, of stopping suddenly in the middle of the road, in order to *think*. Impervious to the hooting and imprecations of motorists, he would stand gazing at the sky, spectacles on nose, mouth slightly ajar, a tweed hat on the back of his head and a long football scarf trailing on to the ground. In this position he would remain for two or three minutes while he worked out the budget and the casting for the next play. Crazy he may have looked, but fool he certainly was not. He knew the secret of being economical without that economy being apparent on stage.

The Wimbledon Theatre has a capacity of 1,700, and nobody these days would think of using it for regular drama. Peter managed it though, by each week putting on big plays suited to that big stage and auditorium. The evening of my first day at work, I was given a costume and pushed on as a farmer in Ugo Betti's *Summertime;* this was followed by *Reluctant Heroes, The Barretts of Wimpole Street* and the old musical romance *Smilin' Through.* The Peter Haddon Company was not in the forefront of the avant-garde, but it made a lot of people happy.

When the spring season came to an end, the company was disbanded, and, having learned the rudiments of my trade, I applied for a fully-fledged assistant stage manager's post at a summer season in Newquay, and got it. Flushed with the feeling that I was now well on my way, and with the prospect of earning a magnificent six pounds ten shillings a week throughout the summer, I suddenly asked Jacqueline to marry me.

She said yes, and we had a swiftly-contrived but rather smart Wimbledon wedding, before happily going off to spend the summer together at Newquay. There were difficulties. Even with Jacqueline working part-time behind the bar at an hotel, we found it quite hard to make ends meet. My well-to-do mother-in-law subsidised us when necessary, but in becoming beholden to her we were opening the door to a certain amount of well-meaning interference in our lives. My own parents still managed to send us £2 a week, but not with a very good grace. Try as they might, they couldn't bring themselves to like their daughter-in-law. Moreover, Jacqueline and I were slowly finding out that we didn't have an awful lot in common, beyond the ability to have a good time.

Meanwhile the sun shone over the happy seaside holidaymakers. Cornwall in those days had not had to devote itself quite so relentlessly to tourism, and Newquay still felt a bit like a fishing town that had come up in the world. The theatre, well away from the sea front, was not dissimilar to the one at Frinton, and the seasonal policy was exactly the same.

The company, however, was run on a much tighter rein. There was a Leading Man, a Character Man and a Juvenile Man, and their three female counterparts. There were two assistant stage managers,

Jennifer Macnae and myself, and both of us had to act in nearly every play. The stage manager also appeared in quite large roles, as frequently did Anthony Cundell, who was not only the director, but company manager and extra Character Man as well. Then there was his wife, Lorna Green, the scenic artist, and on one occasion she had to act too. And that was the lot. We were all kept very busy; especially as, in order to give Saturday-to-Saturday holidaymakers the chance to see two plays in a week, we did our change-over between Wednesday and Thursday. The stage management consequently worked right through the Wednesday night.

Looking back – and, more specifically, looking back over the acutely embarrassing production photographs – that Newquay season should perhaps be recognised as the artistic nadir of my life. At any rate, *so far:* I suppose one must cover oneself against all eventualities.

On the first night of one production – a whodunit – I noticed that the eldest of the three actresses had omitted to take an important prop off with her on her final exit. After the show, I knocked on the dressing-room door.

'Miss Aitken-Brown,' (that was not her name) 'did you realise you didn't take the glass of whisky with you when you went off in act three?'

'Oh, didn't I, dear?' she replied vaguely. 'I'm so sorry. I'll try and remember tomorrow night.'

'Well, please do, Miss Aitken-Brown. It's very important to the plot.'

'Right you are, dear.'

Next night, the same thing happened. When the curtain came down, the applause was tempered with a certain mystified dissatisfaction. 'She's done it again. Go and tell her,' growled Anthony Cundell.

Knock, knock. 'Miss Aitken-Brown?'

'Come in.'

'Miss Aitken-Brown, you did it again. You left that glass of whisky on the sideboard, where everybody could see it.'

Irritation crept into her voice. 'Oh really dear, does it *matter*? I've got an enormous part next week, and there's an awful lot to think about . . . '

A cold sweat started to form at the back of my neck. 'But – Miss Aitken-Brown,' I faltered, ' – you know that glass of whisky is poisoned, don't you? You take it up with you to your bedroom, and you drink it, and you *die.*'

She looked at me briefly in astonishment, and then broke into peals of merry laughter. 'Oh, do I die, dear? Well I never – I had no idea! Well, well. What must they have thought!'

I realised that what she did each week was to underline her part, up to her final exit, and then turn straight back to the beginning in order to start learning it. The rest of the text didn't concern her, and she had no idea of the dénouement of any play in the English language unless she happened to be on stage at the final curtain.

Chapter Four

When my wife and I boarded the Humber ferry at New Holland, birds were singing in the cloudless sky of a warm autumn afternoon. But half way across the estuary a mist began to settle, and gradually developed into a cold grey fog which didn't seem to lift during the entire three months I spent at the New Theatre, Hull.

Neither William Wilberforce's birthplace, nor the Library where Philip Larkin used to work, nor yet the unique green kiosks of the Kingston-upon-Hull Telephone Company brought a smile to my face. These were not happy months. Our digs were cheerless and malodorous, the landlady and her family surly and very poor company. The repertory season at the New Theatre was actually run by the excellent and much-loved Reginald Salberg, but he very seldom made the journey to Hull, being fully occupied at his headquarters in Salisbury. The only way Reggie could get a decent company together up here was by guarded promises of future employment in pastoral Wiltshire.

The theatre itself was managed by a man called Peppino Santangelo, who had started life in the string quartet aboard the *Queen Mary*. Many would have preferred it to have been the *Titanic*. Mr Santangelo would stand dinner-jacketed in the foyer, eyeing the patrons as they came in and turning away those whom he considered improperly dressed. This effectively meant that we played to dismally small houses throughout the season, despite a heavy reliance on thrillers and whodunits.

In those days there was a steady stream of thrillers being presented in London, and in due course they were passed on to the regions. Their dialogue had a music of its own own.

'All right, damn you Inspector, so I *was* there in the morning room . . .'

'I'm afraid it's not a pretty sight – she's been in the water for some time.'

And of course, the immortal 'Is he . . . ?' 'I'm afraid so.'

There was an Agatha Christie adaptation called *Alibi,* in which one of the many suspects, a character called Major Blunt, did little for the plot beyond strolling in and out declaring his belief that there might be time for a whisky-and-soda before changing for dinner. As the Detective Inspector, I finally got to ask him a question, to which the Major, in the printed words of French's Acting Edition, gave the reply:

BLUNT (*sharply*): What do you mean?

I don't think Rex Graham, who played Major Blunt, ever managed to get that line out. Already as he came towards me, his mouth would begin to twitch and he would concentrate his gaze hard on a point somewhere just above the mantelpiece. After waiting a moment, watching his shoulders begin silently to heave, I would deliver my line, and then add under my breath: 'Blunt, sharply', and we would both collapse. It was disgraceful, but we were all working at such high pressure that God-given moments like this provided a necessary escape valve.

The working week of an ASM went like this:

Sunday night, help with the fit-up, place the furniture, decorate the set and make the tea. Monday morning, return anything that had been borrowed for last week's show, then come back and walk around the set for the electrician so that he could focus his lamps. After that, clear up and sweep the stage before going down to the railway station to pick up the wigs and costumes for the afternoon's dress rehearsal, at which I would operate the sound system, arrange the props and handle all the changes in the intervals. If I was also *in* the play, as was often the case, my performance had somehow to be fitted in with all these other duties. That evening the same routine had to be gone through again in front of the public. On Tuesday morning, at the first blocking rehearsal for the next play, I would mark out on the stage the outlines of the set. I might be playing a part in this, too. A production meeting followed, at which a list would be given me of furniture and properties which had to be obtained from store, hired from local shops, borrowed from tractable residents or, as a last resort, constructed by me. I would start on this on Tuesday afternoon. On Tuesday evening there was another performance, of course. On Wednesday morning, a rehearsal of next week's Act I, then a matinee and an evening show. Act II would be rehearsed on

Thursday morning, and by this time the scenic artist would probably be needing my assistance in the paint shop. On Friday afternoon, having rehearsed Act III in the morning, we would do a complete run-through in the new furniture, and there would be a rush to store this away and re-set for the evening's performance. Saturday, by which time every article to be begged, borrowed or stolen had to be in place, consisted of a final run-through, then a matinee and last performance of the present play. After this we would strike the set, store the scenery and furniture and carefully wrap up and label anything we'd hired or borrowed ready for return on Monday, and perhaps get away by two o'clock on Sunday morning.

On Sunday evening we started all over again.

It's not like that now, and in fact there are very few regional theatres that produce work with a permanent company these days. There are strong arguments, both artistic and economical, for the demise of the system. Young actors, though, have lost out immeasurably. In the late 1950s and early 1960s someone spending a year in a really good repertory company would have been able to cut his or her teeth on the different styles of Shakepeare, Congreve, Sheridan, Wilde, Shaw, Coward, Molière, Ibsen and Chekhov, as well as Agatha Christie. The plays may not in all cases have been done very well, but they were done, and no drama training available today can compensate for that.

What was it that finally brought weekly – and in its improved form, fortnightly – repertory to its knees in the sixties? Quite simply, television. Once the audience had been introduced to solid-looking walls, furniture that they didn't know by heart, and a butler who looked like a butler and not a heavily made-up eighteen-year old, the end was clearly not far off.

Because scenery had to be erected and taken down each week, (and sometimes two or three times a night in the course of a single show), solid construction was impracticable and anyway too expensive. Instead, portable 'flats', wooden frames of standard height but various widths over which canvas had been stretched, were used in various combinations to provide the set. For each new show they were overpainted – stencilled patterns on a plain background for Victorian wallpaper, wooden panels for a boardroom scene, oak beams for a country cottage, Regency stripes for opulent Mayfair comedies or adaptations of Jane Austen.

33

Apart from the fact that the set tended to shake a little when anyone shut a door, the only really unsatisfactory feature was the doors themselves. In the scenery store there would be a number of door-flats, that is, flats into which had been cut a framework for a door. These, for convenience, were of a standard shape and size, and consequently so were the doors themselves, no matter whether they were painted to be part of a Manhattan penthouse, a nuclear submarine or a Norman keep.

There was just one refinement. At the fit-up on Sunday night, the Master Carpenter would call out to the Director:

'What do you want on the doors this week – knobs or levers?'

'What did we have last week, Fred?'

'You had levers.'

'All right, we'll have knobs.'

The wigs with which one transformed oneself into old age were my particular source of embarrassment. The gauze foundations of today were considered too delicate (and too expensive) for the wigs we used, and the hire firms sent us monstrosities with inflexible canvas fronts; so that if you raised your eyebrows in surprise, a fierce concentration of wrinkles would appear in the lower sector of your forehead, while the upper area would remain smooth as a billiard ball. Many actors painted their hair white with Meltonian shoe cream or covered it in cornflour rather than be seen on stage in one of these things.

While I was working these sort of hours at the theatre, Jacqueline found little to entertain her in the city, and went back to her mother in Wimbledon, where in any case we would both have to live until I found another job. At the end of February the Hull season at last came to an end, and I boarded the ferry to New Holland.

As the paddle steamer splashed its way across the Humber, the sky began to lighten, and out came the sun.

*

Nowadays, the casual actor is not much to be seen in the streets of Central London in the day time. If he is not in a recording studio telling the general public to buy a sports car or a deodorant, he is probably sitting at home on the telephone, browbeating his agent.

In the late fifties it was very different. From eleven o'clock every morning the area between Charing Cross Road and St Martin's Lane would be stiff with itinerant young actors.

The day would start with coffee and gossip in the Arts Theatre bar, where snippets of news about what was currently being cast might lead to a mass exodus up the road to Cambridge Circus, the abode of some of the less reputable theatrical agents. These people didn't keep a list of clients; when a management rang up wanting someone to fill a minor space in a cast list, the agent would simply wait for the morning stampede up the stairs, select someone who looked about right, negotiate a fairly derisory salary (from which they would immediately deduct ten per cent commission), and instruct the actor or actress where they had to be and when.

After trailing round these offices for an hour or so, those who had not struck lucky would begin to feel they had done enough work for one day, and repair to the Salisbury in St Martin's Lane for a pint and a sausage. Often somebody would come in carrying what appeared to be the script of a new play, and selecting a table in the far corner, would sit and study it with knitted brow, from time to time raising his eyes to the Edwardian chandelier and mouthing silently to himself. This pantomime was not always wholly convincing – on closer inspection the script might turn out to be an old magazine or part of a railway timetable. Second only to actually getting a job, the most important thing was to look as though you'd got one.

Of course in those days a substantial number of actors actually lived in the heart of the West End, *à la Bohème*. One such was the writer/performer Richard Huggett, with whom I once appeared in a show. He invited me to come to supper on Thursday night in his apartment in Old Compton Street, asking me if I liked vegetables. Yes, I said, I was fond of vegetables. The enquiry was repeated, more urgently, the following night. I assured him I found vegetables uniformly delightful. The next day – Thursday – was our matinee day, and between the shows I was wandering along Berwick Street just as the market was closing, and I saw a bearded, cherubic figure on all fours collecting debris from beneath the vegetable stalls. My supper.

Richard's apartment was really a corridor, off which doors into other dwellings had been boarded up. It must have been rather like living in a submarine: he kept books and papers stacked along a third of the space, slept in the next section, and his kitchen/dining/bathing facilities occupied the last bit.

After supper, he invited me to come and meet his neighbour, Diana, who, he said, was very keen on the theatre. Diana was just dressing to catch the last tube home after a hard day. The whip, the PVC boots, the chains and manacles had been stacked in a corner, and she agreed to sit down for a few minutes and share the bottle of wine we'd brought in. I remarked on the fact that the walls and ceiling of the little bedroom were covered in theatrical playbills.

'Well, it's something different for the clients to look at,' explained Diana modestly. My heart went out to her, imagining occasions of enthusiastic congress suddenly being arrested by a shout of 'Gosh, *Donald Sinden*, was he *really* in that?'

Richard, rather indecorously, asked her whether she had had any specially interesting visitors that day. 'Well,' she said, 'there is a man who comes in once a week, regularly at six o'clock. We both have to put on dressing gowns, and I make a pot of tea. We sit on the end of the bed, side by side and watch television for an hour. Then he goes home.' She gave a little nervous half-laugh, covering herself in the event of our finding this afflicting tale hilariously funny.

Actors used generally to drink more in the 1950s. For one thing, very few of us had cars, and for another, pubs were congenially geared to conversation rather than loud music. Soho also had a number of special drinking clubs for actors – Gerry's, run by Gerald Campion of Billy Bunter fame, the Buckstone, and for really serious alcoholics, the Kismet. Membership of these scruffy but friendly haunts was only a few pounds a year, and they were useful places to drop into for the afternoon if you were going to the theatre later and couldn't be bothered to go home in between.

A prevailing condition if not of actual unemployment, then certainly of chronic under-employment, was something younger actors took for granted. Today, the theatre, cinema and especially television requires new young talent all the time, but back in 1957 we felt marginalised. In any given play the central character tended to be a middle-aged authority figure, an MP, a doctor, a schoolmaster or the chairman of a bank.

Very soon the demands of the newly-vocal younger audiences would bring about a violent change. Writers like Pinter, Wesker and Osborne were more to their taste than the star-studied emanations of Terence Rattigan and N.C. Hunter, or the poetic drama of T.S. Eliot and Christopher Fry. In the powerful world of TV soaps, the cosy domestic hearth of *The Grove Family* was being deserted for the stark working environment of *Emergency Ward Ten*. Kind old Dixon of Dock Green had to give way to the younger, tougher and less articulate crew of *Z Cars*. Youth was about to be given its big chance.

But that had not happened quite yet. Most of us sitting there in the bar of the Salisbury were conditioned to think no further than the next Special Week somewhere, playing a small part in *Laburnum Grove* or *Murder at the Vicarage*.

Luckily, there was always a Shakespeare play on every school syllabus, which meant that the local theatre had to do it, and would probably need a few extra actors to flesh out the permanent company. So I found myself dispatched by one of the Cambridge Circus sharks to Canterbury, where I appeared in *Macbeth* as Second Murderer and as Thanes of various counties, and where I lived in a windmill with Clifford Williams the director and Gillian Diamond, who later became a major power at the Royal Shakespeare Company.

While I was there I did, to my grateful surprise, receive an invitation to join the Salisbury Arts Theatre Company – initially as stage manager but, if things worked out, eventually as a fully-fledged actor with a tiny increase in salary.

Jacqueline and I had bought a small Standard car, and drove down the A30 to the handsome cathedral city where I was to spend the next two years of my life. We were delighted with Salisbury, but could find absolutely nowhere to live. All the available lodgings seemed to be occupied by Army personnel, or by the sinister denizens of the Biological Weapons Laboratory on Porton Down.

To begin with, we took a room over a pub near the station for three pounds a week, with an additional charge made for a hot bath. To ensure against clandestine bathing while her back was turned, the landlady had removed the top of the hot tap, and would only restore it upon prior payment of the two-shilling fee. One Saturday night, returning very late and very dirty from striking the set, I felt in urgent need of a hot bath, and not wishing to wake the landlady with a demand for the necessary apparatus, unscrewed the top of the cold tap with the end of a penknife, fitted it on to the hot one, ran a bath and got into it.

The bathroom door burst open to admit a furious woman in curl-papers demanding the immediate surrender of two shillings. I explained to her the impracticability of having such a sum about me in my present situation, but finally had to march, stark naked and dripping wet, along the corridor and get the money from my trouser pocket before she would consent to go to bed.

Next morning we moved out, and after a week of staying in small hotels we could not afford, my mother-in-law advanced us the money to buy a 27-foot caravan, in which we lived for the next eighteen months.

It is one thing to own a caravan, but quite another to know where to put it. Jacqueline was pregnant, the baby was due in August and I did not relish the idea of the three of us having to pass the following winter being shifted on from one badly serviced and perhaps insanitary caravan park to another.

Fortunately, a space became vacant on a small official site behind the Old Castle Inn opposite the Norman earthworks at Old Sarum, and we took it. The elderly landlord of the pub was an entertaining man who had been in the Royal Flying Corps during the First World War, flying Sopwith Camels and, as he put it, 'firing at the Fokkers with my revolver'. The Fokkers finally shot him down, and he was treated, Red Baron fashion, to champagne and a comfortable internment from which he was sent home, after a tearful parting with his captors, in 1918.

Our daughter Juliet was born in London, and alas I was unable to get away in order to be present at the birth (although perhaps I would not have been allowed – the presence of husbands was not then encouraged, and I was to break new ground at Queen Charlotte's nine years later when I witnessed the arrival of my son Sam.) Juliet was a beautiful child, and when a few weeks later she and her mother joined me in Old Sarum, she adapted to caravan life with cheerful tranquillity.

I was, however, becoming very worried about Jacqueline. The disturbing mood-swings had now begun to take on a cyclic pattern of extreme manic depression. She had seen doctors in London, and been prescribed medication, but the drugs seemed unable to arrest the pattern beyond to some extent ironing out the extreme highs and lows. In her depressed state it was hard to get her to do anything much, and I began to be concerned about leaving Juliet with her while I was at work; so I would often drive them in with me to the theatre and deposit them in the communal dressing room, which understandably was not always popular with the company.

Her high periods were much more difficult to cope with. She would wake up in the middle of the night, turn on all the lights, play the gramophone and, in the loud, affected, histrionic tone peculiar to her in this state, would demand food, drink, or a game of cards. In between the peaks and the troughs she was her recognisable self, but such periods became shorter and less reliable as time went on.

I became desperately short of sleep, and went about like a despairing zombie. I no longer went with the others after the show to the King's Arms across the road, but sought a secluded pub on the other side of town and sat morosely over a drink till I had to go home at closing time.

What was I to do? Was I going to have to give up Salisbury – give up the theatre in fact – and devote myself full-time to looking after the family on a weekly hand-out from my mother-in-law? Would I be any good at it? Would I hate them all for it? The girl I was in love with had become a completely other being. How had I got myself into this impossible situation, and why? Romantic St Georgeism? Misplaced altruism? Plain stupidity? I blamed myself, not only for marrying at all, but for subjecting Jacqueline to perhaps the worst possible kind of life for someone in her condition. I blamed her too, and particularly her mother, for having kept me in the dark about her medical history, of which I had now learned something from her family doctor.

In fact, as I started on another drink, I blamed everyone. My parents should have made sure I went to university, like my sister. And another thing – why did we never have a piano in the house? If we'd had a piano, by now I could have been the young Clifford Curzon. Why had the BBC, years ago, turned me down as a filing clerk in the editing library, and thus denied themselves the future services of a brilliant young television director . . .

'Time, gentlemen. Let's have your glasses.'

I think at this time I may have become a bit peculiar myself, and undoubtedly my work suffered. To their eternal credit, Reggie Salberg, his wife Noreen and my other colleagues forgave, and to some extent understood. Jacqueline's behaviour in public could be distinctly embarrassing, and they sympathised.

Matters came to a head when, in a very excitable state and having drunk two or three whiskies on top of her prescribed pills, she took the car keys and threatened to drive with Juliet to London. We had a fight. I made a quick decision, bundled them both in the car and drove there myself, passing wife, baby and problem over to my mother-in-law. She was out for the evening, and I left them in the care of her bemused Hungarian housekeeper, helped myself to a handful of biscuits, and drove straight back to Salisbury.

Chapter Five

I had enjoyed my stint as stage manager, running the shows, making sure the director and cast were happy, and having the presumption after my very short time in the business to train my two assistants. Both of them later became influential television producers and needless to say have never employed me since.

But now I was officially an Actor. Such a transition was not uncommon in those days. Joining a rep company as a student ASM was an acceptable alternative to coming into the theatre from drama school or university, and a good way to learn all the practical aspects of the theatre. If you worked among good people, as in the main I was lucky enough to do, you picked up good habits which would last you throughout your professional life.

For a time, I even felt superior to the drama school graduates, who seemed a bit perplexed by the pace of life. Later I began to see that I should have benefited by their training. For instance, I really regret never having learned to dance, though my dancing has a fundamental awfulness about it that no doubt puts it beyond the cure of any teacher.

Most of the actors I worked with probably never thought very seriously beyond repertory life. There was of course a distinct hierarchy among companies – if an actor made it to the Birmingham Rep, the Liverpool Playhouse or the Bristol Old Vic, there might be the chance of being picked up by a roving casting director from the newly-founded English Stage Company, or Joan Littlewood's Theatre Workshop; but for a lot of people it would just be a lifelong circuit of Sheffield, Wolverhampton, Leeds, Colchester, York and so on. A circuit that was shrinking rapidly – in the early 1950s there were a hundred flourishing repertory companies in the United Kingdom; by 1960 there were only forty-four of them left.

Today, Salisbury boasts a modern well-appointed theatre with two auditoria, spacious foyers displaying art exhibitions, comfortable bars and a nice restaurant. But back in 1957 the Salisbury Arts Theatre Company performed in a converted church hall with no fly-tower, very little wing-space, and nowhere to store scenery, which had to be brought on a barrow from an old garage up the street.

Even allowing for the cramped nature of the operation, I still wonder how Reggie possibly managed to run it with a full-time staff of only nine other people. He himself chose and cast all the plays, but he was a manager, not a director – directors were engaged as part of the company. He ran the office with one secretary. There was an electrician, Stan Astin, and his wife Pauline, who ran the box office. Roberto Petrarca the carpenter and Jean Adams the scenic artist were a sort of joint production management, together with wardrobe mistress Kate Servian. A stage manager and two ASMs completed the full-time force, in addition to which there was a two-day-a-week book-keeper and an elderly front-of-house manager who had been a distinguished actor in one of Reggie's earlier companies, but who nowadays had a tendency to stand in the foyer with his flies undone, so he had gently to be asked to go.

Today's perceived requirements of marketing, publicity, fundraising, corporate entertaining and the rest, mean that there is a far longer list of personnel at the back of every theatre programme. Staff involved with actual *production*, though, have remained at much the same level over the years. The current tally of forty-four at Salisbury is relatively abstemious, but nationally the picture is of an industry that invests far more in promoting its wares than it does in actually producing them.

The artistic policy at Salisbury might be summed up as Varied Middlebrow, with Chekhov at one end of the scale and Whitehall Farce at the other. The less intellectually demanding productions were usually left in the hands of Oliver Gordon, a tall, bald ex-County Cricketer who had fought in many campaigns with the Salbergs, both Reggie and his elder brother Derek, who ran the Alexandra in Birmingham.

Other productions were directed by different actors in the company – little Frederick Peisley, who had begun his career way back in 1904, and had been acclaimed the greatest Puck of his time; Ronald Magill, who became a star of *Emmerdale*, and whom I personally considered to be a finer Archie Rice than Olivier when we did *The Entertainer*; Ian Mullins, who went on to run the Redgrave

Theatre Farnham. I even directed myself sometimes, usually while acting in the play as well: an experience tending to promote schizophrenia.

My particular friend in the company was Geoffrey Lumsden. Born Geoffrey Forbes, he was at Repton with Denton Welch, whose *Maiden Voyage* shows Geoffrey's behaviour even at that age to have compounded warring elements of rectitude and anarchy. Each fortnight while at Salisbury he donated a bottle of Gordon's Gin, to be awarded to the person who, by common consent, had given The Worst Performance In A Really Good Part. I myself won the Lumsden Gin on several occasions, notably when I played the coveted role of Henry Ormonroyd in *When we are Married*: every time I missed a laugh I could hear in the wings the distressed sighing of no fewer than three of the company, each of whom had played the part before, apparently brilliantly.

Years later Geoffrey put me up for membership of the Garrick Club. He himself had fallen on hard times, was in poor health, and went about very little. I promised him that the day I was elected, I would hold a dinner for him at the club, inviting all the people in the business that he knew and loved best. Every so often, he would ring me up.

'This is Lumsden. Look here, are you *in* yet?'

'Not yet, Geoffrey. They warned me it would take a long time.'

'Oh God. Then I'd better just open a tin of baked beans.'

We never did have that dinner. It took me nearly six years to be elected to the Garrick Club, and by that time Geoffrey was dead.

As well as being a fine actor, he wrote a very funny farce called *Gwendolyn* which, after we did it in Salisbury, was bought by the West End producer Peter Bridge, and re-titled *Caught Napping*. Three or four of us in the smaller parts transferred with it when it went to London in 1959, so that my opportunity of working in the West End came sooner than I had ever imagined.

*

Meanwhile, I was constantly on the phone to Jacqueline's mother for a progress report. She hedged, and I began to suspect that matters had taken a turn for the worse. They had. Jacqueline had been taken to the Holloway Sanatorium at Virginia Water and put on a course of Insulin Therapy. She had had to go there once before, Leila now told me. I went down there next day.

Holloway Sanatorium, now abandoned, was a fearsome place, a companion building to the Royal Holloway College along the road, but with its Gothic vaults extravagantly decorated with hideous gargoyles: vicious dragons and simian monsters with glaring eyes and voraciously extended tongues. A curious design theme for a mental hospital, one would have thought; but I suppose an inmate, screaming in the night that he was suffering from terrible hallucinations, would be comforted by the warder's assurance that he could see them too.

I was directed towards what I can only describe as a padded cell, where my wife was sitting on the floor in a semi-cataleptic condition, having just undergone an enormous therapeutic injection of insulin. Conversation was impossible. There was no qualified person around from whom I could seek information, so to fill in the time before my scheduled meeting with Dr McLeod, the Physician Superintendent, I went outside and walked around the hospital grounds.

Mnemosyne, the goddess of memory, is a merciful but capricious lady. While clearing out, from time to time, the mental cupboards in which we store the dusty relics of our remembered past, she may pause in the salutary act of sweeping them wholesale into the bin, and suddenly decide to keep something back, just for fun. It would probably not be the icon we would ourselves select to represent a particular episode, but if she takes a fancy to it she will blow off the cobwebs, give it a polish, even restore the chipped paintwork, and place it in a prominent position where you will see it every time you pass by.

Thus it is with one crystal clear recollection during that whole agonising period. I had been told of a patients' club in the grounds of the sanatorium – a wooden building like a cricket pavilion where ambulant patients, doctors and staff could get together informally over a cup of tea or a game of table tennis – and, wanting someone to talk to, I sought it out. There I was approached by a man who introduced himself as Dr Wheeler and enquired if I were a visitor. I said I was, and having learned my name, he told me he knew about my wife, though he was not himself in charge of her case. He admitted frankly that doctors were still puzzled by the nature of the chemical imbalance that was apparently at the root of her trouble, but discoveries were being made all the time, and he was confident that a solution would quite soon be found. Her very violent behaviour on admission, he told me, had suggested the use of insulin shock treatment – this was unpleasant, he admitted, and he appreciated that what I had just witnessed must have seemed very distressing, but the regimen, in which he said he himself had no great faith, would certainly not be carried on much longer. There was a possibility, he said, that they might try electro-convulsive therapy, but unless its effects were immediately seen to be beneficial, it would be discontinued. What it amounted to was that they were still searching, that I must not expect quick results, but that the condition was undoubtedly containable, if not permanently curable, and I mustn't worry.

Though much of what he'd told me sounded horrifying, I was impressed by by his confidence and grateful for his explanatory advice, and when the time came to meet Dr McLeod I was in a slightly more positive frame of mind.

The Physician Superintendent, a kindly looking energetic Edinburgh man, pulled out a comfortable chair for me, and enquired if I'd had time to look around at all. I told him of my encounter with Dr Wheeler.

'Dr Wheeler?' he said. 'Ah.'

He walked over to his desk, sat down, and picked up a few paperclips. 'Yes. Dr Wheeler.' He started threading the paperclips together rather sadly. 'I'm afraid,' he finally went on, 'he's not really a doctor. A very clever man, and a *nice* man, and would, I think, have made a very good doctor . . . He's a *voluntary* patient,' he assured me hastily, 'and I think he realises that left to himself, he might feel the need to go around persuading people he was genuine, perhaps start treating them in some way, and then, who knows . . . ' he shook his head, and stared out of the window for a moment. 'What did he say to you?' he suddenly asked.

I related the information I had been given as far as I could remember it, and McLeod listened intently, occasionally nodding his head and interjecting: 'Yes. Well *yes*. Well, that's quite right.' He didn't actually add anything of substance, and weeks afterwards, when Jacqueline's ordeal at Holloway had finally came to an end and I went over in my mind the various conversations I had had with the medical staff, I could think of none who had shown the same sympathy, taken the same trouble to explain, or displayed the same apparent grasp of the situation, as the unfortunate *soi-disant* Doctor Wheeler.

Jacqueline did get better, and though still on heavy medication was able, with Juliet, to return to Salisbury. It had been a long business, and in the interim I had been able to rent a small flat off the Wilton Road. Fate decreed that it should directly overlook the local mental hospital, but fortunately this struck us both as wildly funny.

I would be sorry to leave Salisbury. I had latterly made many friends in the Cathedral Close; the writer and illustrator Daniel Pettiward, the organist Christopher Dearnley, and various of the distinctly Trollopian brotherhood of Canons and Prebendaries.

Across the way from the Deanery and the Bishop's Palace was the imposing North Canonry, where lived Sir Reginald Kennedy-Cox, Lord Lieutenant of the County, and Chairman of the theatre board. Sir Reginald was particularly partial to plays about the Armed Forces, and in addition he was a great admirer of a popular actor called George Selway, who came to us as a visiting star from time to time. When, therefore, George was billed to appear in *Morning Departure* (the play about a terminally submerged submarine of which a film was made starring John Mills and Richard Attenborough), Sir Reginald got quite excited, and a decree went out that the Union Jack be flown from the roof of the Playhouse.

Now, we did actually have a Union Jack, and what's more there was a flagpole on the roof, embedded in an old oil barrel half filled with earth. Stan Astin, the electrician and general factotum, was dispatched aloft with the flag to perform this patriotic gesture.

No one had been up there for some time, and a group of seagulls had come to consider the oil barrel an ideal place to lay their eggs. When Stan attempted to get near the flagpole, they beat him off with savage cries, pecking at him and sending him reeling backwards across the roof. Poor Stan had been shell-shocked during the war, and it had left him with a heavy stammer. Hurling the Union Jack from him in disgust, and covered from head to foot in seagull-droppings, he retreated down the ladder as fast as he could, muttering, 'B-bloody George Selway, b-bloody Sir Reginald K-kennedy C-cox, let them f-fly their own f-fucking f-flag . . . '

And I would miss Charlie, the gatekeeper of the Close, who every Monday would stop me with the words, 'How many in the play this week, Timothy?' and if I answered ten or eleven, he would rub his hands delightedly and promise that he and his wife would be along. If, however, I had to admit 'Only four of us I'm afraid, Charlie,' his face would fall, and he would retreat into his little office without another word.

It's interesting to note that though we'd changed our turnover from weekly to fortnightly some months before, patrons still liked to refer to 'this week's show.' Our relationship with the Salisbury audience was a pretty good example of the sort of bonding that was always intended between a repertory company and the people it serves, and which it is impossible for commercial theatre, or even subsidised touring, to achieve. We were a community working for a community, both representing and reflecting it.

My last performance was in John Mortimer's double-bill *The Dock Brief* (one of the most entertaining one-act plays ever) and *I Spy*. I made a quick sortie to Bristol, where I directed *Any Other Business* for Ronnie and Peggy Ann at the Little, and then joined the London cast for rehearsals of *Caught Napping*.

Chapter Six

Peter Bridge, the producer of *Caught Napping*, was a large, affable man who at that time had, I think, no fewer than six shows running simultaneously in the West End. He was a real enthusiast, who engaged well-established stars like Googie Withers and John McCallum, Joan Greenwood, Hugh Williams, Michael Denison and Dulcie Gray. He was quite young, and I always thought he must have had their pictures pinned up in his prep school dormitory; just before Lights Out he would whisper softly,'One day, I'm going to employ you all.'

There was a very great deal going on in the London theatre at that time. In the last few months the West End had seen the openings of Graham Greene's *The Potting Shed* with John Gielgud and Irene Worth (and incidentally my father), Michael Redgrave in *A Touch of the Sun*, Vivien Leigh and Claire Bloom in *Duel of Angels*, Peter Shaffer's first play *Five Finger Exercise*, Robert Ardrey's *Shadow of Heroes* with Peggy Ashcroft, and revivals of *The Iceman Cometh* (Ian Bannen as Hickey), *Cat on a Hot Tin Roof* (Leo McKern as Big Daddy) and *Long Day's Journey into Night* with Anthony Quayle and Gwen Ffrangcon-Davies.

The new musicals included *Irma la Douce*, *Auntie Mame*, *Valmouth*, *West Side Story*, *Candide* and *My Fair Lady*.

The Old Vic, having completed the Shakespeare canon, continued with *Mary Stuart*, *Ghosts*, *Tartuffe*, *The Magistrate* and *The Cenci*. There were visiting seasons by the Moscow Art Theatre, the Teatro Piccolo di Milano and the Düsseldorfer Schauspielhaus; the Royal Court gave us *A Resounding Tinkle*, *Epitaph for George Dillon*, the Wesker *Roots* Trilogy, *Live Like Pigs* and *The Long and the Short and the Tall*, while from Joan Littlewood's Theatre Workshop came *A Taste of Honey*, *The Hostage* and *Fings Ain't Wot They Used t'Be*.

I went to see as many of these shows as I could, but worshipped no particular gods and goddesses among the stars. The Lordly Ones with their names in lights were too far away for me; the people who made me want to get up there and join them on the stage were not the big stars, they were just actors whose outstanding quality had impressed me over a number of performances – John Phillips, Paul Daneman and Derek Godfrey at the Vic, Robert Stephens (not a star at that time), and the young Michael Bryant in *Five Finger Exercise* and as a definitive Willie Oban in *The Iceman*.

Of course there were those I admired at a respectful distance – Ralph Richardson, who seemed on his day to have his own private line to Apollo; Donald Wolfit, whose Lear I watched, spellbound, five times in one season, but who, it seemed, was considered in West End circles not quite *comme il faut*.

I must admit to one actual pin-up. Back in my EMI days, I had fixed above my tape machine a photograph, torn from the Strand Magazine, of the young Dorothy Tutin in a tweed skirt and woollen jumper, sitting on her bicycle among a lot of autumn leaves somewhere. Having seen her in *The Living Room* and *I am a Camera*, I fell in love.

We had no big stars in *Caught Napping*. The cast was headed by George Benson, Raymond Huntley and Leslie Randall. Huntley, unsmiling, lugubrious, grey-suited, spoke only occasionally, and then through closed teeth. One day just after the start of rehearsals I told him I had just seen him in the film *Room at the Top*, and plucked up courage to ask him what it had been like working with Simone Signoret. He paused, and then in a sepulchral murmur replied, 'I'd rather go to bed with a dead policeman.'

Our director was Anthony Sharp, a vigorous pedagogue who cheered us on with phrases like 'Good, chaps! Jolly spiffing!' and was known to be a good play-doctor – particularly of farce, where the placing and strategic grading of laughs has to be built into the structure during rehearsal.

The OED defines farce rather contemptuously as 'a dramatic work intended only to excite laughter', and any attempt to pin it down more precisely will depend on an individual's first encounter with the form. Was it with Feydeau, Goldoni, Ben Travers, Brian Rix or Ray Cooney? They are all very different, and the fact that humour goes out of date very quickly means that there has been no definable continuity of style. Goldoni wrote two hundred and fifty plays which may have made the 18th-century Venetians rock with laughter, but today we are hard put to it to present three of them. The

Aldwych Farces of Ben Travers and others, written to a formula and performed by a permanent team of expert practitioners, had a good innings, but the Ralph Lynn/Tom Walls characters now seem too outrageous, and most of the plays themselves are fairly thin. Brian Rix and his team managed to keep the Whitehall audience laughing with half-a-dozen plays spread over twenty-five years, but this broader, full-blooded style ceased in its turn to amuse, and was modified and given a rather more middle-class look by his erstwhile disciple Ray Cooney.

That leaves Feydeau, whose plays really do seem to me to be timeless. They deal with the enduring stuff of farce. His characters are very serious people with a great deal at stake, obsessed with their own social propriety and the need to conceal their clandestine peccadilloes from spouses, neighbours and employers. Serious social drama is written about exactly the same things.

Alas, I have only ever seen one production of a Feydeau farce that made me laugh as much as I was obviously meant to. This was in Paris, and my moderate French was just about up to it. The play was the little-performed *Chat-en-Poche*, and the plot concerns a rich banker whose daughter wants to be an opera singer. The banker duly commissions the composition of an opera for her, rents the Salon Garnier, and engages a young counter-tenor to sing the leading male role. The father is rather alarmed at the attentions the handsome young man is paying to his daughter – attentions that are warmly reciprocated – until he learns that the lad has sung as a chorister in the Sistine Chapel. To the banker, it follows that the young man is a physical castrato, and he is highly amused at the prospect of the ultimate discovery of this fact, not only by his daughter, but his own wife and the wife of the doctor next door, all of whom have been smitten by the young man, who is, of course, completely intact and having a high old time with all three of them.

At the little Théâtre Daunou the cast played with a desperately serious intensity of purpose, the dictates of social behaviour cloaking the tragic hysteria which almost but never quite broke out. John Cleese was later to remind me strongly of this in the television series *Fawlty Towers*, but it's not an approach we encounter often enough on the stage.

Our own farce opened in Richmond, and went on to Brighton, Streatham Hill and Golders Green before coming in to the Piccadilly.

The Piccadilly is the theatre that everybody thinks is in Piccadilly Circus, but in fact isn't. It is tucked away behind the Regent Palace Hotel, and is unknown even to many taxi drivers. It is a perfectly nice theatre, and I've had some very good times there, but it's a bit big for domestic farce. Besides, there was the weather.

The unusually warm May in which we opened gave way to an even warmer June, and then a blazing July. It was declared to be the hottest summer in living memory. Very few theatres had air-conditioning in those days, ours certainly didn't, and people just stopped going. Instead they lay covering every inch of the London parks, or sat around almost naked on the roasting pavements. On stage, each of us must have lost pounds in weight. There is always a good deal of chasing around in farce – I had to do a lot of it, very fast, the sweat pouring off me, and when the curtain came down, there would be Tony Sharp with a notepad: 'Timothy – jolly spiffing, but a bit faster on the chase, there's a good chap, it needs to tootle along you know.'

Theatres with shows that had opened to brilliant reviews were going dark all around us, and Peter Bridge kept us limping on for thirteen weeks hoping we might pick up some of their business, but of course we didn't, there wasn't any business to pick up. The sweltering summer went on, and by the end of August we had to call it a day.

I can't pretend that my debut in the West End caused a tremendous stir. In fact, technically I had not yet spoken a word on the London stage. My character was called Talky, precisely because he did not talk. He was a bookmaker's runner, and spoke entirely in tick-tack language. I was dressed in a beige teddy boy jacket, drainpipe trousers and a string tie with a toggle, and I lacquered my hair into a heavy overhanging frontal curl which I think was the final cause of nearly all of it dropping out.

*

On the door of the Ladies' lavatory backstage at the Palace Theatre Wellingborough was written, in scarlet lipstick, the message IVE SUGARRED IT FOR ELVIS.

How do I know this? Because we were performing *The Long and the Short and the Tall* there, and the large cast of male soldiery filled both of the men's dressing rooms, so as their Japanese prisoner with quite a lot of make-up to put on, I had to dress in the women's quarters. The Royal Theatre, Northampton, a beautiful 1884 building by C.J. Phipps, to which I went back several times, had chosen to play an additional week at the very unbeautiful Wellingborough Palace, hardly ever used now except occasionally as a cinema. It was filthy dirty, and one night when I was lying on the floor having been shot dead, a small rat (or perhaps a large mouse, I had my eyes closed) trudged disconsolately around on my chest.

Enough of this *nostalgie de la boue*, I hear my reader complain, when is this fellow's career actually going to *start*?

Well I'm sorry, I'm not sure there *is* a career, at least not according to my understanding of the term. Some people are able to decide the path they are going to take, and pursue it faithfully until they reach their chosen goal. I've simply zig-zagged about from one job to another, trying to make them different, and for the most part enjoying myself. I have travelled hopefully, but if I actually arrived anywhere I'm afraid I can't have been looking out of the window at the time.

The three main ITV producing companies, ATV, ABC and Associated-Rediffusion, were now well under way, and on returning to London I fixed up interviews with their Casting Directors – to little effect. When, after telling Dorothy Jane Ward I had recently played a non-speaking bookmaker's runner in a play she wouldn't have seen because it was too hot, I went on to describe my success in mid-Northamptonshire as a Japanese soldier who, of course, didn't speak either, it dawned on me that the interview was not going as well as it should.

So I was back on the road. I didn't take the family; Jacqueline's grandmother, a fierce old lady who lived in Brighton, had just died, and Leila as beneficiary was able to buy some extra property in Wimbledon, in part of which we lived at a peppercorn rent, so they were comfortable. I bought an old black Hillman for £35, and drove around doing a play here, a couple of plays there – Bath, Worthing, Northampton and back to Salisbury – until Bernard Miles at the Mermaid answered my letter (I wrote thirty or forty such letters a week) and asked me to come and be in Brecht's *The Life of Galileo*.

The Mermaid at Blackfriars had opened the previous year, 1959. It stood next to the little Puddle Dock, and was approached down some steps from Queen Victoria Street. The public restaurant above the stage overlooked the Thames, and below it were our dressing rooms, with a small terrace where we used to stand and watch the lightermen adroitly shunting and docking their barges. Sometimes we would applaud a particularly skilful manoeuvre, and the bargee would turn to find himself being congratulated by the Pope, a couple of Cardinals and the Astronomer Royal.

When part of the river was reclaimed to build Upper Thames Street, Puddle Dock found itself a dock in name only, waterless and a hundred yards inland. The theatre was demolished and pokily re-erected beneath a noisy nearby underpass, where no-one could get to it even if they wanted to.

It was a sad end to a long dream. Colleagues often said of Bernard Miles (Sir Bernard as he became) that he was a genius at getting theatres built, but hopeless at running them. That's not entirely fair. He was always a maverick, and shared some of the eighteenth-century piratical qualities of the character he portrayed every Christmas in *Treasure Island*; but he was responsible for some very good productions, and was himself a wonderful character actor on stage and screen. There was not much in the theatre that Bernard hadn't set his hand to at some time or other. In his early days he had worked as a scenic designer and stage carpenter, and went on to act, direct, stage-manage, produce, go into music-hall, and to found with his wife Josephine the first temporary Mermaid in 1951, which opened with a production of Purcell's *Dido and Aeneas* sung by Kirsten Flagstad and Maggie Teyte.

Two years after that, the Elizabethan-stage Mermaid was reconstructed in Cornhill, within the Royal Exchange; and Bernard spent the next six years pursuing the City Fathers, coaxing from them enough money and a suitable site for a permanent building. Initially, he used to put on a dark suit to visit the halls of power, but very soon abandoned it in favour of corduroys and an old sweater. 'Artist at work,' he would explain to us confidentially.

He wasn't at his best in the character of Galileo Galilei, but the production itself was sumptuous, having been borrowed wholesale from the Berliner Ensemble. Bernard was brilliant at doing these deals. During the final week of rehearsals there was great excitement because Brecht's widow Helene Weigel, the great German actress and exemplar of the dramatist's philosophy, was coming to see us.

She watched a dress rehearsal, and afterwards we all sat around on the stage, on tenterhooks, while Bernard asked her for her impressions. She was very charming, complimentary without being effusive; and finally Bernard geared himself up to put the $64,000 question.

'Erm, Helena,' he ventured, 'what about the *alienation effect*? Did you think we got that, all right?'

'The alienation effect?' she shrugged her shoulders and smiled. 'Oh, you shouldn't bother very much about that. It was just a phrase invented by Bert to protect himself from over-indulgent actors.' Thirty years of theatrical gospel, washed away in a matter of seconds.

I didn't have much to do in the play, but it was my first experience of Brecht, and the production went down well with public and critics alike. By the end of the run I had saved enough to buy a slightly better car, so I sold the Hillman for £2 to Stephen Hancock, who needed it to drive his wife Jo and all their luggage back up north. In the middle of Derby, the car blew up. They were fortunately unhurt, and as I said to them afterwards, how else could they have got all the way to Derby for two pounds?

The next play at the Mermaid was a musical about a chimpanzee who goes into politics and eventually becomes Prime Minister. I stayed on for it, and the only thing I can remember about the show is hearing my father, in the audience on the first night, laughing delightedly when I first came on.

At last, I thought. I have finally been accepted as a useful partner in the family business.

Chapter Seven

*I*t was my father who got me my first proper part on television – Charles Hayter in *Persuasion* for the BBC. The Corporation were producing their very first Jane Austen cycle, and my father, who had just been in *Pride and Prejudice* for them, suggested me to the director, Campbell Logan.

In the cast of *Pride and Prejudice* was a young actress named Prunella Scales. Because father was giving a slightly camp performance as Mr Collins, and because he worked fairly regularly for the H.M. Tennent management, an organisation known not to be aggressively heterosexual, Prunella decided that he must be what was termed an Old Queen. Subsequent events caused her seriously to revise that view, but in the meantime she decided to be extremely nice to him, because such people are known to be Very Powerful.

Persuasion was not broadcast live, it was recorded; but in those days it amounted to much the same thing. Each episode was performed straight through from beginning to end, and retakes were prohibitively expensive. When anything went wrong, you just ploughed on regardless; if you really thought you'd made a total mess of a scene, the only way to stop it was by uttering an obscenity straight to camera. Then they really would have to stop and go back, but it wasn't something you could do twice, for fear that your name would be added to a proscriptive list somewhere in the heart of Broadcasting House.

Everything was shot on video camera, nothing on film, and exterior scenes mostly had to be done in the studio. In the designer's efforts to simulate open countryside, the ground always had to rise quite steeply away from the camera, culminating in a hillock with a thick hedge, in order to get over the difficulty of showing the horizon. From behind the hedge, characters would emerge up some concealed steps and enter via a gate or stile. It was impossible to achieve a good open-air acoustic in such surroundings, and attempts to introduce wind or rain could be physically disastrous.

Even in the days when wealthy neighbours used to ask us round to watch Muffin the Mule on their tiny blue-grey screen, it was clear that television was to become the accepted means of family entertainment, and it bonded people together at the bus stop, the butchers' or the doctor's waiting room in communion about whatever was shown at prime time the night before.

As more terrestrial channels were added, though, and the choice became wider, we saw this social bonding slacken. With the addition of cable and satellite, common interest has now virtually become restricted to the two most popular soaps. Viewers are turning away from broadcast television altogether, preferring to watch what they want when they want. The young escape the tyranny of family viewing by taking their videos away to be played in a private world.

It's hard to know what will happen eventually. More and more people are going to be spending their working hours at home with their eyes glued to a screen. When evening comes, will they remain sitting there, ordering up a chicken tikka and while they're eating it choose something to watch from the vast catalogue of television and cinematic material that will soon be available? What will such material be like? The need for quantity must militate against quality. Chat shows, game shows, keyhole actuality, docu-soaps – these are all cheap to produce. Real documentaries come a little dearer, so do sit-coms. The most expensive of all is Drama. Old films can be economical to show – but will there be enough old films left in the libraries, bearing in mind the remarks of the director who recently remade Hitchcock's *Psycho* shot by shot, explaining that his daughter refused to watch anything in black-and-white?

Or, at 5.30, will people turn the thing off with a sigh of relief and go out to meet other members of the human race, at a pub, the cinema perhaps, or maybe at the theatre or some other place of live entertainment? Could it be that television will eventually go the way of the lantern-lecture, the *thé dansant*, canasta and the Tupperware party? An intriguing thought.

*

After going through the Jane Austen canon, Campbell Logan, who preferred to rehearse in a remote church hall in Pimlico in order to be near his mother who always gave him lunch, went on to direct for the BBC a staggeringly boring historical romance about the secret passion of the Earl of Sandwich, called *She Died Young* and sub-titled by the cast None Too Soon. It was set in London in the mid eighteenth-century, where every coffee house was crammed with the notables of the time – Johnson, Boswell, Garrick, Burke, Goldsmith etc.

Sir Joshua Reynolds was discovered at an easel, laying down his brush with the words 'Ha! managed that difficult highlight at last!' This all-purpose character-establishing line can be adapted for use in any artistic biography, viz: 'Ha! managed that difficult transferred epithet at last!' (Keats), 'Ha! managed that difficult augmented fifth at last!' (Beethoven), 'Ha! managed that difficult shouldered architrave at last!' (Christopher Wren) and so on.

Doctor Johnson was played by Robert Atkins, hitherto known to me only as the presiding genius of Regent's Park. I remember seeing him one evening in *A Midsummer Night's Dream*. 'O grim-look'd night, O night of hue so black,' he declaimed as Pyramus, and then as the heavens, apparently in response, burst open, 'Oh Christ, the performance will be continued in the marquee.' I believe that his last appearance in front of a television camera had been in the earliest days of that invention, before the war. As Samuel Johnson he was rather larger than life, but then so was Samuel Johnson. When a particular phrase took his fancy, Atkins would roll it about in his mouth for a while, and then repeat it two or three times until it had lost its fascination for him. This threatened to add many minutes to the play, but in those days this was only a problem if you ran up against the News, which was of course sacrosanct.

Boswell (Robert Urquhart) obviously had to seduce someone in the course of the story, and his chosen quarry was the Bishop of Bath's daughter, played by Prunella Scales. During rehearsals Miss Scales and I had enjoyed a mild flirtation over the Times crossword, and when on the studio day we were suddenly informed that owing to an electricians' strike the recording would have to be postponed until some unspecified date in the future, it seemed natural to invite her to fill the unexpectedly free evening by coming to the pictures. We went to the Odeon, Marble Arch and saw *The Grass is Greener* starring Cary Grant and Deborah Kerr, had a quick snack in South Kensington, then she went home to Chelsea and I caught the District Line to Wimbledon. We didn't meet again for some time.

I was fond of our Wimbledon house, but we never seemed to be there much. Just now we were assisting my mother-in-law in her latest enterprise, a small restaurant in Connaught Street, W.2., which she proposed to run herself. It cannot be said that Leila possessed many of the qualities one might expect for such a pursuit: concentration, stability, an eye for picking staff, and a familiarity with the neighbourhood and its demography. Concentration was not her forte, visits to race meetings and fashion shows prevented her from keeping an eye on her rascally under-manager, and in one single afternoon she engaged an impossibly temperamental chef, a kitchen assistant who hated everybody, and a waitress who drank a great deal of gin and dropped trays. Leila had not, I think, ever been near Connaught Street before, and had no idea who lived and worked there, or what they might like to eat.

The madness of the scheme appealed to me, and I offered to decorate the place for her. She was adamant that the design should be 'contemporary', which meant the midnight blue, lime green and mustard yellow that had been the uniform of the late fifties. I'd once heard that a dining room should be decorated only in the colours of things you can actually eat, which seemed to rule out dark blue; but she insisted, and it finished up looking like a rather dubious massage parlour. It required very subdued lighting, and I made sure it got it.

To my total bewilderment, the restaurant became very popular, made money and Leila later sold it to another restaurateur at a considerable profit.

The painting was done in the evenings after rehearsals for my next stage appearance, in the Whitehall farce *Simple Spymen*. I was to play the elderly Army Intelligence Officer, Colonel Gray-Balding. I was twenty-seven. More cornflour on the hair.

The play was just finishing its three-year run at the Whitehall, and being re-cast for a twenty-six week tour of England and Scotland. A long time to be away; there were two or three weeks where I could commute from home, and there would be some Sundays when I could get back, but it would put a strain on our already restless domestic situation.

I had been up to Northampton again to play the lead in *All for Mary*, and then to Manchester to appear briefly in *The Plough and the Stars* for Granada TV, and I was very conscious of not spending enough time with my four-year-old daughter, who most days was collected from nursery school and taken back to Leila's new house in Putney, where Jacqueline, not being good at being left alone, spent most of her time.

It was I suppose natural for her to regard her mother as the best guarantor of her welfare. Leila was materially a very generous person and would, I think, have been quite content to support the whole family permanently, if she thought it best. I saw that there might be a real danger of this happening if we did not somehow assert our independence.

Jacqueline had been unable to do any paid work for the last couple of years, but I was earning enough for the three of us to live on, modestly, as long as I didn't mind working out of town. The trouble was that because I wasn't around much, her mother's personality and very up-beat lifestyle proved too strong for Jacqueline to resist.

Of course it wasn't purely a material problem. Since her breakdown, things had never got back to normal between us. I don't mean that the ordeal had changed her significantly, nor do I think had it essentially altered my own feeling towards her. It was a more gradual process; we were beginning to look much more closely at each other, and recognising that we were two very different people. There had been no violent demonstrations of incompatibility; we could manage to jog along all right, but we both knew we weren't getting much out of our marriage.

I was being excluded, and so I excluded myself; classic psychological behaviour. It was partly why I went ahead and signed up for this long tour of Eastbourne, Brighton, Southsea, Oxford, Bristol, Leeds, Manchester, Coventry, Wolverhampton, Streatham Hill, Golders Green, Exeter, Bournemouth, Nottingham, Liverpool, Stockton-on-Tees, Glasgow, Edinburgh, Newcastle, Stratford-on-Avon, Blackpool, Wilmslow and back to Brighton. Nearly all of these were 'No.1 dates', theatres that now only slip in the odd week of drama between six-week runs of musicals, so that such a tour would be impracticable today, even if you could get actors to agree to stay on the road that long.

Andrew Sachs and John Slater took over the parts played in London by Brian Rix and Leo Franklyn. I already knew Andrew slightly, and I'd met the elderly Company Manager Bertie Parham. He and I occasionally shared lodgings; and it was in Leeds, I think, that I drew his attention to something that had caught my eye in our landlady's Visitors' Book, in which some of the distinguished performers had added after their names the initials 'L.D.O.' Was this some sort of obscure decoration or qualification, I asked?

Bertie shook his head. 'Coded information for future guests,' he explained. 'Landlady's Daughter Obliges.'

Touring is currently experiencing a come-back, but theatrical 'digs' today are much harder to find than they were forty years ago, when every actor was armed with a national catalogue of landladies, the great names of the touring circuit: Mrs Treacy in Nottingham, Mrs Cairns in Edinburgh, Mrs Mundy in Glasgow, Mrs Hellewell in Blackpool, Mrs Blakemore in Wolverhampton and so on. Probably the most famous of them all was Manchester's Mrs Mackay, of Astra House (the Home of the Stars) in Daisy Avenue. Her brilliant malapropisms were renowned throughout the profession. 'I've got that Allan Cuthbertson coming next week,' she told me.' I hear he's a bit pendatic.'

I used to press her about her famous guests, and she confided that an archeologist from Israel had once stayed with her while making a documentary for Granada, and had actually shown her the celebrated Deep Sea Rolls.

When years later she had managed to enlarge her business by purchasing a mortgage on the house next door, someone asked her mischievously whether her rival boarding-house proprietors down the road had been able to effect a similar deal. She pursed her lips. 'Oh no love,' she said, 'they didn't have the cholesterol.'

We played in some beautiful theatres, to fairly large audiences, and to a reception that did not seem to vary much from place to place. Brian Rix and his writers were accomplished craftsmen, they knew where the sure-fire laughs would come, and the director Wallace Douglas just had to follow a blue-print.

This was still the epoch of the British bucket-and-spade holiday, and at our first three seaside dates whole families, having abandoned the beaches at six for boarding-house tea, washed the sand from their crevices and turned up at the theatre in pleasingly large numbers. For us, too, it was almost as good as a holiday; the weather was beautiful, and I swam, walked the South Downs and went over on the boat to wander around the Isle of Wight.

In August, just after the start of the tour, I received a postcard from Prunella Scales, saying that they had at last succeeded in recording *She Died Young*, and that she was sorry I hadn't been available for my original part; she'd missed doing the crossword with me. I wrote back saying I was sorry too.

The fourth week of the tour was at Oxford. Now, I had no idea that Prunella, who was in a play called *Whiteman* (the first ever production of the Prospect Theatre Company, with which I was to become closely involved) would be at the Oxford Playhouse that week, nor had she imagined that I would at the same time be playing at the New Theatre, now the Apollo. It was a total coincidence.

The weather still continued charming. She had a day off, we met for lunch at a pub, then went down to Folly Bridge and took a punt on the Isis. She talked about her boy-friend Robin, and I told her a bit about Jacqueline. It was a lovely and perfectly innocent afternoon. At the end of the week I went on to Bristol, but we continued a correspondence – jokey, superficial, carefully not touching on the thing that we both knew had begun to happen to us.

Chapter Eight

Carefully perhaps, but not quite carefully enough. We were both sufficiently accomplished letter-writers to be able to read between the lines. A few weeks later, when she had finished *Whiteman* and was rehearsing a new play called *The Marriage Game*, I asked her to come up to see me in Manchester, and she did. Then *The Marriage Game* began a six-week tour, and we contrived a series of Sunday assignations at crossing points in our two schedules. If she had been playing in Bristol and was about to move on to Sheffield, and I had just left Manchester and was going on to Coventry, we would meet in Birmingham; if she was travelling south from Leeds to Brighton, and I was going in the opposite direction from Bournemouth to Nottingham, we would rendezvous in Oxford. We had a lot of energy in those days.

Of course, for my Streatham Hill and Golders Green weeks I would live at home, and I had not quite decided whether to try and carry on as though nothing had happened, or whether that would be foolish. It was essential that Jacqueline and I should have an honest talk about what we saw as our future, and I began to rehearse this in my mind.

When I got home, there was someone sitting in the kitchen whom I had never seen before. He seemed thoroughly at home, and greeted me cheerily. Jacqueline explained that he was looking for temporary accommodation in the area, so she had rented him our spare room. One thing, I could see at once, had led to another. He was called Roger. Roger the lodger. I say I say I say. My delicately-prepared scene seemed inapposite for the music-hall. Later that evening – when Roger had gone out – we sat on the bed and agreed that, in the present state of play, it would be best for us to go our own ways for a while. We should see how we felt at the end of the year. It was perfectly amicable, and we felt closer to each other than we had for a long time.

The tour continued. As autumn turned to winter, we moved further north. The Grand Theatre Blackpool, where we played twice on Christmas Day, had booked us in for two weeks; and as the intervening Sunday was New Year's Eve, I thought I would travel up to London for a party Pru was giving in her Chelsea flat, and come back to Blackpool on Monday morning in plenty of time for the show.

It was a splendid party, and I stayed the night. However, when I woke at seven the next morning the ground was buried under a foot of snow, which was still falling heavily. I listened to the news. There were no main line trains out of Euston at all.

Aircraft were grounded. Desperately, I rang Paddington. Western Region trains were severely curtailed, but some were still running, and in those days there was a service from Paddington to Birkenhead, so I thought if I got there, crossed the Mersey to Liverpool and caught a train thence to Preston, I might be in with a chance.

There was a train at ten past nine, and I boarded it. The snow showed no signs of abating, and our progress was continually dogged by frozen points, but we finally got to Birkenhead at about four o'clock. I just caught a ferry, but when I got across the water there were no taxis at the landing stage, so I ran all the way to Lime Street. The snow was falling harder than ever. At Lime Street a train was indeed advertised for Preston, but officials didn't seem confident about it. Eventually, at about twenty to six, it pulled out and crawled painfully as far as Ormskirk, where it shuddered and gave up.

I didn't know Ormskirk at all, but I tramped through the thick snow of its dark and deserted streets until I came to a garage, in the forecourt of which stood a taxi with chains fitted to its wheels. I found the driver, and begged him to drive me to Blackpool. He thought I was crazy, but in the end he gamely said he would have a go.

We hadn't gone more than a couple of miles when we ran into a snowdrift. That was the finish; it was already a quarter to seven and I ought to have been at the theatre in ten minutes. We ploughed our way back to a pub and I rang Bertie at the Grand and told him what had happened. He was very cross indeed, and rightly so. My poor understudy, Maurice Baring, who was actually a retired ballet dancer and absolutely terrified of acting, would have to go on for me. Before I could wish him luck, Bertie slammed the phone down.

We managed to turn the taxi round and get back to Ormskirk, where I found a bed. The next day, the snow had cleared somewhat, and the trains were running. The first thing I did on arrival in Blackpool was to buy a bottle of champagne and deliver it to Maurice, who had apparently been brilliant, despite the fact that not more than a couple of dozen patrons had been able to brave their way to the theatre.

I had committed the worst sin in the book. Absolutely nothing, short of death or the most serious illness, excuses anyone from missing a performance. I've never done it since. Of course I should never have risked going to London; I was deeply ashamed of myself, and my colleagues didn't let me forget it for several days.

*

When the tour was over, I found a bed-sitter and moved in with my desk, a cup, a few plates, and a handful of cutlery. We had decided finally to part, and the easiest plan was for me to let Jacqueline divorce me for adultery with a person unknown. I would not contest this, and I would let her keep everything in the house. We would agree a level of maintenance, and I was to have free access to Juliet. It was what we both wanted, and there was no problem about it. I didn't want sides being taken among our friends as to which of us was to blame; if it were advertised as being all my fault it would save a lot of trouble.

So I made myself as comfortable as I could on the top floor of a house in Turnham Green belonging to a Mr and Mrs Pritchard. Mr Pritchard, a kind man in a Fair Isle sweater, used to meet me at the bottom of the stairs when I was going out, tell me I was looking tired, and ask if my bowels were working properly. 'I never have any trouble myself,' he would tell me proudly. 'Seven thirty every morning, set your watch by me.' Just out of interest, I tested him for a couple of days; he was absolutely on the dot.

Prunella's introduction to the theatre – and indeed her early experience – had been quite different from mine. On leaving school she had gone directly to the excellent but short-lived Old Vic School. This was originally situated in the Waterloo Road above the dressing rooms of the Old Vic itself, and in the space that I later came to know well as Rehearsal Room 'A', she was taught by Michel St.Denis,

George Devine, Glen Byam Shaw, Litz Pisk and Jani Strasser. Her first actual job was at the other Old Vic, in Bristol, as an acting ASM. She did a pantomime season in Huddersfield, appeared in two films, *Laxdale Hall* and *Hobson's Choice*, and then joined the cast of *The Matchmaker* for the 1955 Edinburgh Festival, transferring to the Theatre Royal Haymarket and then to Broadway.

While in New York she attended classes at the Herbert Berghof Studio with the great American actress and teacher Uta Hagen, who was to become her lifelong guru. Back in England, Pru went to Stratford for the 1956 season and then joined the Oxford Playhouse Company under the direction of Frank Hauser.

All this had brought her into contact with people, conditions and attitudes markedly different from those to which I myself had become used. She set to work gently divesting me of the rather buttoned-up, determinedly middle-aged, useful-character-actor persona which I seemed to have designed for myself, and encouraged me to think more imaginatively and more selectively about what I really wanted to do. As she was pretty well supporting me at this time, I could afford to take her advice.

Pru lived in a spacious third floor flat in Flood Street, Chelsea, with three other girls who were extremely tolerant of my more than occasional presence. During the day, after my visit to the Labour Exchange, I sometimes did odd jobs about the flat – papering the lavatory, putting up shelves – and became a convenient repository for all the gossip. As each of the girls returned from work, they would pump me for news of the others, and I'd try to satisfy them without giving away too many secrets. 'I think Mary's got a new boy-friend,' I'd tell them, 'she's reading a lot of very strange books.' 'Joan's chucked her job, but she's bought a very expensive skirt.' '*Wait* till you see what Enid's done to her hair.' It was bliss. A friend of the whole group, called Douglas Dryburgh, had a spare room in his own flat round the corner in Tedworth Square, and so I listened to the last of Mr Pritchard's matutinal performances, said goodbye and hauled my few belongings over to Chelsea.

This was 1961, and the warm, heady wind of that decade was already gently beginning to blow. People in the streets looked happier, more aware of themselves. It was suddenly all right to question authority. For years the mandarin self-assurance of Harold Macmillan had made any serious criticism of the Government seem unpatriotic and distasteful. Now, circumstances seemed to demand it. The succession of security crises in the early sixties was greeted by an ecstatic Press delighted suddenly to be let off the leash.

It was treat after treat. First the Portland Spy Ring scandal, which resulted in many officers of the Underwater Warfare Establishment being sent to prison for long periods. Then George Blake of MI6 was exposed as a double agent working for the KGB, and he, too, went to jail. The Government had hardly had time to recover from Blake when it transpired that information had also been passed to the Russians on a regular basis by an Admiralty executive officer, John Vassall, who may or may not have been enjoying a homosexual relationship with a junior minister.

But the best was yet to come. A liaison between the Minister for War John Profumo and the call-girl Christine Keeler might have gone unremarked but for the fact that one of Miss Keeler's other clients happened to be the Russian Defence Attaché. As it was, an M.P. called George Wigg felt himself obliged to ask a question in the House. Quite what Mr Wigg fancied these three people talked about in bed is difficult to imagine, but the fat was fairly in the fire. The Prime Minister asked Profumo whether there was any truth in the allegations. Profumo said that there wasn't, and was subsequently found to have lied. The lie was popularly supposed not only to have brought about his own downfall, but that of Macmillan himself, as well as hastening that of the whole Conservative Government. In more recent years we have observed that a minister's 'being economical with the truth' no longer need have catastrophic results, and I've always felt that poor Mr Profumo suffered from having been born ahead of his time.

It is often said nowadays that 'if you remember the sixties, you weren't *in* them'. I don't know what this means, quite. I may not have been 'in' in the sense that I wasn't stoned all the time. I never offered people a flower at a tube station with the instruction to smile. I didn't go to Khatmandu thinking I was doing the residents a favour by singing to them and eating all their rice. I loved the Beatles, but I missed out on the Rolling Stones, and the kaftan which in a misguided moment I bought in Carnaby Street hardly came out of the wardrobe.

I did, nevertheless, identify with all that was going on. At the time, I felt that the establishment of comprehensive schools, in an effort to clear up the class-distinctive anomalies of the education system, was long overdue. The sexual revolution of hippiedom cleared the air of a lot of silly inhibition – even if the sharing of common ground between the genders often meant sharing clothes, hairstyles and identities.

The cardinal thing of which I became aware was that we had to concern ourselves with the welfare and interests of other individuals, other sections of society, other races, other nations. Very often this manifested itself in absurdly pretentious and impractical ways, but the impulse was right, and it did bind all sorts of unlikely people together in a woolly but agreeable liberal concensus. Of course, we didn't have to *do* anything. We applauded Marcuse's mobilisation of the student body to revolt against capitalism, and we identified with the outraged opposition to the Vietnam War. At a safe distance from Parisian students and American Servicemen, we felt pleased with ourselves for giving them the nod of moral approval.

In this sunny climate, even the Labour Exchange seemed a brighter place. Instead of a dingy confrontation with weary bureaucracy it became a congenial Friday morning club, where one met old friends and strolled with them across Chadwick Street to drink a little of the Government's largesse.

In fact I quite missed those Friday mornings when I got my next job, an invitation from the Everyman Theatre Cheltenham to go and direct, unsurprisingly, *Simple Spymen*. Pru and I booked into a hotel during rehearsals, because it was here that it had been arranged I was to be found *in flagrante delicto* for purposes of the divorce.

The prior arrangements had been conducted in the most civilised manner between myself and the enquiry agent employed by Jacqueline's solicitor. There had at first been some difficulty about his getting to Cheltenham, and I suggested that perhaps I could save him the trouble by providing evidence that could be noticed by the chambermaid, from whom he could later obtain a statement.

No, that wouldn't do at all. Hotels, he told me, gave strict instructions to their chambermaids that they were to see and hear nothing – they didn't want their staff going off to give evidence in the divorce court when they should have been making the beds. So we finally fixed a day when the agent could come and surprise us, but unfortunately the earliest train he could catch from Paddington would arrive just after Pru had to leave the hotel to go up to London for the day. However, this apparently was in no way a problem. The physical presence of 'Miss X' as he insisted on calling her, was not obligatory – nor, for the matter of that, was mine. 'Twin indentations on the pillow will suffice,' he said, 'though perhaps an item of ladies' night apparel would just serve to clinch matters.'

I checked the train for him, we exchanged cordial wishes, and the next day Pru went out to Marks and Spencers and bought a matter-clinching class of nightgown. The following morning I draped it over the bed, thumped the pillow twice and went to rehearsal.

In the fullness of time my decree nisi came through. The only small rift in the amicable relations that existed between all parties was when Leila, suddenly down on her luck, brought a case against me to raise the maintenance I was paying her daughter. I was perfectly ready to increase it a little, but Leila, having been misled about my financial situation, demanded much more, and we went to court. Charles Ettinger, my solicitor, an old friend from the law department at the Polytechnic, had briefed a young man named Greville Janner, later a QC, then a distinguished MP, and now in the House of Lords. He was very good, even then, and we won our case.

Jacqueline and I remained in touch until, years later, she re-married and she and her husband went to live in South Wales. Her health gradually deteriorated, and the various medications she was prescribed seemed only to produce more and more troublesome side-effects. In 1995 her unhappy life came to an end in a hospital in Pontypool.

Our daughter Juliet went to Pru's old boarding school, Moira House in Eastbourne. We saw her regularly during the holidays, and when she left school she came to live with us for some years before setting up on her own. She married a teacher, and has two children, and they are all wonderful, but I regret more than anything in the world the years of my daughter's life that I lost; that essential time between the ages of five and ten, when a father and daughter should be such companions and discover all manner of things together. Those years are irreplaceable, and I feel them as a great hole into which even now I stare blankly, every time we meet.

Chapter Nine

*P*eter Hall, in 1960, had done something which publicly and professionally was about to alter the whole concept of classical theatre in this country.

As the young heir apparent of the Stratford Memorial Theatre, he had suddenly found himself, with the departure of Glen Byam Shaw and the gentle stepping aside of Anthony Quayle, in charge of the place. He set to work to convince the Stratford Governors of three things: first, the need for a permanent acting company in place of the current seasonal engagement of stars and supporting actors, ('My heritage is made up of ghosts and legends', he told the press); second, that this company should perform not only at Stratford, but in an associated theatre in London, all the year round, both in classical and modern work; and thirdly, now that the long-drawn-out plans for a National Theatre were at last coming to fruition, this was the moment to put in a parallel request for public subsidy. Stratford, at that time, had to generate all its own income.

The important artistic argument was that every actor in the new company would be equally at home with modern text and classical verse. One would inform the other. So the Royal Shakespeare Company, as it now was, bought a lease on the Aldwych Theatre in London, to which some of the productions from the previous year's Stratford season would be transferred, to be slotted in with the modern repertoire.

Before long it began to be felt that there were not enough auditoria for everything the company could and should be producing under its new mandate. In 1962, an experimental RSC season of new plays, mixed with a few revivals, was presented at the tiny Arts Theatre in Great Newport Street. I managed to get a part – three very small parts really – in the first play of the season, *Nil Carborundum* by Henry Livings. It was, I thought, a very funny though rather chaotically written mockery of life in the Air Force, that suffered by comparison with Arnold Wesker's very successful *Chips with Everything*, which dealt with the same subject and opened at practically the same time. Our play was distinguished by a memorable performance by Nicol Williamson as a frantic, cowardly, mendacious RAF cook.

I hadn't imagined that this would lead to anything further with the company, so I went straight from this to the New Theatre, Bromley, to play Lord Augustus Lorton in *Lady Windermere's Fan*. While I was rehearsing, Clifford Williams, with whom I had earlier shared a windmill in Canterbury, sent me the script of a play called *Afore Night Come*, which was to be the third play in the RSC Arts Theatre season, and offered me a small part. I read it, and cheekily thought I was quite well suited to another much better part, so I wrote to Clifford saying so. To my immense surprise, he agreed. The part I turned down was played in the end by David Warner, so that was all right.

David Rudkin's *Afore Night Come* was one of the most astonishing plays to emerge from the confused but exciting tangle of new writing being produced, or striving to be produced, in the various small experimental theatres that were opening all over London. The play is set in a Worcestershire pear orchard at picking time and, in what feels at first like a documentary on rural labour, we are introduced to the resident workers: Spens, the foreman, Mrs Trevis, who packs the fruit, and the local, closely-knit team of regular pickers. Three supplementary piece-workers, a Birmingham teddy boy, a sensitive and embarrassed student, and a loquacious elderly Irish tramp join what Alan Brien in his review called the Stone Age Mafia.

The pickers move among the trees with their pouches full of pears, unload them to be packed, and go off again. Banter is exchanged, but as the day wears on this gives way to brooding resentment directed against two of the strangers. Work slackens, there is a growing feeling of unease in the orchard. The sky threatens thunder. Picking, by popular consent, is abandoned in favour of cutting up bicycle tyres to make strips for binding the trees. Knives come out, and the slashing of tyres goes on relentlessly while the Irishman sits and complains about the headache that has prevented him from doing any work. The foreman quietly slips away to attend to something else. One by one, others of the group drift off, leaving only the three men with knives. The stage darkens as a helicopter looms overhead, spraying pesticide, and the men seize hold of the Irishman and ritually decapitate him behind a tree. The body is cleared away, the foreman returns, the siren sounds the knell of parting day, the ancient gods of the Black Country are assuaged, and the men put their coats on, mount their bicycles and go off home.

That the play made such an impact was to a great extent due its director. None of the cast, which included Peter McEnery, Freddie Jones, John Nettleton and Doris Hare, had ever come across anything quite like it before. Clifford tackled the play one layer at a time; the mechanics of pear-picking, the social milieu, the psychological condition of the characters and lastly the elusive poetry of the dialogue. It was difficult for me to emerge from rehearsal each afternoon still beneath its dark influence, catch the train to Bromley, put on white tie and tails and try to scintillate in *Lady Windermere's Fan*.

Not unexpectedly, before the opening night the playwright found himself in conflict with the Lord Chamberlain's Office. People used to be very scornful and resentful about the Lord Chamberlain, but at least he wielded an institutional form of censorship, which kept at bay those sometimes deliberately destructive people who sought to have productions stopped through private prosecution. I knew only one of the Lord Chamberlain's Readers, a charming and liberal-minded man who always made a distinction in sensitive areas between what was natural and what he felt to be gratuitous.

He could not, however, in any circumstances permit the word *fuck*. A number of characters in the play – Spens, the foreman in particular – used the word rather a lot. There was some argument over this, but in the end Rudkin suggested the substitution of an invented word, *firk*. This was agreed, and the alteration made in the prompt book each time it occurred. As spoken in Worcestershire dialect the words were of course indistinguishable. His Lordship surely must have known this and enjoyed the joke.

Not having been asked to be in any more of the plays in the Arts Theatre season, I looked around desperately for something that might offer me a regular salary and allow me to stay put for a while. I had done two or three things on radio, and loved the medium. Could I perhaps join the BBC Drama Repertory Company? I applied for, and was granted, an audition. I had no difficulty in selecting the usual variety of texts to prepare – Shakespeare, Oscar Wilde, John Osborne etc., but I wanted also to find something that was original and funny, and here my invention failed me until one day, browsing in a second-hand bookshop, I accidentally knocked to the ground an early edition of the St John Ambulance Manual for First Aid. It fell open at the chapter *Rules for the Recovery of a Person Suffering from Electric Shock*. I picked it up. (*1*), it said, *Turn off the source of supply*. It went on to advise: (*2*), *Insulate yourself from the floor. If you are not wearing rubber-soled shoes, stand on a piece of ordinary plate glass or oiled silk. Hay or straw is also effective*. It was irresistible. I rewrote the chapter in the form of a First Aid lecture, included it in the audition, and romped home.

I spent a very happy year in the Drama Rep. In those days there were forty-two of us, including among the older members some of the great names of radio's Golden Age. As well as actual Drama, we were used for all manner of things: documentary features, stories, poetry programmes, satirical comedy, schools broadcasts, variety shows, and every aspect of the World Service. It was wonderful to work on such a vast range of material, and to speak aloud some of the best writing in the English language. It also gave me the chance to play a number of handsome, lusted-after juveniles – an opportunity for some reason rarely afforded me in other media.

Over the years, the Drama Rep was scaled down, renamed the Radio Drama Company, and in 1998 virtually scrapped – retaining simply a core of six graduate students as a form of in-field training. Among the profession there was a lot of breast-beating about this, in which I didn't absolutely join. One of the great advantages of radio is that it is rehearsed and recorded over a period of a couple of days or so, and therefore a producer can call upon very distinguished and well-known actors to fit a broadcast into their very busy schedules. To a great extent these actors were being kept out of radio by the large and ubiquitous forces of the Rep. There was for a long time an assumption that microphone technique was a very special art that could only be learned slowly by a gifted few, but now that this myth has been exploded, and casting is more general, I'm sure radio drama is the better for it.

The BBC Club, which occupied the ground floor of the Langham building opposite Broadcasting House after the closure of the famous old hotel and before the opening of the present one, was the lunch-time haunt of the Features Department, a remarkable collection of many of the best, and some of the most eccentric, minds in this country: poets, philosophers, historians, economists, scientists, political thinkers and senior journalists. Louis MacNeice was still in the Department when I was there, with Terence Tiller, Laurence Gilliam, Douglas Cleverdon, Nesta Pain, Joe Burroughs – a tweed-jacketed, whisky-imbibing assembly of formidable intelligence.

There were some intellectual heavyweights among the Drama Department, too: Martin Esslin, Hallam Tennyson, H.B.Fortuin, Michael Bakewell, and the legendary R.D. Smith. Legendary because of his unorthodox behaviour during a production; you might find one morning that half your part had been given away to someone Reggie Smith had just met in the bar of the George round the corner, who was down on his luck. On the day of an important rugby match Reggie might well pop off to Twickenham in the middle of a recording, leaving matters in the hands of his trusted studio manager.

I have one particular memory of Reggie's unfailing kindness to fellow professionals. When I was working at the Royal Theatre, Northampton, the Artistic Director was Lionel Hamilton, who, by 1963, had been there for seventeen years. He was very popular and did his job so well that most people, including Lionel himself, assumed he would be staying for the duration of his working life. However, a new appointee to the theatre's Board of Directors had got wind of Lionel's domestic arrangements – he lived with a male chiropodist – and felt that the theatre's civic educational role was jeopardised by such a person being allowed to continue in such a position. Somehow this man talked the rest of the Board round, and in September 1963, Lionel was relieved of the post he had held for so long.

As well as a director, he was an actor – of, it must be said, the Old School – and I went up to Northampton to see the last night of his final production, *An Ideal Husband*, in which he also played Lord Goring; somewhat too old for the part, and with quite a lot of rather orange make-up, but speaking the Wildean epigrams impeccably. Two days later, Monday, I happened to be walking down St. Martin's Lane, when I saw a rather bemused-looking man carrying a raincoat and a suitcase, standing outside the Salisbury and wondering whether or not to go in. It was Lionel. I went over, took him inside and bought him a drink. He confessed that he no longer knew anyone in London, but had come up to find work and somewhere to live. Apart from holidays, he had hardly been out of Northampton for seventeen years. He was in despair, and there was really nothing practical I could do to help. Suddenly I caught sight of Reggie Smith at the bar. I brought him over, introduced the two men and explained Lionel's present situation. Within minutes, Reggie had found him a broadcast for the following week, given him the name of someone who might have a flat, and invited him to a one-day match at Lords'. In short he had handed poor Lionel a new lease of life.

*

Pru had been attending a series of classes given in London by the American director Charles Marowitz, as a result of which he asked her to be in a play he was putting on for a series of Sunday nights at the British Drama League in Fitzroy Square. This was an intriguing four-hander called *The Trigon*, by James Broome Lynne, and there was in it the character of a pathetic over-age boy scout which Pru flatteringly felt would be ideal for me. I was still under contract to the BBC, but I could manage it if we rehearsed in my free evenings.

Charles and I met, and eyed each other warily. He was a tall, dark-bearded, Method-trained, iconoclastic New Yorker, who seemed to live entirely on the sustenance provided by something called a Chocolate Whippsy. To Charles, 'BBC Drama Rep' were the three dirtiest words in the English language. For my part, I had a lot of difficulty stomaching his rehearsal terminology. 'I think you should exchange a focus with Anthony' he would say. 'You mean you think we should look at each other?' I would reply testily. To his proposal that we bring about a 'physical reorientation', I would ask if he meant he wished me to *move*.

Things carried on like this for a few evenings until we both started to laugh. I think in the end Charles learned a little from me, while I learned an inordinate amount from him, for which I shall ever be grateful. The play aroused a certain degree of interest, the critics were very generous about the performances; and there was talk about a revival, which indeed came to fruition the following spring.

I could have stayed on at the BBC for a second year if I'd wanted to, but *The Trigon* had revived my appetite for the theatre. At last I had found myself a decent agent, Ronnie Waters of Al Parker Ltd., and he put me up for a part in Robert Bolt's new play *Gentle Jack*, to be produced by Tennents. I was summoned to read for the part of Hubert, the village idiot.

Auditions for this prestigious management were very smart affairs. The girls arrived in expensive dresses, the men in suits. I thought, this is ridiculous, I really can't turn up in a suit as the village idiot. I rang my father, as a Tennents habitué, for advice. He saw my point, but advised caution. In the end I threw this to the winds and arrived at the stage door of the Haymarket Theatre in a pair of patched trousers, an old green pullover and grubby plimsolls.

The stage door keeper was most reluctant to let me in, and only did so after a lot of telephoning. There was a row of chairs backstage, on each of which sat an actor in a suit. I sat at the end of the row, under their curious and resentful gaze. My turn finally came, and as I walked on to the stage there was an audible gasp from the darkened auditorium. No supplicant had appeared like that in front of 'Binkie' Beaumont and his associates, ever. I needn't have bothered to speak my lines; the part was mine as soon as I walked on to the stage.

Gentle Jack was a strange, allegorical piece, and the fact that it was not judged to be a success when it opened at the Queen's was I think due mainly to the mistake of casting Dame Edith Evans in what was not actually the central role of the play. The real protagonist was the character played by Michael Bryant; but Dame Edith's status, billing and gorgeous costumes skewed the audience's perception of the dramatic argument. Dame Edith knew this, and was unhappy, but when she voiced her concern to Binkie he just sent her off to Hardie Amies for another £500 worth of pink paper taffeta, of which there was more than enough in the production already.

Another apparently curious piece of casting, which, however, was on its way to working brilliantly, was Kenneth Williams in the role of Jacko, Michael Bryant's Dionysic alter ego. Kenneth began playing him as a playful, destructive androgyne, which was chilling and absolutely what was needed for the play. But during the prior-to-London fortnight at Brighton he was got at by *Carry On* fans who couldn't make head or tail of the play and appeared to feel that Kenneth had cheated them. Self-confidence was never his strong point, and he started camping up the performance, which of course distorted the play even further.

The director, Noel Willman, was a gloomy man made more gloomy by each of these difficulties. He conscientiously patrolled the dressing room corridors every evening after the curtain fell, with notes on the night's performance. John Phillips and Noel Howlett, two very senior and distinguished actors who shared a dressing room would, when they heard their director coming upstairs, run and lock themselves in the gentlemen's lavatory. Willman would knock on the lavatory door, but there would be no sound from within. 'Come out', he would call. Then, 'Listen, I know you're in there. I've got some notes for you. John. Noel. Come on. Don't be silly.' After a moment he would sigh and give up, and as they heard his steps retreating down the stairs the two of them would tumble out, giggling like schoolboys.

I was sorry that this should be the only chance I had to work with Edith Evans; I had admired her so much in the past, and this play showed her neither at her best nor her happiest.

On the first night she gave us all book tokens, and during our final week (not so very long afterwards) she invited us into her dressing room so that she could sign the books we had bought. On the flyleaf of mine, she wrote, 'To Timothy Webb, with best wishes, Edith Evans.' I thanked her, and took it away to my own dressing room up three flights of stairs. A few minutes later there was a knock at my door. It was Dame Edith's faithful dresser.

'She went and put the wrong name on your book, didn't she,' she said. 'I was watching her do it. Give it here, I'll get her to change it.'

I told her it was all right, it didn't matter a bit.

'No, give it me,' she insisted. 'She might see it on the posters, and remember, and then I shall get it in the neck.'

I surrendered the book, and minutes later it came back with two neat lines through the word 'Webb' and the name 'West' penned underneath. The correction was initialled 'E.E.', like a cheque. I still treasure it.

One other thing had happened during the rehearsals for *Gentle Jack.* Pru and I had decided we wanted to spend the rest of our lives together, so in the October of 1963 we got married, with just two witnesses, at Chelsea Registry Office. After a family lunch at Prunier's (alas, no more) we departed for a slightly-less-than-two-day honeymoon at the Compleat Angler in Marlow.

Foolishly I was quite unaware that this was probably the most celebrated venue for illicit weekends in the entire Home Counties. You could interleave every menu with copies of your marriage lines, and cover the stairs in confetti; but the waiter would still murmur with a conspiratorial wink, 'I think *the lady* has already retired *upstairs,* sir.'

Chapter Ten

We spent our first married Christmas with Pru's parents at their cottage in Abinger, near Dorking. Although scarcely more than thirty miles from Charing Cross, Abinger and its surroundings still feel like real country. This is very much due to the strict vigilance of Patrick Evelyn, the descendant of the great 17th-century diarist John Evelyn of Wootton, and heir to the considerable Evelyn Estate. He is very much in evidence locally, and there is a distinctly feudal feel to the whole area.

I adored Pru's parents, who welcomed me into the family in the most heartwarming way. Her father, John Illingworth (Pru had professionally used her mother's name of Scales, for the sake of euphony) was an ex-army officer, who had been pensioned off under the Geddes axe in 1929, had re-enlisted for World War II, was for a time a salesman for Tootal Fabrics, and now worked for a local insurance company. He was a pacific, self-effacing man, determined to avoid taking sides in any question of conflict until he had studied the matter fully. A friend was once telling us a terrible story of someone she knew who had gone into a Kenyan Game Park, and who, having very foolishly got out of his car to offer an elephant a bun, was picked up bodily by the said elephant and dashed to the ground, breaking his skull. We all expressed dutiful horror and sympathy except John, who held up a hand in gentle remonstrance, saying: 'Yes but my darling my darling my darling my darling. Look at it from the elephant's point of view.'

Pru's mother had written some successful children's books, and had been an actress before she married John. At one time a member of William Armstrong's Liverpool Playhouse company with Robert Donat and Marjorie Fielding, she now displayed her talents occasionally for the Westcott Players, a local amateur group run by Greville Poke (who became chairman of the English Stage Company) and his wife, the actress Patricia Laurence. Pru's mother got on very well with my own mother, and provided a source of advice and comfort when my father for a time found himself a little friend in Paddington, and my mother went off to work as a personal assistant to an elderly retired solicitor in Cheltenham. This situation didn't last long – my parents were back together again within a few months, in a small cottage between Brighton and Hove, where they spent the remainder of their lives.

Richard Briers and Pru were currently recording a very popular television sit-com by Richard Waring called *Marriage Lines.* I was in one episode, playing the man who sold them their flat. As I read the script I was beginning to feel that this character was quite interesting enough to become a regular member of the team, until I reached Richard's line, 'Poor Bob, he's gone to South Africa for *seven years*,' so that was me out of the way. Fortunately I was still doing a lot of radio, which kept me going until further news came about the proposed revival of *The Trigon*. The astonishing tidings were that no less a person than Binkie Beaumont had agreed to produce it. The bizarre mental picture of Beaumont, great mogul of the West End establishment and elegant high priest of traditional showbiz, in partnership with Marowitz, the seditious black-sweatered consumer of Chocolate Whippsies, defied the imagination.

Things were indeed not easy between them, and were not helped by the presence of Binkie's American co-producer Margaret Hewes. Hewes had been responsible for choosing our designer, an elderly artist called Sir Francis Rose, who went about Brighton in a scarlet-lined opera cloak with a silver-headed cane. He had a fascinating past. Known at one time as the Plaything of Paris, rich gifts had been showered on him plentifully by sundry older admirers. He had known Gertrude Stein, and for him she had inscribed the words 'A Rose is a Rose is a Rose' on all his teacups. He was reputed to have been in bed with Ernst Roehm in Munich in 1934 on the night of Hitler's surprise round-up of dissidents, and fled through the sky-light and over the rooftops. Altogether an unusual choice of designer for a play set in a conventional first-floor flat in Crouch End.

He was a rather alarming man in many ways; his temper would suddenly spin out of control and he would squeal exotic obscenities at all and sundry. On the night of our first performance at Wimbledon, where we opened, he suddenly turned up in the wings with three canvasses that he had painted himself, and demanded to be allowed to hang them up on the set. The curtain, in the current fashion, was already up when the house came in, and the performance was due to start. Waiting in the opposite wing, I could hear raised voices.

STAGE MANAGER: Sir Francis, no! You cannot go on the stage. The audience is already in – the performance is about to start!

SIR FRANCIS: Damn the performance! Damn the performance! Bum, bum, BUM!

We played a week in Wimbledon, a week in Brighton, then Binkie decided the best place for us was the Arts, where we played for three weeks, and that was it. In the meantime, the RSC had decided to include a revival of *Afore Night Come* in their Aldwych season and, as I wasn't available, had cast someone else in my original part. I don't know what happened next exactly, but they suddenly decided they didn't like my replacement, and grabbed me back ten days before the opening.

I stayed on with the RSC until 1966. At the Aldwych, as well as the Rudkin play, I understudied the part of Goldberg in Harold Pinter's *The Birthday Party* – a part I didn't actually get to play for another thirty five years – played the Doctor in Roger Vitrac's *Victor*, a lunatic schoolmaster in *The Marat/Sade*, Pilia Borza in Marlowe's *The Jew of Malta*, Master Page in *The Merry Wives of Windsor* and, in David Mercer's short play *The Governor's Lady*, a Colonial Governor who gradually turned into a gorilla.

The season, which included Samuel Beckett's *Endgame* in addition to those mentioned, had its philosophical genesis in Peter Brook's Theatre of Cruelty programme, and became known in the media as the Dirty Plays Season. Emile Littler, a Governor of the RSC and a member of its Executive Council, issued a press statement deploring the Company's artistic policy, finishing with the words, 'I don't know what the Arts Council think of these wretched Aldwych plays, but as a taxpayer I resent my money being spent in this manner.'

Littler's behaviour provoked a sharp rebuke from his Chairman, Sir Fordham Flower, accusing him of disloyalty and improper conduct. However, Peter Cadbury, of the ticket agency Keith Prowse, threw in his lot with Littler, as did Sir Denis Lowson, the ex-Lord Mayor of London, who was also an RSC Governor. Others on the Board, however, expressed total support for Peter Hall. The battle was taken up gleefully by the press, and each new cry of disgust provoked a flurry of activity at the theatre box office, though presumably not at the Keith Prowse bureaux, where patrons must of course have been demurely turned away. A sober and responsible note was finally struck by a consortium of drama critics who, in a joint letter to *The Times,* expressed their belief that the Company and its present work were 'an absolutely vital ingredient in our theatrical life, and indeed serve a much wider national purpose.'

I loved the Aldwych. It was always bursting at the seams, trying to cope with the demands of four or five designers and as many lighting designers, in a repertoire which required a change-over practically every night. Some of the productions had come from Stratford and, having been designed for that much larger stage, had to be modified and chopped about for London. There was precious little wing-space, and storage must have been a nightmare. The different smells associated with each play – peat from the floor in *Afore Night Come,* sweat from the bodies in *The Marat/Sade,* fresh scene-paint from Ralph Koltai's Gruyère-cheese-like set for *The Jew of Malta,* which was always getting chipped – had no chance to disperse before they were augmented by the next.

I shared Dressing Room 4 with John Nettleton, Ken Wynne, Bryan Pringle, Michael Williams, Clifford Rose and Paul Dawkins, though of course we were not all there on the same nights. Paul Dawkins had joined the company to play Spens, the foreman, in *Afore Night Come,* and he was superb in the part, but the directors weren't at all sure what to do with him for the rest of the season. He had been given the very thankless role of Admiral Martin del Bosco in *The Jew of Malta;* thankless because he had only one scene with one very boring speech, and made more thankless because for this brief appearance he had to apply a moustache and beard, and put on over his doublet and breeches a steel breastplate, greaves and brassets and a helmet with a huge yellow plume.

It took him rather a long time to get into all this, and we knew it would also take him a while to get down the stairs to the stage in all that armour, so we always felt apprehensive about his actually making his entrance in time. Paul was constantly laying plans to give up the profession and make his fortune with some brilliantly useful invention, about which he would discourse in great detail, holding a liberally-charged glass of Bell's whisky in one hand while struggling to buckle his greaves with the other.

'Gas-driven road vehicles,' he would declare. 'It's got to happen. Balloons on the top of cars. Producer-gas; we had it in the war, we can have it again.'

'Paul, you've had your call, you know; hadn't you better hurry up?' one of us would say, helping him with his greaves.

'The Edinburgh Police Force,' he would continue, 'has already expressed strong interest. In fact, I expect to hear from the Superintendent of their Motorised Section tomorrow morning.'

An urgent call from the prompt corner, and we would clamp his grotesque helmet over his brows, push him out of the door, hear him clump sedately down the stairs and hope that he got there.

At the next performance, we would ask how things had developed with the scheme.

'Producer-gas? No. Political problems. A tie-up with the oil companies. No. *Jigsaws.* Jigsaws for hospitals. Mass-produced, very cheaply, I'll get a grant from the NHS – '

'Mr Dawkins on stage please, Mr Dawkins on stage *at once,* please.'

Clatter clatter clatter. We would listen to the tannoy, and after a pause we would hear a résumé of Paul's speech being delivered by the unidentifiable voice of some attendant knight. After a moment the door would open, and there would be Paul.

'Bugger. Missed it again. Yes, as I was saying, save the nurses a lot of trouble entertaining the patients . . . Not much point in my staying for the curtain call, do you think?' he would muse, peeling off the beard and moustache, 'I mean, no-one's actually seen me this evening.'

Paul was not asked back the following season. I went once to his flat in Putney, which he had papered throughout with the first four books of the Old Testament, written in ball-point pen on Bronco toilet paper. His wife moved away and he began to drink quite heavily. I think he did a little work as an extra on television, but nothing in the theatre, and the last time I saw him he was living in a hostel for the homeless in Charing Cross, where I heard shortly afterwards that he had died.

*

John Blatchley's production of *The Merry Wives of Windsor*, the last main play of the Aldwych season, was directed, perhaps mistakenly, as a pantomime, with sets and costumes by the cartoonist André François and pit-band music by Malcolm Williamson. Pantomime is all about big things, freely expressed – love, hate, joy, terror – whereas *Merry Wives* is essentially a comedy of parochial bourgeois attitudes. Bill Alexander's 1984 production, set in the keeping-up-with-the-Joneses 1950s, hit it exactly right.

So in spite of a first-rate cast that included Brenda Bruce, Elizabeth Spriggs, Ian Richardson, Clive Swift and a Mrs Quickly by Doris Hare who wasn't entirely happy with Shakespearean text but who, when she forgot her lines, would put her hands on her hips and say 'I warrant you!' very loudly, the show was taken out of the repertoire quite quickly. So quickly, in fact, that when poor John Blatchley returned from something he'd been doing in the United States and took some influential friends to the Aldwych to see his production, they found themselves watching *The Marat/Sade* – nobody had thought to inform him.

Of course *Marat* was the great hit of the season, and they crammed in as many performances as they could. I personally find the play a fair old load of rubbish, though a wonderful opportunity for an imaginative director; and Peter Brook rose magnificently to the challenge. So much has been written about (and by) Brook, that any further attempt of mine, based on very limited experience, to examine his methods and beliefs would be impertinent. I will only say that working with him was an unforgettable experience, and one to which I was at first reluctant to give myself fully.

Possibly a director's greatest attribute is a low boredom threshold. Peter Brook possesses the lowest on record. He is never completely satisfied with himself, his actors, or the theatre in general. His need is constantly to innovate – if something seems to work, he fears it must already be out of date, and a new and more powerful means should be found to convey the same thing, or perhaps not the same thing, maybe something better and more surprising. This can be exhausting for all concerned, but very often the struggle is rewarded by a piece of work that comes to be recognised as a milestone in the development of the theatre.

He became co-director of the Royal Shakespeare Company in 1962, and brought, from the *Theatre of Cruelty* season, a group of actors –

Glenda Jackson was one – who became the nucleus of the *Marat* company.

These people were already well-versed in his ways of working, and the rest of us who were brought in to swell their ranks were sometimes made (though never by Brook himself) to feel like interlopers and heretics. Most of us were playing the inmates of the Asylum at Charenton, and my instinct would have been to seek medical guidance about specific forms of lunacy and the way they manifested themselves, before deciding on a characterisation. The chosen course among the Theatre of Masochism Group, as they were known by some, was to explore their own personalities for violent traits that could be developed and exaggerated to the point of dangerous madness.

This was certainly an exciting process to watch; and Brook fed and encouraged it, only calling a halt when one girl, simulating an epileptic fit, seemed on the point of succumbing to a real one.

After Brook's radiant *Midsummer Night's Dream* of 1970, he founded the Centre International de Recherche Théâtrale, moving away from text-based theatre towards mime and other cross-cultural forms before eventually settling at the Théâtre des Bouffes du Nord in Paris. The English theatre is the poorer for his self-imposed exile.

*

The preponderance of *Marat* and *Jew of Malta* performances at the end of the Aldwych season meant that for the last six weeks Glenda Jackson, Tony Church and I, who were to be in the coming Stratford season, had to drive up there after the performance on most evenings in order to rehearse the following morning, and then get back to London for the show at night. The Company put us up at the Arden Hotel, and paid for a table d'hôte supper when we got in at 1 a.m. One night, I considered that after having worked a 14-hour day I was entitled to half a bottle of claret with my meal. For fully eight months, a battle about who should pay for this wine continued to be waged between the RSC Financial Controller and myself. In October I finally capitulated and brought to his office, in lieu of money, an identical half bottle of wine. This apparently threw the annual audit into deep confusion, and I was delighted to hear it.

The previous Histories season had been a triumph, and it must have been difficult to know how to follow it. Paul Scofield was coming to do *Timon of Athens* in the autumn, and Peter Hall was planning a *Hamlet* with David Warner. *The Jew of Malta* was being brought up from the Aldwych to play back-to-back with *The Merchant of Venice*, Eric Porter playing both Shakespeare's Jew and Marlowe's villainous prototype. There would be a revival of Clifford Williams' ever popular *Comedy of Errors*, and the season would begin with the not-often performed *Love's Labour's Lost*, directed by John Barton.

Central to Peter Hall's idea of building a company that dealt equally well with classical and modern texts was a defined attitude to verse-speaking. When he formed the Royal Shakespeare Company in 1960, the first person he took on board as Associate Director, with a special responsibility for training the company in the speaking of verse, was John Barton. John had been two years senior to Peter at Cambridge, but they had both come under the influence of the foremost authority on Shakespearean text, George 'Dadie' Rylands. Both men had acted in Marlowe Society productions for Rylands, but whereas Peter Hall emerged from Cambridge as a natural director, Barton appeared at first as the non-executive academic of the organisation.

The old-fashioned style of verse delivery, wherein meaning was sometimes sacrificed to music, had largely been superseded in recent years by a directly opposite approach. 'Look, loves,' the young Shakespearean star of the 50's seemed to be saying, 'the chap wrote this play in 1603 – I can't help that. In those days they wrote in verse, for some reason, but don't worry, stick with me and you'd never know.'

A new approach, a new philosophy, was certainly overdue.

The most important thing I learned from John Barton was that the verse you speak says *exactly* what you mean. Your character's feelings, desires and intentions could be conveyed fully and truthfully only by those exact words arranged exactly in that form; any alteration at all would manifestly detract from your intention. I loved working with John on his production of *Love's Labour's Lost*, and also on a dialogue between Socrates and Alcibiades in an experimental programme he devised as a prototype for the more far-reaching work on the Ancient Greeks which has now come to fruition as the mammoth Anglo-American project *Tantalus*.

John's otherwise remarkable brain always seemed to have difficulty in monitoring the behaviour of his limbs. He was incapable of crossing a large room without bumping into its one single item of furniture. If there was a small object standing by itself at the far end of a shelf, somehow he would manage to knock it off. Actors remember him walking round and round the rehearsal stage in the Conference Room at Stratford, his notebook in one hand and in the other a chair on which he would occasionally sit for a moment to give notes. The only other object on the stage was John's coffee cup, which he had set down in the middle of the floor, and forgotten. Those present watched in breathless fascination as John's gyrations took him nearer and nearer the target, until the joyous moment when he set one leg of the chair inside the coffee cup and sat down, to a spontaneous round of applause.

Always a heavy smoker, it may be that his disconcerting practice of chewing razor blades during rehearsal was an attempt to wean himself away from the nicotine habit. If so, it clearly didn't work; he was happily able to carry on both activities simultaneously all the time I was there.

In those days there were a number of actors at Stratford who were employed simply as spear carriers, attendant lords; those that will do to swell a progress, start a scene or two. Among these was an elderly man with the face and bearing of an infirm, shuffling old bishop, who had become accepted as a perennial member of the company. His name was Terence Greenidge. Terence had left Oxford in the early thirties with high honours, and had been acclaimed as possessing one of the finest minds of his year. I don't know much about his early days, but at some point he had suffered a very serious mental breakdown, and doctors had performed a frontal lobotomy. This, though it had put an end to any thoughts of a serious academic or theatrical career, left him capable enough to carry out whatever he was called upon to do in the season, and he did it with an unfailing good grace. Living friendless and on his own, he needed people to talk to; and discovering that we shared a passion for old railways, I proposed a Sunday outing to explore the abandoned track of the old Stratford-on-Avon and Midland Junction line.

It was a beautiful day; we took some sandwiches and a bottle of wine, and with the aid of maps and photographs we traced the path of the old railway, identifying the sites of previous stations, level crossings and signal boxes. As we walked, Terence told me of a film he had written and directed while an undergraduate; it was the very funny story of a fiendish plot by the Master of Balliol and the Pope to kidnap the Prince of Wales, and starred Elsa Lanchester and Terence himself (then, I'm told, a strikingly handsome young man). He possessed the only extant copy of the film, which he had shown to the entire Stratford company last year, to their great delight.

The things that much concerned Terence in his life were necessarily few, and Income Tax was not among them. Over the years he had got into the habit of destroying unread the dozens of letters and forms sent to him by the Inland Revenue authorities. I didn't find out about this until much later, but shortly after the end of our season together, representatives arrived at his one-room flat in Arden Street to take possession of property to the value of what he owed in back tax. The furniture and fittings belonged to his landlord; he owned virtually nothing beyond his clothes and a few books, including a slim privately-printed volume of his own poetry, *Girls on Railway Stations*. They took those.

In boxes stacked in the bookshelves they found three reels of film. They took those too.

Chapter Eleven

*T*he season stretched on into late November. Fog settled on the Avon, the male swans performed their ritual autumn battle for supremacy, the American tourists went home. We lit a fire in our rented cottage in Tredington and began to think about the future.

At this time, the newspaper critics were being very kind to me. They seemed to like what I did within the company, and commented on my versatility. In the last eighteen months I had played a young Worcestershire pear-picker, a Venetian Jew, a solid Windsor burgher, a disabled Maltese pimp, a lunatic, an elderly Syracusan merchant, a country parson and a gorilla. Now, it's all very well to be versatile in a repertory situation – you can have a rather thin time of it if you're not – but when you hope to convey a clear image of yourself to the profession at large, it actually counts against you.

Also, I had made a dispiriting discovery. James Laurenson, Michael Pennington and I had a very long gap between entrances in the second half of *Timon of Athens,* and we used to fill in the time by going up to the company offices and searching through the waste paper bins for confidential information about future planning, casting, salaries etc. In the days before photocopiers, the secretaries typed all correspondence that had to be circulated on to stencil paper for the Gestetner machine, and after use the perforated stencils were screwed up and thrown away. They were still legible though, and, particularly towards the end of the season when next year's plans were being hatched, the bins yielded a rich fund of information.

Among one such plentiful harvest we found a chart, upon which was listed all the names of the present Stratford company, divided into five columns labelled A,B,C,D and E. The 'A' list was of the undoubted stars of the season, Paul Scofield, Eric Porter, Janet Suzman, Glenda Jackson, Ian Richardson, Peter McEnery. 'B' embraced the principal supporting actors, 'C' was one category down from that, and 'D' one further down still. The 'E' list was the walk-ons, a classification that for reasons of financial restraint and common humanity has long been abandoned.

I found my name listed among the 'D's – useful people for filling a small part. I was appalled. I'm ashamed to say I can't remember in which column my two friends had been placed, but I do recall sitting brokenly in that darkened office, clutching the chart and querulously appealing for justice. It was a scene from a Woody Allen movie. ''D'?' I whimpered. 'Do they really mean 'D'? Well, obviously I wouldn't have expected 'B' – but I did think 'C' at least – is that unreasonable? 'D' . . . I mean, for God's sake, 'D' . . . !'

If this was a true indication of my future within the RSC, it would be time, I thought, to move on. I had already been asked back to the Aldwych to play two small parts in Peter Hall's production of *The Government Inspector*, but nothing else had been suggested. For a little while, I would wait and see.

So I duly waited and saw, but apart from a dramatised reading of Peter Weiss' *The Investigation*, the RSC had nothing further to offer me, and in March we parted company. I was probably being arrogant, but it troubled me that I was finding the parts I played too *easy*; I knew that acting shouldn't be easy, and I wanted some challenges.

I'u had for a long time been friendly with the director Toby Robertson, who had been a contemporary of Peter Hall and John Barton at Cambridge, but had gone his own way, and with Richard Cottrell and Iain Mackintosh was now running Prospect Productions, a company based in Cambridge but with a grant from the Arts Council to tour the country. Prospect were keen on literary theatre: they had just done an adaptation of *Howard's End,* and were now embarking on something rather more complex – a play about the life and work of Dr Samuel Johnson, told in his own words and those of Boswell and others. It relied very much on the device – later used to great effect by David Edgar and Trevor Nunn in *Nicholas Nickleby* – of letting characters set a scene by speaking narration about themselves and their situation, so that the play could at will break all the unities of time, place and action.

Toby came to lunch in our little terrace house in Barnes, and told me about it, and I was excited by the idea of joining the company. I was offered the not terribly interesting part of Sir John Hawkins, one of Johnson's duller biographers, and to go with it, a nice part in Anouilh's *Thieves' Carnival*, with which the Johnson play would run in repertoire.

We began rehearsals. The actor who was supposed to play Johnson was not there – indeed there seemed to be some secrecy about his identity. I was asked to read in for him. He wasn't there the next day either, nor did he appear during the rest of the week. The part was very substantial, Johnson being on stage practically throughout the play, and the rest of the cast were growing very uneasy. Finally Toby turned to me one morning and said briefly, 'Well, I suppose you'd better do it.' So I did. Thus began a sixteen-year involvement – with occasional intervals for rest and refreshment – with the Prospect Theatre Company. I never found out the name of the mysterious absentee thespian; indeed, I secretly began to doubt whether he ever actually existed. If he did, and if he still does, I should like to thank him very warmly.

*

'Isn't it terrible,' I observed to Richard Briers, sitting in his living room around the corner from Queen Charlotte's Maternity Hospital, 'that in these days of medical research, nothing really has been discovered to relieve the pain – the *trauma* – of childbirth?'

'Terrible,' agreed Richard, pouring another whisky for us both.

'I mean,' I went on, stretching out my legs and leaning back in the armchair, 'there's Pru – she's been in there nearly thirty hours now; I've gone through all the heavy breathing with her, I've read to her, she keeps getting contractions, but nothing *happens*. In fact, they told me not to expect anything to happen for ages yet. That's why I came over here.'

Richard, whose house by reason of its position served periodically as a rehabilitation unit for expectant fathers, made a little generous noise expressive of welcome, though in fact it was ten o'clock at night and I had already been there some time.

'Obviously she expects the discomfort, *obviously*, I mean – well, just a small one, thank you – she's read all the books, we've been through all the Erna Wright thing, it's just that to keep thinking it's going to come, you know, and then it *doesn't* . . . I'm going to watch it though, when it does come. Pru's gynaecologist – he's the Registrar – has overruled the Matron, and I'm allowed in. I'm not going to miss it, believe me.'

Meanwhile Pru, being wheeled toward the delivery room, was giving the nurse a list of phone numbers – our house, my parents, my agent – where I might possibly be found. Finally, as she was being placed on the table, she gasped, 'Try Richard Briers . . .'

I got the phone call, ran across Goldhawk Road and into the hospital. As I got out of the lift, a nurse threw a gown over me, added a cap and mask and pushed me into the presence. I was just in time to see a shapeless purple object emerge, and unroll to become this entirely new person called Sam, apparently complete and very clearly of the male sex. It was miraculous. I was ecstatic.

'Very good,' I said. 'No retakes.'

I arrived sleepless at rehearsal next morning, and we went straight into Act Two, to hear Julian Glover (of Lower 2B, Bristol Grammar School, now playing James Boswell) saying: 'Sir, if you had a child, would you bring it up?'

Myself (as JOHNSON): 'Why yes, sir, I would, but I must have all conveniences. If I had no garden, I would make a shed on the roof, and take it there for fresh air. I should feed it, and wash it much, and with warm water to please it, not with cold water to give it pain.'

BOSWELL: 'But, does not heat relax?'

JOHNSON: 'Sir, you are not to suppose that the water is to be *that* hot. I would not *boil* the child.'

The play showed the Great Cham in every mood – expansive, boorish, paternal, melancholy; his devastating wit and unconquerable prejudice covering an awful inner loneliness and religious despair. The axis of the play was of course his relationship with Boswell, who in Julian's hands was not the simple toadying Scots hanger-on sometimes portrayed, but a warm, intelligent, sometimes naive, essentially lubricious, always entertaining companion. The partnership was very dear to us both, and we repeated it over the years in three different versions of the play on stage, and one more on television.

Richard Cottrell directed *Thieves' Carnival*, the other play in the repertoire. There are often problems with Anouilh in this country, but Richard's production contrived to be neither sentimental nor arch. Ben Pearce Higgins had written some attractive music, played on the clarinet by Julian Farrell, and this at one point required Martin Potter, Julian Glover and me to dance. Bill Drysdale, a very nice choreographer, was called in for the occasion.

'Now, Tim,' he began cheerily, 'this is very simple – just like walking, really. Sway back on the first beat, and on the third, step forward with your left foot – no, *left* foot . . . all right, we'll do something even simpler . . . '

He began to smoke rather heavily, and to look very tired. On the fourth day, he didn't turn up, and we never saw him again. I don't think we got it right once, during the whole tour.

Some years later, though, I was staying at Mrs Mackay's boarding house in Manchester, and came down to breakfast one morning to find Bill Drysdale sitting at the table buttering a piece of toast.

'Hello, Bill,' I said. 'Remember me? Timothy West, *Thieves' Carnival?*'

The knife dropped from his nerveless fingers. 'You're not', he whispered faintly, 'in *Ragtime* for the BBC?'

'No, no,' I said. 'I'm doing a serial for Granada.'

His perspiring face broke into a warm smile, and he stood and gratefully shook my hand.

The initial tour of the two plays was very gentle: Brighton, Cambridge, Oxford, Nottingham. It was a very happy time, I think, for everybody. Julian wooed – and subsequently married – the lovely Isla Blair, who was playing Fanny Burney and the ingénue daughter in *Thieves' Carnival*. The Cambridge contingent enjoyed themselves. There was a strong academic flavour about Prospect, predominately light-blue – the Company Manager had read medicine at Cambridge, and the master carpenter mediaeval Latin – and we were entertained by various members of King's College far into the night.

After Nottingham we were given a fortnight off before starting on a second tour, and Pru and I went to Deya in Majorca, where one night we sat in Robert Graves' garden and watched a play he had written about cannabis-smuggling on the island. The smugglers were the heroes of the play, and many of the performers, a mixture of villagers and regular tourists, were agreeably stoned throughout.

It was the only visible chance we had for a holiday, though it meant leaving the recently-weaned Sam behind with our young nanny (Pru cried for him every morning for about half an hour, and then gradually cheered up). It seems extraordinary now, looking back, that throughout our boys' childhood we were always able, even when earning very small salaries, to afford reliable live-in help while we went out to work. Often when we were both working abroad and had the children with us, whoever we had helping us at home would be able to come too. Since those days the equation between parents' earnings and the cost of engaging home help has gone crazy. How young couples manage today I simply don't know; what I do know is that a lot of those mothers who are capable of doing valuable jobs, just cannot afford to work.

Our new tour was to be longer, and now consisted of three plays: a slightly rewritten version of the Boswell/Johnson; a new play by David Grant, *The Gamecock;* and Shakespeare's *The Tempest,* in which I was to play Prospero.

Prospect's production ethos was determined by its mission to tour, and to tour to theatres of very different sizes. (We played, for instance, adjacent weeks at the Sunderland Empire, with a capacity of 1,574, and Sir Nicholas Sekers' little theatre at Rose Hill, Whitehaven, which holds 120). Consequently there was always very little scenery and usually even less in the way of furniture. In all his Shakespearean productions, Toby Robertson took to heart Shaw's recommendation that poetry makes its own scenery. Production money was spent on costume, lighting and music, but the onus was on the actor to deliver the text and tell the story in an exciting way. (Quite speedily, too; the audience had to be able to catch their last buses.)

These constraints didn't bother me at all, in fact I welcomed them. Particularly in the case of *The Tempest,* where I have always felt Prospero's magic island to be of small compass, the spirits to be a very modest labour force, and the power they wield distinctly limited.

Prospero's own magic knowledge (conned from old books, when he ought to have been governing Milan) is finite and, I think, waning. He rejoices, to begin with, in the exercise of his magical powers, but is always conscious of the sands running out, and must somehow learn humility, forgiveness and the courage to re-think himself as an ordinary fallible mortal.

The budget provided for a total of nine weeks' rehearsal for the three plays. This works out per play at rather less than the usual four weeks' rehearsal allowance in this country. It's not much. The National and Royal Shakespeare Companies might stretch to six weeks, or even eight. On the other hand, the fifteen *months* allotted by the Maly Theatre of St Petersburg seems to me over-generous.

There is in the UK an institutional parsimony about rehearsal time, affecting all the performing arts. British orchestral musicians are the best sight-readers in the world, simply because they have to be. A television actor may be required, at 8.30 in the morning, to jump into a conjugal bed with someone to whom he's never said hello. In radio drama, it seems to be believed that actors turn up at the start of a recording, slit open the envelope that contains their script, and read from it happily for the first time. A member of the BBC Radio management recently, when implored that more studio time be scheduled for rehearsal, retorted,'Rehearsal? When I call for a plumber to mend a dripping tap, I don't want him to *rehearse*, I want him to mend it.'

For the stage actor who is rehearsing a new play, the statutory four weeks tend to follow an established pattern:

First week: Everyone else seems to be wonderful, but you yourself don't know what you're doing, and you can't think why on earth they've cast you.

Second week: You start to see daylight, but at the same time begin to realise that the play itself simply doesn't work.

Third week: You find that the play is in fact perfectly all right; the problem is that the director doesn't know what he's doing.

Final week of rehearsal: It becomes blindingly clear that the rest of the cast are in league to sabotage your performance.

The technical rehearsal: Your designer, who spoke so well at the read-through, is now revealed as a certifiable lunatic.

The dress rehearsal: Likewise, the stage management are a gang of incompetent morons.

Then comes:

The First Night, and this brilliant play, superbly directed, exquisitely designed, sensitively played by a uniformly matchless cast, is delivered to an audience apparently made up of disenchanted eskimos.

The next morning, though, when the newspaper reviews appear, you remember that actually the audience had been splendidly perceptive and more than ready with their laughter. Yes, come on, they'd had a wonderful evening. So why are these idiot critics trying to maintain that the show was rubbish?

A word about critics. For the good ones, and there are several, I have a lot of sympathy. Editorial constraint, and particularly the habit lately adopted by some newspapers of heading up a review with a qualitative logo or star-rating so that the reader doesn't have to bother with the ensuing copy, has devalued the reviewer's job, while at the same time increasing, to I believe an unwished-for extent, his or her influence over the box office.

For a long time I used to read and collect my notices, and was surprised, looking back over those I've kept, to see how much more space the reviewer was given by his or her editor even thirty years ago. Further back than that, we read of James Agate demolishing a play in the morning's press, and the same evening enjoying a convivial supper at the Ivy with the play's author, director and star. This can only have been because he had been given sufficient space to be detailed and specific – and perhaps helpful – in his criticism.

As far as personal notices are concerned, I no longer expect very much. This is simply because most of the critics I respect have been around for quite a long time, and so have I. It's unlikely that I can do anything further to surprise them, and they do need to be constantly surprised. After all, how many *Hamlets* must they have seen? How many *Cherry Orchards*? How many *Private Lives*?

I personally can not imagine anything worse than having to go to the theatre four nights a week. What do they get paid, I wonder?

Chapter Twelve

Ronnie Waters, of the theatrical agency Al Parker Ltd. of Mount Street, Mayfair, eventually started making preparations for his retirement and passed me on to his assistant, James Sharkey. In time, James left Al Parker, took over another agency for a while, and then set up on his own; but through all these moves he continued to look after me professionally until his own retirement thirty-three years later.

I don't believe in all that time we ever had an argument, much less a real quarrel. Sometimes a faint sound that might have been a groan was discernible over the telephone when I told him I wanted to go and do yet another new play at Southampton for £170 a week, but there would be no open hint of reproach. He took the view that, while films earned the money, and television was necessary for popular exposure, an actor's real business was with the theatre, and it was essential to maintain a balance.

In 1967 that balance was very much easier to hold than it is now. Television in this country grew out of the live theatre, so initially the only actors available were theatre actors (the cinema world having rather turned up its nose at this new medium which clearly could not last), and if you were competent on the stage you were assumed to be able to adjust yourself perfectly well to the small screen.

Nowadays we are breeding a strain of actor specifically for television – people who simply look and sound right, because vernacular filmed drama demands absolute naturalism. A senior producer at the BBC has gone on record as saying he dislikes employing people who have worked in the theatre or, indeed, have ever been to drama school. This is not only unfortunate for those he would term 'stage' actors, but equally unfair to the TV soap celebrities who would like to do some theatre work for a change. Trevor Nunn or Adrian Noble are not going to be very impressed when they learn that P.C. Smith, Nurse Jones or Leading Fireman

My first stage appearance: Bristol Constabulary 'C' Division Christmas Pantomime, 1943.
The anxious-looking group at the bed are my mother, sister and self.

My mother, Olive Carleton-Crowe,
early in her stage career.

A publicity picture of my father,
Lockwood West, c.1932

T.W., Shanklin, Isle of Wight, 1939.

With father, mother and sister Patricia, South Ruislip, Middx., 1947.

Redland Hill, Bristol, 1940. Our back garden is one of those on the right. The trams were shortly to be withdrawn, and replaced by the no.7 bus.

The Polytechnic Student Players' production of Terence Rattigan's Harlequinade. *T.W. in crumpled tights R, crosses swords with subsequent writer and broadcaster Tony Bilbow.*

Jacqueline.

The Box Office Manager, Frinton.

Two of my early benefactors:
(1) Lionel Hamilton, here seen as Malvolio, Northampton, 1959.

(2) Reginald Salberg, at the Salisbury Arts Theatre, the same year.

The Summer Season at Newquay, 1956, 'perhaps ... the artistic nadir of my life... so far.'
Gordon Daisley as the Detective Inspector performs one of many similar arrests, while his
Sergeant, T.W., lurks discreetly in the shadows far left. I have forgotten the name of the actor
seated foreground, whose expression suggests that we may have got the wrong man.
A moment towards the end of the play...

The Royal Shakespeare Company in the Sixties: (1) John Barton.

(2) Clifford Williams.

Official RSC Publicity during the 1964 'Dirty Plays' Season tended to be rather solemn, so we thought we would compose our own Christmas card. (L. to R.), Peter McEnery, Geoffrey Hinsliff, Henry Woolf, Morgan Sheppard, Robert Lloyd, T.W., Freddie Jones.

The Prospect Theatre Company.
(1) Artistic Director Toby Robertson.

(2) Associate Director Richard Cottrell.

The Tempest, *Prospect Theatre Company, 1967. T.W. as Prospero.*

MARKETING
WEEK

AUGUST 29, 1980 40p VOLUME 3 NO.26

Timothy
West:
Can
marketing
save the
Old Vic?

The answer was 'no'.

Seventies retro-chic: The family on tour, Melbourne, 1972.

Robinson were cast in their rôles simply *because* of their lack of stage experience.

In the United States, it is broadly true that if you want to make a career in the theatre, you must live on the East Coast; if you prefer to work in the cinema, of course you must base yourself in the West. Attempting to combine the two involves two homes and an enormous number of 3,000 mile flights. Our geography in this country presents no such problem. It is possible for our actors to work in all media, sometimes during the course of one day. The only advice I ever feel qualified to pass on to drama students is to take full advantage of that possibility.

So, in 1967, I was able to do quite a lot of television work without turning my back on the theatre. Drama was very much the mainstay of television production, and there was a much higher percentage of single plays – requiring therefore a higher turnover of actors – than is the case today.

There was a 60-minute play entitled *Life for a Life*, for ATV, to be transmitted live, which I remember particularly. I was engaged to play a leading part in it without actually having met the director, which I thought rather odd. We had the first reading of the play, sitting round a table at the company's Elstree Studios. As I delivered my first lines, the director looked over in blank amazement before covering his face with his hands, a posture he resumed each time I began to speak. When the reading finished, he came over to me.

'Was that all right, Shaun?' I asked nervously.

'No,' he replied candidly. 'Why did you play him Welsh?'

'Well . . . his name's Ossie Williams, and he says 'i'n it?' and 'look you' and so on . . . so I thought, perhaps . . . ?'

'No, no. He's a cockney.'

'Is he?'

'Obviously.'

'Oh. Oh. Well. All right.'

For the rest of the day's rehearsal, I played him with an East London accent, though it didn't sound right to me. It didn't sound right to Shaun either. At lunch-time he took me into a corner.

'No, you haven't got him at all.'

'Well, Shaun, it's only the first morning; give me a little time, I think I'll get there. It's a very well-written part.'

'Well, yes, it *is*!' he said firmly, and went off to get his lunch.

It went on like that, every day. Jack Hedley was playing the other main part; Pauline Collins and Lewis Fiander were also in it, being splendid, and everything the three of them did brought a warm smile to the lips of our director. I had never felt like this since joining the profession. In fact I had never felt quite like this since primary school; why could my mother not write a note saying I had a pain in my tummy, so that I wouldn't have to drag myself to Elstree to undergo another day's punitive rehearsal?

Somehow we got through the two weeks, and arrived at the day of transmission. Shaun, having decided it was pointless to try further, just let me get on with it, eyes lowered in silent disapproval. After the final camera rehearsal, we sat in the make-up room being powdered and checked over before transmission, and Shaun came in.

'Good, Jack. Terrific performance. Pauline, yes, I love what you're doing. It's very funny, Lewis, keep it just like that.'

He came to my chair, and sighed.

'It's still not working, is it?' I growled.

He sighed again, more deeply. 'No,' he admitted. 'No, it isn't. Do you know,' he added wistfully, 'who I really wanted for this part?'

'No?' I said. 'Does he live nearby? We've got – let's see – twenty-eight minutes; I could give him a ring, what's his name?'

His eyes misted over, and he struggled to choke back the emotion as he whispered the words, 'Charlie Drake.'

I'm afraid I was so angry that I went into the studio and played the whole thing Welsh.

*

Prospect mounted two more tours in 1967: George Farquhar's comedy *The Constant Couple*, which was very well received on the road and then came in to the West End and died, and Richard Cottrell's adaptation of Forster's *A Room with a View*.

It was on this latter tour that I stayed in the worst digs I had ever come across, in Newcastle-on-Tyne, where a trade fair or something had used up all the tolerable accommodation. The sheets were damp, the room filthy, the breakfast disgusting, the landlady uncivil and her tariff preposterous. There were four of us from the company staying there, and on the Friday night we held a council of war.

My father had told me of a traditional response by touring actors in his day; they used to nail a kipper to the underside of the dining room table. We did better than this. On the Saturday morning we went out and purchased a pair of such fish, and while the two girls held the landlady in the kitchen arguing about the bill, Neil Stacy and I unscrewed the back of her rexine sofa, inserted our kippers, and screwed it back again. On the sleeper that night, going back to London, we raised a glass to our pisciform avengers, and only regretted that we wouldn't be around to witness their effect in a week's time.

At the end of the year, I was invited back to Bristol – not to the Little Theatre, nor the huge Hippodrome, where we'd been with *Simple Spymen*, but to the beautiful Georgian Theatre Royal, home of the Bristol Old Vic Company.

The play was an adaptation by James Saunders of Iris Murdoch's *The Italian Girl*; a kind of Gothic Rabelaisian farce very stylishly directed by Val May, and enormously enjoyable to do. The audience liked it as well, and we brought it in to the West End the following year, to Wyndham's Theatre.

Wyndham's, in Charing Cross Road, stands back-to-back with the rather larger Albery Theatre (originally the New). Both houses were at this time owned by Donald Albery; and just after we opened, construction began on an overhead bridge linking the two theatres, so that one stage door would serve for both, with a consequent saving on doorkeepers and firemen.

The bridge formed a short passageway between one floor of dressing rooms in the Albery Theatre and those on the equivalent level at Wyndham's, and we could see that this might be made to serve a further purpose. A show at either theatre with a particularly large cast could theoretically spill people across the bridge to occupy spare dressing rooms on the other side.

Richard Pasco, whose brother I was playing in *The Italian Girl*, grew very incensed at this idea, which had in fact never actually been suggested by the Albery management. This, however, only served to feed his growing suspicion that our small cast – Elizabeth Sellars, Jane Wenham, Christopher Guinee, Deborah Grant, Imogen Hassall, Richard and myself – were the probable future victims of a secret and injurious managerial plot. It takes one paranoiac to recognise another, and though publicly I will not admit to the condition, preferring the term 'galloping sensitivity', yet there exists a kind of freemasonry among the afflicted which enables us to spot the symptoms in others. In his perturbation about Donald Albery's dark designs, I recognised Richard as a brother sufferer on no ordinary level.

The Festival Ballet was booked into the Albery for an eight-week season – exactly the sort of emergency that Richard feared. In the event, the large company of dancers was perfectly well accommodated in their own theatre. One Saturday morning, however, Christopher Guinee and I came in and cleared out Richard's dressing room, carefully replacing all his belongings in a vacant room one floor up. His own room we dressed for a fictitious ballerina named Jennifer Maclaren, whose name we put on the door, providing her with spare ballet shoes, a tutu, a tray of resin and good luck greetings including telegrams from her parents, her boyfriend and her dog Hamish. For good measure we added a signed photograph of Christopher Gable, and some satsumas in a bag.

As a joke, it was a disaster. At four o'clock Dickie Pasco came into the theatre, and a minute later an eldritch shriek assailed the ears of the Saturday-afternoon bookshop-browsers in Cecil Court.

Our unsuspecting Company Manager scurried up the stairs to find his apoplectic leading actor wordlessly pointing to the desecration of his dressing room, his worst fears foully confirmed. Sheepishly, Christopher and I owned up and admitted we'd got a bit carried away; but it was some hours before the essentially kind and generous Dickie could bring himself to smile.

On the positive side, access through to the other theatre meant that on Saturdays, when our two matinees began at different times, it was possible to go on to the Albery fly-floor or down to the wings, and watch a little of their own show.

The ballet season had been followed by John Osborne's *Hotel in Amsterdam*, starring Paul Scofield. Scofield, once he was settled into a run, famously enjoyed chatting and playing games with other actors when it didn't actually interfere with what was going on on stage. At one point in Osborne's play he had to walk off into the bedroom, leaving the stage empty for a few moments before re-entering; and he would fill this off-stage time by exchanging a few words with whoever had come across the bridge that afternoon.

He never seemed in a hurry to go back on, and we started to

prepare weekly jokes to entertain him, little tableaux becoming gradually more and more elaborate. One week we brought in a trestle table covered with a white cloth, on which reclined Kate O'Mara (who had taken over from Imogen Hassall), naked and garnished with salad. Paul came over, made some appreciative remarks, helped himself to a radish, dipped it into the salt in Kate's navel, and sauntered back on stage with it.

After this, their company manager asked us to stop.

Imogen Hassall's tragically short life resembles the plot of a Jackie Collins novelette. The daughter of the distinguished poet, librettist and biographer Christopher Hassall, Imogen was brought up in a literary/theatrical environment in Bristol. She was extremely, and marketably, beautiful; and as an aspiring actress she immediately became sidetracked into areas which required modelling bezazz rather than acting talent. She made a number of fairly inconsiderable films, and was seen partnered by a predictable succession of playboys, some of whom treated her very badly indeed.

The kind of work in which she was involved brought her little satisfaction, but she was unable to summon the commitment necessary for the serious theatre. She wandered, uncared-for and confused, from one job to another, from one man to another. She seemed increasingly bored with her part in *The Italian Girl*, allowed her concentration to wander, and a few weeks into the London run she pleaded a nervous breakdown and left the cast.

A little while later, we read in the papers that Imogen had taken her life by swallowing a massive overdose of sleeping pills. We were all devastated, not I think ever having truly believed in the nervous breakdown, and wondering whether any of us could in some way have prevented the tragedy. She was only in her late twenties.

The play continued to run throughout the very warm summer of 1968, much of which I spent commuting between London and a little cottage we had taken outside Chichester, where Pru was appearing in a play by Peter Ustinov, *The Unknown Soldier and his Wife*, at the Festival Theatre. Then I got a call from the BBC to play the conductor Hans Richter in a film about Richard Wagner, and suddenly had to spend my days in London having tuition in conducting and, more alarmingly, trying to learn the trumpet.

The young Richter was Wagner's secretary at the time in which the story was set, and had to conduct the chamber orchestra in its famous Christmas morning performance of *The Siegfried Idyll* outside Cosima's bedroom at Tribschen. Also, there having been no-one else to do it, he had to play the 8-bar trumpet part himself. Our film showed him working on it and improving to performance standard, and they lent me a trumpet and told me to start practising.

I rang a friend of mine who plays the trombone, and asked him how long it took to become proficient. About three years, he said. I said, well, this is for Friday.

How does a beginner practise the trumpet in a quiet cul-de-sac in Barnes in the middle of summer, when everyone has their windows open? After a number of complaints, I drove to the middle of Wimbledon Common, walked some way into the undergrowth, sat down on a log with my trumpet and my music. Before I had got two notes out, a Ranger appeared on horseback and told me music was forbidden in the Park. I felt flattered by his use of the word 'music', but there was nothing for it but to pack up and go. That night I drove down to Chichester after the show, turning off down a cart-track, getting out after about half a mile and settling down among the stubble of a newly harvested field: a lone figure trying to capture the secret of the embouchure, sadly blowing away in the moonlight.

Chapter Thirteen

*I*t was when, coming to the edge of the twelve-inch-high Chichester stage one night, she experienced an absurd feeling of vertigo, that Pru realised she might be pregnant. So indeed she was, and it was clear that without further ado we must find a bigger house to live in. Toby Robertson and his wife lived in Wandsworth, backing on to a sort of Pooteresque park with a goldfish pond and a rose garden – we couldn't afford anything like that, but on our way back from visiting them we saw For Sale notices outside a tall rather forbidding-looking Victorian house, and I bullied Pru into buying it. We've lived there happily ever since.

Joe, our second son, was born at King's College Hospital, Denmark Hill, on the evening of 1 January 1969. Our doctor, having anticipated that again there would be some delay, went home to Barnes for supper, and almost immediately had to speed back across South London, arriving just too late to witness the birth, and with quite a lot of curry on his chin.

It is a good plan, if possible, to organise things so as not to have your baby on New Year's Day. The hospital seems rather depleted, and the few staff who are there look exhausted. Then for many years you will have to hold noisy children's parties whilst you and the other parents are nursing hangovers. Later on, you may find it advisable to book into a hotel for the night while your offspring takes over the house for a party of his or her own, and you will return to find your marital bed full of earrings, if nothing worse.

The house we bought had been converted into a number of individual bed-sitting rooms, with other facilities dotted haphazardly around, so that original bedrooms had become kitchens, intended kitchens had been put to use as bathrooms, and obvious bathrooms were doing service as broom cupboards. All the plumbing and all the wiring had been contorted to suit, and we laid out £3,000 – a vast sum – for a comprehensive firm of builders to put things in order. This meant that for the first three months Sam and his nanny lived up on the second floor while the rest of us camped in the basement. Meetings between the two parties were hard to arrange. Meanwhile, the builders lived in luxury on the ground floor. The first thing they built was a very solid tea-bar for their own use; they had their post delivered to the house, and they brought in quite a number of their own personal effects, including their wives.

Very soon the luckless householder had to wrest himself from this apogee of domestic comfort, and put up with the hardship of a 5-star hotel in Manchester for most of the next four months.

Big Breadwinner Hog was an eight-part serial for Granada Television written by Robin Chapman and directed by Mike Newell and Michael Apted. Basically, it was an underworld thriller involving three different families of villains: a big-business cartel, with enormous financial and political resources, an old-fashioned Kray-style strong-arm gang, and a very young, very bright band of rich kids out to take over the empires of the other two groups. The leader of this last faction, played by Peter Egan, was called Hog, and it was Robin Chapman's proposition that someone with Hog's brains and imagination must necessarily succeed in rising to the top of the criminal world, as long as he is prepared to be completely ruthless. Granada were nervous about the idea, but finally gave it the nod.

The other thing the writer was concerned to show was the detailed and long-lasting effects of physical violence. In the James Bond style of thriller, people you don't care about are casually shot or knifed, die, pass out of frame and are forgotten. In *Hog*, the gang member who had acid thrown in his face in Episode 1 still wore the bandages until Episode 5, when they came off to reveal shocking disfiguration. Robin Chapman wanted to rob screen violence of all its machismo glamour, and show only the cruelty and the pain.

Perhaps it was a rather sophisticated attitude for the tabloid press to take on board. An outcry greeted the first episode, and there were DO WE HAVE TO WATCH THIS? headlines on the front of the more excitable papers. To their shame, Granada capitulated. While the first two or three weekly episodes were being screened, we were still finishing making the last couple, and the producer was now instructed by his overlords to water down whatever remained to be shown.

The original ending to the whole thing was, I thought, brilliant. Hog, having destroyed the heavy mob and taken over the big criminal corporation, has arrived at the very top of the pyramid. He has achieved his ambition. What is there left for him now – except the fear of being unseated? Can he trust his lieutenants? Does he know what forces may be mustering, beyond even his very considerable control, to destroy his empire? Will the police, for all his precaution, stumble on some piece of evidence that will undo him?

The police in fact have no such evidence, but they know their man. They know Hog will have to be so careful about his every move that he will virtually cease to be a danger. The spirit is already destroyed – it will not be long before someone sees to it that the body is too.

It was apparently felt that the public might see this ending as an endorsement of the criminal life: just look at Hog's superb office, his expensive suit, his attractive secretary. So Robin was told to come up with a more conventional dénouement. The police had to find something left behind at one of Hog's earlier raids which positively identified him as the culprit, and arrest him. This was what finally went on to the screen. It was a very disappointing anticlimax, which I thought patronised the viewers' intelligence.

That aside, Granada was an exciting place – the canteen was crammed with interesting and famous people making many different kinds of programmes. Round the corner, the old red brick building which had once housed the London and North Western Railway Company's horses was now a studio theatre, called the Stables. Here a regular company performed plays which, if deemed successful, would then be televised. Half-way up Quay Street was a club called The Film Exchange, a regular watering hole patronised traditionally by television personnel on one side of the room, and by the legal fraternity from Manchester's Crown Court on the other.

The Crown Court gave its name to a regular series produced by Granada, in which each week a different and fictional criminal case was tried before a professional judge with a jury made up of members of the public. The accused, the witnesses, barristers and solicitors were all played by actors, and though all the circumstances of the case were scripted, the actors playing the two leading counsel had to compose their own closing speeches to the jury. Faced with this task, an actor took his or her responsibilities very seriously indeed. If, after an outpouring of rhetoric of which you had been rather proud, the jury found against you, it was very hard not to take it as a slur on your acting ability.

I never got to play counsel myself, but I used to listen to the injured comments of those who did, afterwards in the Film Exchange.

'I don't think they were *listening* . . . there was one old boy who was practically asleep, and that woman in the green jumper just kept staring at the camera. When I made the point about Baker not possibly being able to hear the scream above the noise of the television, there were a couple of them staring out of the *window*. That poor woman – think of it – Holloway for ten years; even if she gets out in five, she's lost the best years of her life . . . no, I won't have a drink, I'm too upset.'

Then I used to move over to the other side of the room and listen to the *real* barristers.

'I say, hard luck about Jenkins. What did he get, fifteen?'

'Fifteen without remission. I knew it was no go as soon as I saw we were up before bloody old Broomfield. You playing golf on Saturday?'

'Afraid not, old boy. Daphne's got some sort of a garden fete in Prestbury, I promised I'd go along and rattle a tin. Cheers.'

'Cheers.'

*

The Prospect Theatre Company by the end of the decade had grown in scope and stature; there were smart offices off the Charing Cross Road, and productions were financed under a new scheme, the brainchild of the Arts Council Touring Department, called DALTA (Drama and Lyric Theatres Association). This was really an incentive to Local Authorities around the country to buy up, and do up, their ailing touring theatres, for which they would be rewarded by prestigious seasons of drama, opera and ballet.

All in all, the idea worked very well, and was largely responsible for our now having such beautifully restored regional playhouses as the Theatre Royal Newcastle, the Lyceum Sheffield, the Birmingham Hippodrome, the Theatre Royal Nottingham, the New Theatre Cardiff, and several others. In the coming years, of course, the programming strategy at these theatres changed significantly; the growing supply of big musicals compensated for the shrinking availability of large-scale drama and dance product. About the only offering that remained constant was opera.

Back in 1969, however, we at Prospect were being looked after very well. A tour of large- and middle-scale theatres had been arranged for a 30-strong company, performing in repertoire Shakespeare's *Richard II* and Marlowe's *Edward II*, after opening at the Edinburgh Festival. Prospect had for the last few years provided a centrepiece for the official Festival, and this year were asked to perform, not in one of the city's theatres, but in the Assembly Hall of the Church of Scotland.

We arrived in Edinburgh on a stormy Sunday afternoon. Atop the rain-lashed Mound, the austere figure of John Knox glared down in disapprobation as we passed nervously through the granite portal into a dark, chill, unwelcoming vault. Hundreds of musty-smelling hymn-books were piled against the walls. Towering above us in gothic majesty loomed the Moderator's seat. A stage had been built, and scaffolding and lighting equipment was spread around, waiting to be erected – but were we *really* going to do a play here? *Two* plays, one of which began with two men, Edward and Gaveston, kissing each other on the lips in full view of the audience? What would they think?

Well, we soon found out what one person thought: a certain Councillor Kidd, who demanded that the Chief Constable investigate this 'shocking and filthy' production. 'Can you blame me,' he asked the city at large, 'when I see two men kissing one another? It is the sort of play that Edinburgh does not want.' Benedict Nightingale, gleefully reporting this in the *New Statesman*, wondered what Edinburgh would have preferred: 'an Edward who greets Piers Gaveston with a slap on the back . . . as a rugger captain might welcome the return of a scrum-half unfairly dropped by the selectors?' Kidd's remarks chimed with the opening Festival address given from the pulpit of St Giles Cathedral by that guardian of public virtue, Malcolm Muggeridge, who launched an attack on the moral laxity of contemporary writing. Muggeridge's address did wonders for box-offices all round the Festival, while Councillor Kidd assured us of capacity houses for *Edward II* every night.

The two kings were played by Ian McKellen, and he was rightly acclaimed for two remarkable performances. I was cast as his antagonist in both plays – Bolingbroke in *Richard* and Mortimer in *Edward*. An extra responsibility for the actor playing a duo of parts sharing more or less the same dramatic function, is to make them as different from each other as possible. Ian had already refined his performance as Richard in an earlier production – an unassailable king by divine right, aloof, superior, but then descending, when finding himself unaccountably dashed from power, into self-pitying histrionics. Ian found Edward only gradually, I think, in rehearsal, but emerged finally as a much more extrovert, sophisticated king; where Richard promenaded serenely with the effortless grandeur of regal omnipotence, Edward lurched about with a restless, dissatisfied energy. Where Richard crumbled in defeat, Edward gave as good as he got, a formidable warrior in adversity.

Bolingbroke I treated as a politician rather than as a soldier, and this again was partly a consideration of balance. As Mortimer, I was clearly called upon to do some rather butch acting, with sword fights and a love scene with the delectable Diane Fletcher; so as Bolingbroke I might perhaps be more Machiavellian, concentrating on being everything that Richard was not, and doing the opposite of whatever he did. If the king was being supercilious with his followers, I would treat mine with humility; if he deliberately neglected his P.R. appeal, I would take extra care with mine. If he waffled, I would be decisive, if he raged I would keep my temper; if he distractedly threw himself around Westminster Hall, dressed in his white shift, I would stand perfectly still, wearing black.

We turned out to be the major success of the Festival, and had a great time. The rain stopped, and I remember only the sun twinkling on the Firth as we sat outside the Cramond Inn, and warm balmy nights cruising up to the Mound in Diane's open-top Sunbeam Tiger with the moon – on which Man had now set his proprietory foot, and which consequently we had almost begun to think of as an inventive installation by Strand Electric – softening with silver the forbidding outline of Edinburgh Castle.

Good times though they were, one couldn't but be conscious of the negative attitude towards the Festival displayed not only by the tight-fisted City Fathers but by Edinburgh citizens generally, many of whom made a practice of moving out of town for three weeks and letting their properties to Festival visitors at an exorbitant rent. There was a distinct feeling that the annual event, instead of celebrating Edinburgh, occurred in spite of it. John Drummond, in his book *Tainted by Experience*, gives an entertaining but disturbing account of his factious years as Festival Director, at the end of which his advice to his successor was: 'Hold it in Glasgow.'

We took *Richard II* abroad, to Vienna and then Bratislava. This was an interesting time to visit Czechoslovakia; not many weeks before, the Russian tanks had entered Prague, and President Dubcek had been brutally removed from power. There were still a number of Russians about, although they had to conceal their nationality to escape the burning hatred of the nationalistic Czechs.

The film *Doctor Zhivago* had started a fashion in England for black Russian-style coats with fur sleeves and collars, worn with matching hat and muff. Toby Robertson's wife Jane had very unwisely chosen this guise in which to wander the streets of Bratislava. Passers-by, presuming her to be the mistress of a very senior member of the Politburo, threw stones at her, and she had to retreat very fast back to our hotel.

Of all the members of British Equity to bring to Czechoslovakia in this time of conflict, Paul Hardwick, who played John of Gaunt, was perhaps the most unfortunate choice. Paul looked so exactly like Leonid Brezhnev that he was indeed subsequently cast as the Russian leader in a television film, and the similarity was compounded by Paul's wardrobe of double-breasted grey suits, the recognised uniform of the KGB. On his arrival in Bratislava, he walked cheerily into a bar and ordered a vodka. All conversation stopped, while a group of purposeful-looking men advanced on Paul, and motioned him to come with them round the back of the building.

Paul instictively grasped the situation, and, not knowing any Slovak, hastened to explain himself in German. This, however, was a bad move – the undercover Russian officials in the city always spoke in German to disguise their identity. The situation looked very bad indeed, until he remembered he had his smallpox vaccination certificate, in English, in an inside pocket, and that luckily convinced them he was nothing more dangerous than a strolling player.

It was understandable that the Bratislavans in their present circumstances should hardly extend a welcome to any overseas visitors; however, on the night of our first performance at the Nova Scena Theatre, everything changed dramatically.

Richard II seemed to them to be their own story; that of the overthrow of their national government. Richard was a portrait of the hero Dubcek, Bolingbroke the disgraceful puppet president Husek. At the curtain call people stood, wept, shouted slogans, threw flowers at Ian's feet. The authorities were dismayed, we were hustled out of the theatre into a bus and back to our hotel, which we were not permitted to leave. The next day our hotel was changed, and we were told that the press conference which had been arranged was cancelled. We were virtual prisoners for the rest of our stay in Bratislava, on a diet of overdone lamb chops surmounted, for some reason, by a fried egg.

Back in the U.K., we continued our DALTA tour, recorded both plays for television and came back to London for a very successful season at the Piccadilly. Immediately it was over, I started rehearsals for *Abelard and Heloise*, by Ronald Millar, directed for the John Gale management by Robin Phillips.

This account of the twelfth-century theologian Peter Abelard's tragic love-affair with his pupil Héloïse, and her subsequent seclusion in the convent at Argenteuil, sent the audience away congratulating themselves on having undergone a profound spiritual experience, whereas actually what the play offered was a tantalising compound of sado-masochism, incest, *folie de soutane*, and most important, perhaps the first nude love-scene to be played on the West End stage.

The two artists concerned in this were Keith Michell and Diana Rigg, playing the title roles. Keith was understandably nervous about the scene. 'I can't guarantee always to look as though I'm in love with her,' he complained to the director. Indeed to appear so every night, with two matinees a week, would demand an act of heroic priapism, even with the visual encouragement of a naked Miss Rigg. Keith solved it by finding different ways in which to sit.

Our prior-to-London tour began, unusually, in Exeter, where Diana received a few reproving letters from scandalised residents, and one request from a military gentleman in Tavistock for an article of her underwear. Five weeks later we opened at Wyndham's Theatre to rather dismissive notices which did nothing to discourage the public; it turned out to be an immensely successful production.

There were, in addition to the main characters, six monks and six nuns, and Robin Phillips had these figures form a frozen presence around the edge of scenes in which they were not involved; six motionless monks framing the convent, and as many stationary nuns positioned between the pillars of Notre Dame.

The weather in June was very hot, and the nuns got into the habit of getting into the habit with nothing at all beneath it. One night, however, there was a thunderstorm, and the rain beating down on the roof started to come through on to the stage, gradually soaking the immobile nuns wet through. By degrees, each chastely-draped member of the sisterhood was metamorphosed into an erotic ebony statue, every contour and every crevice intricately sculpted. Watching each other, they began to laugh. The audience began to laugh too. It was unfortunate that Keith, lying in bed downstage, was so placed that he was unable to see the regrettable exhibition behind him. The scene being played was a particularly poignant, one could say painful, one; Abelard having just been castrated by agents of Héloïse's uncle. At this point in the play, Keith Michell was not generally accustomed to hearing roars of laughter. My character, an old priest (yet more cornflour), had come to comfort Abelard, and sitting beside the bed, I could observe it all. The merriment swelled. Keith's eyes blazed with baffled fury. His voice rose, ringing with emotion. Where would this end, I wondered? I made a decision. Interrupting Abelard in mid-flow, I said very firmly, 'Peter. Peter. Peter, *stop*. I think you should look behind you.' Keith glared at me; clearly I was party to whatever this plot was to expose him to ridicule, but he finally did as I suggested. He fell back on the pillows, shaking with laughter, and we might as well have abandoned the play at that point.

There are in certain plays what have become known in the profession as 'house-counting parts' – characters who sit facing downstage for quite long periods, listening, but not actually doing very much. Given reasonably good eyesight, this affords an actor, if he or she so wishes, an opportunity to assess the size of the audience: particularly useful if one is on a percentage of the box office, but in any case giving an idea of how well the show is doing.

Such a part was Gilles de Vannes in *Abelard and Heloise*. In the first act I had a chance to conduct a fairly accurate survey, and back in the dressing room I would convert this into the estimated monetary value of the house. My room-mate John Warner would then write the figure clearly on my bald head. While I was sitting down in Act Two, Diana had to kiss the top of my head, and she would memorise the figure and check it with the box-office return which, being on a percentage, she would be handed each night. If I was within £50 of the correct figure she would buy me a drink afterwards; if not, it would be my turn.

The time passed very happily, the more so because I had been able – unusually – to obtain an early release from the play to go up to Edinburgh to do two more plays for Prospect, just for the Festival.

To replace individual people during a run is an inconvenience for the producer and director, for the other members of the cast, for the wardrobe department and for the publicity people, so I was therefore being a bit of a nuisance. At one time, a long stay in a West End run was just what most actors wanted. Nowadays, however, agents will usually try to negotiate the option of an early release for their clients. Nobody can tell in advance whether a show is going to succeed or not, and agents, who are necessarily cynical people, need to think of their clients' future. Better to have a fixed date on which they can leave, than be kept hanging on tenuously while houses dwindle, waiting for the fortnight's notice of closure but unable in the meantime to plan for other work.

There is another consideration. During the run of a play the London audience will change rapidly, the cognoscenti giving way to the more casual theatregoers, then to office outings and to coach parties, and finally almost entirely to the foreign tourists who make our cultural life possible in London, but upon whose perfect under-standing of English it is not always reasonable to rely. To many actors, after having collected a few nice personal notices after the opening night, the grass soon begins to look greener elsewhere . . .

At Wyndham's Theatre, as I write this, the producers of the three-handed play *Art* have adopted a very successful policy of changing the entire cast every twelve weeks, thus attracting first-class replacements each time, with strong audience appeal. The constant injection of new blood keeps this very attractive play going, and everyone is satisfied: audiences, actors and management.

Up the road and round the corner from Wyndham's, at the St Martin's Theatre in West Street, the strategy for *The Mousetrap* is rather different. Alongside the wooden boards displaying the original reviews by Ivor Brown, George Bernard Shaw and William Hazlitt, a list is posted once a year bearing the names of a group of actors who will be guaranteed employment for the next twelve months. As the cast assemble for their first rehearsal, each actor will be asked the date of his or her birthday, so that it may be celebrated among the company when the time comes. Nothing short of death or a direct hit on the St Martin's Theatre can prevent that celebration.

People, and I actually know some of them, go to *The Mousetrap* once a year, and compare performances. As others might talk of John Gielgud's Hamlet, so the older patrons will boast of having seen Richard Attenborough as the original Detective-Sergeant Totty, and argue about the different qualities brought to the role when Derek Blomfield succeeded to it in 1957. Tourists from the United States and elsewhere return to the St Martin's year after year – a pilgrimage, like going to Westminster Abbey or the Tower of London.

Now, I am not one to sneer at success, and I congratulate the executors of Peter Saunders, the original producer, on a miraculous achievement; but all the same is it not a great pity, at a time when so few of the smaller theatres in London remain available for use by freelance producers, that the valuable 550-seat St Martin's should have remained out of commission, so to speak, for over forty years?

What we need in the London theatre more than anything is the equivalent of Off-Broadway, small theatres where straight plays of not universal appeal can be produced, paying the actors and staff less than commercial salaries and charging the customers a good deal less than commercial seat prices. Fringe theatres do this, of course, but they all work on a limited-run basis, a system that softens the effect of failure, but militates against success.

At the moment, a play that is commanding full houses at, say, the Hampstead Theatre and is turning people away every night, probably won't have paid off its production costs after six weeks, because the theatre only has 120 seats. Now, you can't extend the run, because you have another show coming in for which you've contracted the actors; you've rehearsed it, advertised and sold tickets for it. So what do you do about your present success? Do you transfer it into the West End? There may be big problems – the actors have only been engaged up to the closing date at Hampstead, and they're probably going on to something else. There may not be a suitable West End theatre available – at least not one on which your tiny Hampstead set is not going to look ridiculous without being entirely rebuilt, which you can't afford. Even if you overcome these problems, you have to accept that the play you produced for your Hampstead patrons will now be marketed differently and aimed at perhaps a very different audience, who may receive it in a very different spirit. This need not, of course, necessarily be bad news, but it does need thinking about.

In New York, the Broadway and Off-Broadway theatre districts are more or less geographically differentiated, whereas in the heart of the West End the subsidised and the commercial, the 'serious' and the boulevard, the experimental and the traditional, the classic revival and the popular musical jostle together, occupying what premises they can. Something for everybody, indeed, and all offered – apart from the musicals – at much the same range of prices.

For the discerning theatregoer, guidance around this multiplex may be needed. To some extent, this is provided by the Good Housekeeping Seal of Approval that is deemed to attach to transfers from the Royal Court, the Almeida and the Donmar Theatres, enabling tickets for their shows to be purchased with a confidence that often appears not to be shown for a similar kind of play when produced by an independent commercial management. This is unfortunate. Such independent producers are thus driven to concentrate on ever 'safer' product, and so theatres come more and more to target a specific section of the London audience, now beginning to see itself as divided into two separate watertight compartments: one for 'serious' plays, the other for musicals and pot-boilers.

Chapter Fourteen

In 1970, I seem to have been allowed to follow an outrageous pattern of cut-and-run. I left *Abelard* early, in order to go up to Edinburgh for a revival of the Boswell/Johnson play and Toby's production of *Much Ado About Nothing*. The latter play was then going on tour, but I didn't go with it; instead I went back to London to be in Harold Pinter's production of James Joyce's *Exiles* at the Mermaid. However, by the time plans were made to transfer this to the Aldwych, I had already gone to Spain to film *Nicholas and Alexandra*.

Exiles was a remarkable experience. Joyce's only play had been seen only once in London, in 1950, and had acquired the reputation of being unplayable. Ezra Pound told the author, 'I don't believe an audience could follow it.' Bernard Shaw, who thought it obscene, actually managed to prevent an earlier production in London. The 1918 premiere, in Munich, was a disaster. Now, Pinter, with a brilliant performance by John Wood in the central role, displayed it as a fascinating and painful verbal examination of human feelings.

There are, I think, very few directors in this country better than Harold Pinter. An actor himself, he thinks in actors' terms: does a performance ring true? And if true, is it clear? Then, only if it is both true and clear, is it *interesting?* As a playwright himself, his chief responsibility as a director is to the author's intention: is the play being delivered to the audience? Of course, cynics will say that as both an internationally famous dramatist and a distinguished actor, he has no need to make his mark as a director, no need to stamp his work with the words 'This, you can see, is a Harold Pinter Production'. So much the better, say I.

The Sunday morning after *Exiles* finished, I flew to Madrid to start work on the Sam Spiegel blockbuster *Nicholas and Alexandra*, the story of the last days of Czar Nicholas II and his family before they were massacred in the cellar at Ekaterinburg.

It should have been a really remarkable film; it had everything going for it, huge budget, fine director, brilliant cinematographer, first-class art direction, amazing costumes, excellent cast. Everything but the script. Distinguished screenwriters came and went: a scene here, a couple of pages there, a rewrite further on. The result was that the story lacked a proper focus, it was like a man backing too many horses in the same race. Were our sympathies really supposed to be centred on the Czar and his retinue, or were we invited to see it also from Lenin's point of view? Or Kerensky's? And then there was Rasputin . . .

It was, nonetheless, an exciting picture to make. Ian Holm, returning delighted from a day's filming outside Madrid, told me,'I've just done something I've dreamt of since childhood. What making movies is really about: climbing over the tender of a moving locomotive with a gun in my hand, and holding up the driver!' I was playing the unfortunate Dr Botkin, the royal physician in whose care had been placed the haemophiliac Czarevitch, and who stayed with the family to the bitter end, being gunned down with the rest of them. Consequently I was there at the Sevilla Studios for rather a long time, and saw the coming and going of various British character actors in the standardised uniforms and facial hair of the different senior political officers.

One day, such a person came into the almost empty studio canteen, just as I was starting on my lunch.

'Hello, Timothy,' he said. Now, people tend to call me Tim rather than Timothy, unless they're cross with me; so I concluded that beneath the beard, moustache and pince-nez must be someone with whom I had simply done a quick broadcast, or Sunday recital, probably some time ago. I welcomed him to Madrid, and asked how long he would be with us. About eight days, he said.

'Oh, good,' I replied graciously. 'Well, they're a very friendly unit, I think you'll have a good time; have you somewhere nice to stay?'

'Yes, quite nice,' he said.

'Good,' I said again. There didn't seem much else to say, so I said I'd see him around, and sat down to eat my lunch. As the man made his way towards the far corner of the canteen, I rose helpfully to warn him that he was about to seat himself at Sam Spiegel's private table. 'I say,' I began – and then choked. There was something about that figure, the shape of the back of his head.

He turned. 'It's good to see you, Sir Laurence,' I added lamely.

They all turned up, one after another. Michael Redgrave, Harry Andrews, Irene Worth, Eric Porter, John Wood, Michael Bryant, Alan Webb – an astonishing cast. Janet Suzman (very movingly) and Michael Jayston were the eponymous couple, several of the young princesses later matured into well-known actresses, and it was a special pleasure for me to work alongside that fine and courageous actor Jack Hawkins, on the last picture that he made.

On returning to England, I received a message from Charles Marowitz, asking if we could meet to talk about an idea he had just had. Charles, together with the producer Thelma Holt, was now running the Open Space in Tottenham Court Road, a basement fringe theatre doing some very interesting experimental work.

I went to see him in his flat near the Zoo, where he still lived on Chocolate Whippsies with a series of very tall blonde actresses. His idea was to dramatise Oscar Wilde's essay in duologue form, *The Critic as Artist*, and to stage it inside a gauze box at the Open Space, with me as the Oscar character. Charles had never read a word of Wilde until someone brought him the collected essays while he was in a New York hospital recovering from a minor operation. He had immediately become hooked, and when we started rehearsals, combed the rest of the author's work in search of extra lines to help justify some physical activity.

'I've just found a great line about *smoking*,' he told us one morning. 'Listen to this: "Every man should have an occupation of some kind."'

'Brilliant, Charles,' we said. 'Where on *earth* did you find it?'

Marowitz' readiness to be made fun of was disarming and deceptive. He actually did a superb job in synthesising the dual nature of this piece: on one level a mannered, epigrammatic debate on the superiority of criticism over creation, and on the other, the passionate seduction of a beautiful young man by his intellectually brilliant senior.

Even allowing for the probability that the critics would naturally be generous about a play that was generous about the critics, it was very well received and, I still think, a remarkable piece of work. One person, however, was very upset by it – the mother of Peter Davies, who played the young man whose seduction at the end of the play I gave every indication of having accomplished. The distraught lady left the theatre without staying to see Peter, and went straight home to Taunton. On the following Sunday, Peter had to go down there to placate her, armed with photographs of myself closely surrounded by my wife and children.

*

The director John Dove told me he categorises actors as being either Red Wine or White Wine. It's a valid classification. Michael Gambon, Anthony Hopkins and Albert Finney are Red Wine; Ian Richardson, Derek Jacobi and Nigel Hawthorne are White.

Having by now done quite a bit of Shakespeare, reasonably successfully, I thought perhaps a Red Wine part such as Macbeth, Richard III, Brutus or Shylock might come my way: however, I wasn't entirely prepared – at the age of thirty-seven – for Toby Robertson to offer me the Gevrey-Chambertin rôle of King Lear. After thinking it over very carefully, and discussing with Toby the pros and cons, I thought I would draw the cork and try my best to finish the bottle.

Quite apart from considerations of energy, I believe there is a strong reason for thinking of Lear as being younger than his own (very unreliable) assessment, 'four score and upward, not an hour more or less'.

Nearly every one of Shakespeare's tragic protagonists – Antony, Macbeth, Hamlet, Leontes, Coriolanus – commits some sin, fault, error of judgment or dereliction of duty in the first act of the play, and spends the next four acts suffering for it. In more cases than not, this offence involves prejudicing the natural and social order of things – the worst sin in the Shakespearean book.

So it is with Lear. If you make it obvious that he is too weak to retain office at the beginning of the play, then his division of the kingdom (admittedly injudicious, considering the personalities involved) is basically reasonable, and the tragedy will become simply that of an unfortunate victim of filial ingratitude.

It's much more than that. Lear intends his abdication to be conditional; he wants to relieve himself of the responsibility of king-ship while retaining the nominal power. His is the action that splits Britain apart, and leaves the stage littered at the end with corpses, including his own. An ordinarily great playwright might have let

Lear experience the agony of suddenly realising his culpability in the final act; not so Shakespeare. He decrees that the banished king shall lose his wits, so that only vague intimations of his fault creep through the fog of his madness, and even at the end of the play he is not properly aware of the terrible thing he has done.

What about Lear's madness? I have always believed that as Shakespeare clearly wrote so much from personal observation, Lear's deranged behaviour – and Ophelia's too – must have been drawn from life. The unfortunates who served as his models, though they were then described simply as 'mad', would have been suffering from conditions to which we would now give clinical names. So I phoned my G.P. to ask if he could put me in touch with a specialist in geriatric medicine. The specialist in turn gave me the name of an authority on senile dementia. He turned out to be a relative of Michael Hordern. I rang him.

A very abrupt voice answered, and as concisely as I could, I told him what I wanted and asked if I might come and see him.

'Forget about senile dementia,' he snapped. 'Lear has arterio-sclerosis.'

'Arterio-sclerosis – are you sure?' I ventured. 'How do you know?'

'Because I've *read the play*, that's how. It's a recital of the classic symptoms. Hardening of the arteries produces a psychoneurosis. *Hysterica passio*. Periods of lucidity interspersed with periods of delusion, the latter growing gradually more frequent and more pronounced. Fits of extreme anger. Occasional physical sensations of inward turmoil; women afflicted with the disease used to imagine their womb was racing around inside them: 'How this mother swells up toward my heart'. It's all there. Read the play.'

Well, it was only a theory, but it held enough water to use as a syndrome on which to base Lear's stage behaviour. That's all one needs, really; a case study that seems to fit the bill. The actor has to feel he has authority for what he's doing, and that there are a few guide-lines to enable him to believe he's being medically consistent.

Once again, we opened in Edinburgh, at the Assembly Hall, in August 1971. Toby's production (one of his best) was very stark; a bare stage, everybody costumed in creamy-white wool, all similar, no pre-judgments to be made about any of the characters, lighting very bright and fairly constant, snatches only of music. Very energetic, and we all got very hot, me especially. Seven *Lears* a week is a lot; an Edinburgh doctor prescribed salt pills, for which I was grateful.

Next door to the Assembly Hall, and connected to it, is a fifteenth-century building that has been renovated for use as the University Students' Hostel, its two-foot-thick walls painted white, and the monastic-looking cells furnished with a desk, chair and just-about-adequate bed. This being the University vacation, the rooms were free, and most of the *Lear* company were staying there, as well as Pru and our two boys Sam, now five, and two-year-old Joe.

I think this may have been the time when the seeds were sown of Sam's future mode of life, and which doomed his parents' hopes of his becoming an estate agent, a chromotherapist or a systems analysis consultant. He had a splendid fortnight, padding downstairs in his pyjamas and dressing-gown to watch bits of the play, being taken to the different Festival events round the city, watching the street buskers, jugglers, fire-eaters and sword-dancers, and going up to the castle for the tattoo. He listened to the Lone Piper. 'Did you like that?' I asked him. 'No,' he answered, still clapping enthusiastically, 'but it must be very difficult.'

After Edinburgh, we went out on the road, and we added a production of *Love's Labour's Lost*, which we played in repertoire, thus easing the burden of quite so many *Lears* in a week. The comedy was a wonderful contrast – designed by Robin Archer as a sixties hippie commune. Carl Davis set the love poems of the four young men to music, in different styles: Berowne had a Sinatra-type ballad, the bookish young King a Gesualdo madrigal pastiche; Longaville, the eldest, did a sort of Noël Coward Latin-American number, with bongos, and Dumaine a rather wistful little song that might have been written by Paul McCartney.

I played Holofernes as a tweedy, bottom-pinching minor public schoolmaster, and Ronnie Stevens, the Fool in Lear, again partnered me as the pedantic curate Sir Nathaniel. 'A very good bowler', another character says of him; so of course we had a cricket-match on stage.

We went to Venice with *Lear*, to the Biennale, playing at the beautiful Teatro la Fenice, later the victim of a mysterious, or perhaps not so mysterious, outbreak of fire. To take a solo curtain call from between huge velvet curtains parted by two uniformed flunkies in powdered wigs is an exhilarating experience, slightly modified by then going up to a chilly, uncarpeted dressing room and trying to wash in cold water. But then Italy's theatre managers are not alone in deciding on which side of the footlights they prefer to spend their money.

After Venice, Wolverhampton. I booked into a small commercial hotel near the railway station. Having been quite lavishly entertained by the Grand Theatre management after our first night, I asked not to be called the following morning till nine o'clock.

Almost, it seemed to me, as soon as my head touched the pillow, I was awoken by a gargantuan woman hurling open the curtains and banging a tea-tray down in the least accessible corner of the room.

'What – what?' I stammered, only fifteen percent awake. 'Is it really nine o'clock?'

'No,' replied the giantess, 'it's only ten past seven, but I thought I'd better call you now in case I forgot later.'

I was at an hotel in Bristol recently – quite a large one – and arrived in the evening after the dining room had closed. Feeling hungry, I consulted the Room Service menu. It described a lot of those imitation Hawaiian dishes with little umbrellas stuck in them, but at the foot of the page, beneath the heading '24 HOUR MENU' was some cold meat and salad, which was what I really wanted.

I picked up the phone. 'This is 309,' I said. 'I'd like some cold roast beef and salad, and half a bottle of the house Burgundy.'

There was a pause. 'Ah, that's on the twenty-four hour menu, isn't it,' a voice said doubtfully.

I agreed that this was so.

'Ah, well, we don't go on to the twenty-four hour menu till half-past eleven.'

Chapter Fifteen

At one time Bristol's King Sreet, the cobbled way leading from Prince Street down to Welsh Back and the Floating Harbour, was the pride and joy of my adopted city, and was regularly depicted on biscuit tins and, snowbound, on Christmas cards. Hitler had spared its timbered houses, some of which date from 1633 and include the famous 'Llandoger Trow', the inn where Daniel Defoe met Alexander Selkirk and formed the idea of writing *Robinson Crusoe* and where Robert Louis Stevenson is supposed to have put together the first part of *Treasure Island*.

Opposite the inn is a beautiful old row of almshouses built for merchant seamen, and down the street stood the old Bristol Library, among whose regular readers were Coleridge, Southey and Walter Savage Landor. The handsome Coopers' Hall (1776) stands next to the Theatre Royal, which opened that same year.

Alas, today, at least on Friday and Saturday nights, the street is virtually a no-go area for law-abiding citizens. Nearly every building has become a bar or a night club, from which bouncers fire a fusillade of youthful bodies into the roadway; no car can safely be parked, and patrons emerge from the theatre to tread their way gingerly through blood, vomit and broken glass. Why have the Council permitted this to happen? These facilities are necessary for people to enjoy themselves, they say, and better to concentrate them where there are no residents. But there *are* residents still living in the almshouses. What the Council means is that there are no residents *of influence*.

Back in 1972 things, though sometimes noisy, were very different. The old red lightship moored on the quay at the far end of the street served as a rather tatty but popular bar. The Old Duke, opposite the Llandoger, was, and still is, a widely-recognised jazz venue. The much-loved Italian restaurant and bar, in which Renato Borgnana and his family have been providing succour for the theatre people for as long as I can remember, was often alive into the small hours. But King Street was a happy and friendly place.

The old theatre, which I was to come to know very well, had just undergone a major reconstruction. The perfect Georgian auditorium was of course left as it was, but the cramped Victorian foyer was cleared away, a box office and three bars were housed in the newly acquired next door building, which also allowed for improved dressing rooms and a vastly enlarged stage area; and a smaller studio theatre was built in the basement.

Val May, the then Artistic Director, had chosen to christen the new main-house stage with an original musical adaptation of Pinero's *Trelawny of the Wells*. The plot, dealing as it does with bringing new theatrical ideas into old theatrical buildings, could not have been more appropriate to the occasion; and the technical staff, presented for the first time with masses of space and up-to-date equipment, rose to it magnificently. The audience gasped as Hayley Mills, playing Rose Trelawny, ran on the spot while a seemingly endless street of shops passed across the stage behind her, and as an entire fully-dressed Victorian drawing room evaporated piecemeal without any apparent human agency, leaving Ian Richardson to finish his number on a vast empty stage before an enormous blue cyclorama.

It was a delightful show, with a charming score (his best, I think) by Julian Slade, and it was a huge success. In fact, the run was extended, which meant I had to leave before the end because – again trying to cram in too many things – I was due to go to Australia, where Prospect had been invited to do *Lear* and *Love's Labour's Lost* for the Adelaide Festival followed by a ten-week tour.

For this there were a number of cast changes; Timothy Dalton replaced John Shrapnel as Edgar and Berowne, Fiona Walker's two parts were taken by Jill Dixon and Delia Lindsay, and Sheila Ballantyne supplanted Caroline Blakiston as Goneril. As Lear, I had been cursing the fruit of Caroline's womb regularly for some months, with the result that she was now well and truly pregnant with my god-daughter Charlotte, and didn't want to leave England. Happily, Pru was also able to join the company, as the Princess of France; and we brought our two boys and their nanny, Kelly, who became very popular with the unattached males of the company.

The BOAC flight in those days (Heathrow-Zürich-Dubai-Calcutta-Singapore-Perth-Melbourne, with connecting flight to Adelaide) took about 36 hours, during which time I had picked up a very painful throat infection which felt steadily worse as the hours wore on. When we got to Melbourne, a doctor in North Adelaide was contacted who said he would see me in his lunch hour, and when we landed there was a car to take me out to his surgery.

I had hardly slept on the plane, and dozed groggily in the car until we arrived at the doctor's house. The door was opened by a very pretty nurse who appeared slightly dishevelled and somewhat taken aback by my arrival. 'Oh, we didn't expect you quite so soon,' she apologised, pushing a stray lock of hair back from her forehead. She glanced behind her, and a young man appeared at the end of the hall, just finishing buttoning up a white coat, beneath which he was apparently trouserless. Clearly I had interrupted something of importance to them both.

He took me into his surgery, looked at my throat, sprayed it and wrote out a prescription. I thanked him and got up to leave, venturing the comment that I was so sorry to disturb him in the middle of his, um, his – time off.

'No worries,' he assured me cheerily, 'my wife' – indicating the nurse – 'was just fixing lunch.' Thereupon he took off the white coat to reveal a perfectly respectable pair of knee-length khaki shorts.

Adelaide is an attractive city, laid out in 1836 by South Australia's first Surveyor-General, Colonel William Light. The square mile of the city proper is indeed square, bounded by four broad avenues named simply the North, South, East and West Terraces. Beyond each of these terraces lies another mile of open parkland, providing space for golf courses, tennis courts, a racecourse, botanic gardens and a zoo. In Colonel Light's time the parkland would have provided the military with a clear view of marauding Aborigines, who could be picked off in a leisurely fashion as they emerged from the undergrowth a mile away.

Today, the South Australian Aborigine has a better time of it than his counterpart in some of the other Australian States. His land rights, and his educational and employment prospects, were a primary concern of the late Don Dunstan, the much-loved South Australian Premier to whose imaginative energy the splendid Adelaide Festival Centre was chiefly due. When we arrived in 1972 the complex had not yet been completed; we played at the more conventional Her Majesty's Theatre.

Beyond Adelaide's green belt lie the suburbs – single-storey houses with their own little gardens, accommodating altogether a population of a little under a million, but covering an area about as large as Greater London. Beyond that again, going inland and to the north, is the Barossa Valley. Settlement in the Valley started in 1842 when a group of Lutherans emigrated from Germany to avoid interference with their religious beliefs. The old stone cottages and farm buildings, and particularly the many little churches, look like a faithful reconstruction from a book of nineteenth-century Prussian photographs.

The German families nowadays, some of whom speak 'Barossa Deutsch', are much involved in making the wine for which the Valley grapes are so prized. Our company was invited out to Seppeltsfield, where the current family of Seppelts laid on a delicious al fresco lunch, with beautiful wines, which went on and on way into the afternoon. Eventually we were carried back to Adelaide to do *King Lear*,

'And, to deal plainly,
I fear I am not in my perfect mind.'

From Adelaide we moved on to Sydney, playing at the fine old Theatre Royal in Castlereagh Street, a regular touring venue for the J.C. Williamson Company, Australia's leading theatre producers, known down the years popularly as 'The Firm'.

The Williamson saga is virtually the history of commercial theatre in Australasia, beginning in 1874 with the engagement at the Theatre Royal Melbourne of the American couple Maggie Moore and James Cassius Williamson in a piece happily entitled *Struck Oil!* After acquiring the Australian and New Zealand rights of *HMS Pinafore* from Richard D'Oyly Carte, in order to play Sir Joseph Porter himself, Williamson settled in Sydney and plunged into management, purchasing the rights to each of the Gilbert and Sullivan operas as soon as they opened in London, and bringing over international opera companies, American musicals and Sarah Bernhardt's full French company to satisfy the then almost insatiable appetite of the Australian audience.

The Firm survived the recurring tribulations of drought, disastrous land speculation and bank failure, the Depression, Talking Pictures, two world wars, the death of its founder and two subsequent changes of management, but had eventually passed into the hands of the New Zealand chain-store owner Sir Robert Mackenzie, who by the time we were playing at the Sydney Theatre Royal in 1972 was preparing to pull out of the entertainment business and had already begun selling off all the Williamson theatres.

The freehold of the Royal had been sold to developers who wanted to pull down the theatre and build an office block. Their plans met a lot of public opposition – that same year Her Majesty's along the street had burned down, and the Royal was now the city's only substantial theatre. A Save the Theatre Royal Committee was set up to persuade the developers to incorporate the existing building within their design. Eventually they did agree to include a theatre, but insisted it would have to be a brand new one.

So, on Saturday 29th April 1972, at the end of the performance of *Love's Labour's Lost,* it was my melancholy task to deliver a valedictory speech before the curtain fell for the very last time.

I was only grateful that we'd been rather a success in Sydney; it would have been awful to end the theatre's history with a flop. It was an extraordinary night; people stayed in the auditorium till dawn, singing, crying and throwing streamers. When I cleared out my dressing room I helped myself to an old framed J.C.Williamson notice which sternly forbade the bringing backstage of cooked food, alcohol, fruit, animals or visitors, on pain of dismissal.

They did get their new theatre, which is a tribute to the energies of the Committee, to the many people like Sybil Thorndike who had played in the old building and sent messages of support, and indeed to the developers themselves. It opened in January 1976; I've since been inside, and it is a perfectly nice modern theatre.

It's not the same, though. In the late 19th and early 20th centuries, if you wanted to build a theatre in your town, you didn't go to a local architect; you went to the man who built theatres nationally: W.G.R. Sprague, or Frank Matcham, or Bertie Crewe. When I go into one of their theatres, either as actor or auditor, I am fairly confident that I shall be able to hear and be heard, see and be seen, from all parts of the house. Certainly there have been some excellent smaller theatres built over the last ten or twenty years, again usually by theatre specialists, but some famous larger examples leave a great deal to be desired.

Chapter Sixteen

After Sydney, we did a quick dash up to Brisbane for a Sunday recital, staying with some cousins of Pru's in the Queensland backwoods. 'You deserve a bit of peace and quiet after Sydney,' they told us. The kookaburras woke us at five, then the cowbells started, and shortly afterwards all six children jumped on their individual ponies and rode round the house, whooping. In the penthouse of the Sheraton Hotel overlooking Sydney Harbour we had enjoyed perfect tranquillity, nor had we needed each morning to inspect the underside of the lavatory seat for snakes.

It was a kind thought, however.

We played two weeks in Melbourne, then flew home. Or rather, our plane sat on the runway opposite the observation gallery while our hosts waved, laughed, then shrugged good-humouredly, then their smiles became rather glassy and finally, as dusk was falling, they unobtrusively slid away. After a little while, we were turned off the plane, and accommodated in a nearby hotel for the night. Next morning, having lost twelve hours, we took off for Hong Kong, Bangkok and Teheran.

There was a long pause at Teheran, and after a while an announcement informed us that we were going to be offered free drinks from the trolley, courtesy of BOAC. Now if you are travelling Economy Class, that announcement always signifies bad news, and I peered out of the window to see an entire port-side engine laid out in pieces on a large tarpaulin, surrounded by a group of local mechanics, scratching their heads.

Once again we were turned off and taken to an hotel, this time at gunpoint, having had to surrender our passports. At some uncongenial hour we were herded back to the ailing aircraft, and this time we got to Frankfurt before one of the toilet outlets sprang a leak. It was at this noisome juncture that the cabin crew came round with questionnaires asking for passengers' comments. They must in all cases have made interesting reading, but what most concerned the Prospect management was the financial consequence of our now being thirty-six hours late. When we finally landed it was Wednesday afternoon, and we had to open in Cardiff the following Monday.

The whole company had lost two days of their holiday entitlement, and these would now have to be paid for as travelling days. A lengthy legal wrangle ensued, at the end of which BOAC finally settled with a good grace, and asked for a photograph from *King Lear* to enlarge and put in their window above the legend 'BOAC Takes Care of You.' Our Administrator chose the picture of Gloucester having his eyes gouged out.

But Pru and I had fallen in love with Australia, and have since made many friends in its different cities. We have each been back on a number of occasions, and indeed at one point considered settling there. It was the result of the 1987 General Election in this country that drove us to think of it quite seriously, but by that time we thought we would probably no longer be welcome – perhaps no longer be admitted; Australian acting was doing very well, thank you, without any assistance from the Poms.

The *Lear/Love's Labour's* tour finally came to an end in June with a short season at the Aldwych Theatre, which had been temporarily vacated by the RSC. A whole year had passed since our first day in the rehearsal room, and now I was anxious to re-establish contact with the mechanical media. The film director Alan Clarke was making a TV film about Horatio Bottomley, the MP for Hackney, Editor of 'John Bull' magazine and tireless swindler, and asked me to play him.

Bottomley struck me as rather admirable in a frightful way. During the 1914-18 war, he ran the 'Victory Bonds' scheme; each bond was sold for a pound, the bulk of the money went to buy munitions, and a draw was held at the end of each month, the holder of the winning ticket earning a substantial cash prize.

Although the names of the monthly winners were given to the press, it seemed on each occasion impossible to trace them in person. The authorities became suspicious, and eventually Bottomley was charged with embezzlement and brought to trial. The judge asked him: 'Mr Bottomley, how do you justify taking these hard-earned pounds from members of the public who believed that they were thereby contributing to the war effort, while in fact you were misappropriating the prize money for your own use?'

Bottomley's reply is memorable. 'Well, my Lord, wherever a thousand people are in competition to win a single prize, nine hundred and ninety-nine of them are going to be disappointed. What difference does one more make?'

During the trial, a daily adjournment had been permitted to allow Bottomley to drink a pint of champagne – the only bodily sustenance his vast bulk enjoyed at this time. Eventually he was found guilty, and sentenced to seven years' imprisonment.

BOTTOMLEY: I was under the impression, my Lord, that it was sometimes put to an accused person, 'Have you anything to say before sentence is passed on you?'

THE JUDGE: It is not customary in questions of misdemeanour.

BOTTOMLEY: Had it been so, my Lord, I should have had something rather offensive to say about your summing-up.

He served only five of his seven years, and emerged from Maidstone Jail at the age of sixty-seven. Finding himself abandoned by his commercial, political and journalistic companions, he embarked on a lecture tour beginning in South Africa, but nobody wanted to know. His old associate Peggy Primrose, an ex-Windmill Girl, persuaded a reluctant Vivian van Damm to give him an engagement in his next *Revuedeville* programme. It was, predictably, a disaster; the Windmill audience had come to look at the girls and laugh at the comedians, and they booed Bottomley off. He collapsed in the wings, was taken to Middlesex Hospital, was discovered to have cerebral thrombosis, and died a few weeks later.

After going to Paris to make a minor contribution to the film *The Day of the Jackal*, I was back in Bristol to play Sir John Falstaff in both parts of *Henry IV* for the Bristol Old Vic.

The two *Henry IV* plays have together been declared the greatest work of dramatic literature in the English language. The central character in the chronicle is England herself, and the story is that of the struggle – geographical, material and spiritual – for her possession. Shakespeare reveals to us a rich panorama of English life: the Court, the barons, the country gentlemen, the travellers, the towns-folk, the tavern-dwellers, caught up in the national turmoil as the guilt-ridden Henry IV is striving to put down the rebellion organised by the very people who helped him to the crown, whilst at the same time fearing for the future of the kingdom in the hands of his wastrel son Prince Hal.

What lifts the story from the general to the particular is the complexity of its father-son paradigm. Henry despairs of his son Hal, comparing his filial qualities unfavourably with those of the rebel leader Harry Hotspur; while Hal, estranged from his true father, feels more comfortable with the attractive dissipation of his father-substitute Falstaff.

Who is Falstaff? The great Boar's Head scenes in Part One have a comic energy unsurpassed anywhere in Shakespeare, and of course audiences need to love him, and be sad at his final inevitable downfall. However, his unscrupulous acceptance of the sacrifice of his tattered recruits, allowing them to be cut to pieces for his own personal profit, is by no means comic; it is simply another example of the vicious self-interest that to some extent motivates very nearly everyone in the play.

It seems to me that Sir John must essentially be a 'gentleman', by which I mean of course that he must have been brought up as such. The fact that he has been allowed to get away with things for so long suggests to me that there is some old school tie, tattered and beer-stained now, which has afforded him some sort of indulgence. I see his relationship with Hal as an unwritten contract: he will provide the Prince with entertainment, adventure and a diversion from his proper responsibilities, in return for food, drink and protection.

In Part One this arrangement works well, and fairly effortlessly. Part Two, however, brings a profound change. Falstaff, particularly, fails to fulfil his side of the contract. He is letting his anxiety about the future show through; his jokes are less funny, his trickery more laboured, he gives way to fits of resentment and melancholy. He feels Hal growing away from him, and the old magic is not there to draw him back.

Throughout Part Two, there is a profound feeling of ageing, of bloodlessness, of a general running-down, that makes the play very difficult for a director to handle. Shakespeare must have seen this danger when he decided to introduce, half way through the play, one of his most attractive and entertaining characters, the aged Justice Robert Shallow. Beneath their gentle comedy, these autumnal Gloucestershire scenes have a sad, elegiac quality, a sense of life coming to an end. Even the imagery employed by Falstaff in describing Shallow, 'a man made after supper of a cheese-paring', 'for all the world like a forked radish', is drawn from the *end* of a meal.

In Part Two the King is tired, in fact is nearing death. The rebels are tired, too – no longer is there a sanguine, heroic Hotspur to lead them into battle, no warlike Douglas or potent Glendower to lend their forces; only a group of dry, political malcontents: Hastings, Mowbray, the Archbishop of York. Their very defeat is accomplished not by glorious triumph of arms, but by a despicable piece of treachery. Hal himself is somehow *less* of a person in Part Two, in retreat from his former self, but not yet the assured young ruler we see in *Henry V*.

The two plays need to be seen one after the other, ideally on a single day. Part Two on its own can be tiresome.

*

I had been invited to join the Boards both of Prospect and of the little Open Space, and was learning quite a lot about the intricacies of managing those two very different operations. Also, I hadn't done any directing for quite a long time, and so when out of the blue came an enquiry from the manager of the Forum Theatre, Billingham, near Middlesborough, asking whether I would like to put together a company for a season of plays of my own choosing, I said yes.

It was very much a sideways step, and possibly mad, but my so-called career has been punctuated by several such crab-like reactions; it seems that whenever I'm getting on perfectly well with something, I immediately want to have a go at something else. I've no idea why.

Billingham-on-Tees is not one of the premier beauty spots of North East England. There was an attractive village here once upon a time, and the church boasts a handsome Saxon tower. This was before the advent of ICI, who surrounded the area with chemical works, laid enormous overhead pipes along the sides of the main road, and belched into the air clouds of small particles which then rained down on the inhabitants and took the paint off their motor-cars.

For allowing this to happen to their community, the Local Authority was handsomely recompensed through the rates; and a new pedestrian centre was built, with an hotel, a technical college, some shops, a school, a Chinese Restaurant and what was intended to be the social heart of the development, the Billingham Forum. The

131

Forum is an enormous leisure complex, housing a swimming pool and ice rink of international competition standard, with squash and badminton courts, boxing rings, cafeterias and bars. Oh, and a theatre.

When the place first opened in 1967, the idea was to encourage cross-fertilisation among the various users of the building, so that all-in wrestlers might sit down with patrons of Opera North and compare their different evenings over a companionable gin-and-tonic. After a while, the management accepted that they were perhaps being unrealistic, and went off in the other direction, keeping the theatrical milieu as distinct as possible from the other facilities. So while badminton players trod their linoleum-paved way up to a large matey bar equipped with formica-covered tables and a juke-box, the theatregoers were treated to carpets, soft lights and a cocktail lounge with reproduction Jacobean furniture and little nuts in the ashtrays.

When I arrived, I felt strongly that the pendulum had swung back a great deal too far. Men were feeling they shouldn't go in without a collar and tie, women stayed away if they were wearing trousers. Children didn't come in anyway, because the fearsomely-uniformed commissionaire used to tell them to go away. 'They rip up the seats,' he told me. The regular patrons had shrunk to a small knot of middle-aged couples who drove over from Durham or Bishop Auckland; I saw no evidence of an indigenous Billingham audience at all.

On the credit side, however, here was a well-designed theatre, with a very large stage, upon which liberal resources had been lavished by the local Council. A resident production manager and two full-time carpenters were salaried above the line, all the year round, and there was enough timber in the workshop to build a small housing estate. The Administrator, Les Jobson, was an experienced theatre manager, and he seemed to have virtual control over both programme and finance. There was a Board, but few of its members attended any performances; what kept one of them away was his fear that the swimming pool would somehow overflow and drown him as he sat in the stalls. The architect's working drawings were produced, showing the water level in the pool to be well below that of any part of the theatre, but this failed to convince him. 'I'm not taking the chance,' he said firmly.

Les' overall budget must have been generous. I never enquired the figure, as it was no direct concern of mine, but producing a season of plays with a resident company is a much more expensive operation than taking in a mixture of touring shows on a weekly basis. I wasn't at all sure how it would go down with the audiences I had encountered on each of my preparatory visits, but Les assured me we didn't need huge attendances to cover ourselves, and advised me that fairly large-scale plays were what worked best in that space.

No doubt because none of them had ever been to Billingham, I had managed to engage a very strong company: Keith Drinkel, Pete Postlethwaite, Julian Glover, Elizabeth Counsell, Veronica Lang, Carol Gillies, Trevor Martin, Robert East, Lynn Farleigh, Graham Seed, Roland Curram, Siobhan Quinlan. My ASMs were Lynne Miller, who went on to be a leading character in *The Bill*, and Bryan Brown, who became a major Australian film star.

I don't know where they all found to live. There was a student hostel, whose corridors were patrolled hourly by a janitor with a bulldog. God knows what depravity the two of them imagined might be taking place behind the bedroom doors; the two-foot-wide beds with their slippery nylon sheets would have defeated a Casanova. I endured the hostel myself for a week or two, the Billingham Arms being far too expensive, and then managed to rent a dilapidated bungalow on the outskirts of the town, with an outside lavatory, from which the paper was stolen daily by the neighbours.

The company rose enthusiastically to the challenge of putting the theatre on the Billingham map, finding a new audience, and just getting to know the people of the town. I chose to open the season with the British premiere of Joseph Heller's only play, *We Bombed in New Haven*, a satirical fantasy about a lone American airman's reluctance to be involved in a nuclear raid on Constantinople.

Not exactly a frolicsome inauguration to the season, and in fact it's not really a very good play, though its surrealism is nicely intriguing and there is much rich black comedy in the vein of his *Catch 22*. My main reason for choosing it was to attract some of the younger people of the area, particularly the students of the local technical college to whom I talked on my first visit and who, if they ever went to the theatre, found it irrelevant and frivolous.

In the Eastern Counties particularly, people were reacting with fury and dismay to the installation of American SAC bases on British

133

soil, with their sinister B52 bombers flying off over the coast, daily to practise their appalling missions, so the play did make an impression. Attendances fell a long way short of what I personally would have wished, but Les Jobson said they were better than he had expected – which didn't exactly fill me with confidence.

At all events, the next offering was intended to redress the balance. I wanted to give Pru a production (she is actually a very good director, and certainly more fastidious than I), and I wasn't sure when Billingham had last seen a Restoration play. So we did Congreve's *The Double Dealer*; it worked spendidly on that stage, and the attendances crept up. It was Pete Postlethwaite's first – and perhaps only – introduction to Restoration Comedy. Pru asked him how he felt in his costume. 'Like a lorry driver in drag,' he told her.

The Double Dealer was followed by my own production of *The National Health*, for which we achieved what was held to be the miraculous figure of 62%. Peter Nichols' naturalistic observation of daily life and death in a public ward, interleaved contrapuntally with a hospital-soap-opera account of the loves and tribulations of the medical staff, was one of the great National Theatre successes of the late 60s, but hadn't been done very often since, because of the very large cast. At Billingham we could manage it with ease: including our Theatre in Education team, we were currently employing thirty-two actors. *The National Health* is a really remarkable play, I think, and when Richard Eyre was in charge of the National Theatre I asked him whether he thought the piece might be due for revival. He felt it now to be out of date; in 1968 it looked at the NHS's failure to achieve its declared objectives; to today's audiences those objectives are so much further from being achievable that the play might come over as pure fantasy.

We had next hoped to do a rather interesting new play by Benn Levy, which I felt needed a very powerful leading actress and which Benn felt needed a Star. The kind of person he was talking about would take one look at the Billingham Arms, shriek, and demand to be driven straight back down the A1. The kind of operation in which we were engaged was hard to explain to someone in his position, so in the end negotiations broke down and Derek Goldby instead directed *Major Barbara*, a play that hadn't had much of an airing lately, with Lynn Farleigh in the title role and myself as Undershaft.

By this time, we were making friends in the town; people stopped us in the street to ask how the show was going, and sometimes actually came to see for themselves. I was invited to a reception given by the Mayor of Middlesborough, and met a Mr Hitchens, the head teacher of a State primary school in the Cleveland Hills; a blunt Yorkshireman, he told me he had written a musical about Council corruption in a New Town and asked me if I'd like to hear some of it. I heard myself agreeing to this proposal, and so he made an appointment for me to drive over to his school the following Tuesday afternoon at 3.30.

He greeted me just as most of the children were coming out, declaring 'Come with me, there's a piano in 4B – there's a homework class going on, but I'll tell them to keep quiet. Come on.'

About twenty disconsolate children raised hostile eyes from their books as we entered the classroom. Their teacher glared at them menacingly. 'Now this is Mr West – say good afternoon to Mr West.' The greeting was mumbled morosely by four or five of the assembly, while Mr Hitchens settled himself at the piano and opened his score. 'I'm going to play some music on the piano,' he cautioned his charges, 'and happen I'm going to *sing*. So shut up, all of you, and get on with your work.'

He played a few chords, then launched into a romantic number in the style of *West Side Story*. Indeed, his voice suddenly and surprisingly assumed the rich transatlantic tones of Edmund Hockridge in the show's original London production. '*I have all-the-time-in-the-wooorld –* ' he sang soulfully, ' *– to make love to you . . . I have all-the-tiime-in-the-wooorld to make you care* RAYMOND SEABRIGHT I SAW THAT you disgusting little boy, stand up, hands on head, I'm going to write to your mother, *As I walk down the street, I can feel my heart beat* RIGHT, SHARON PENFOLD YOU TOO, UP YOU GET . . . '

The book and lyrics were terrible; the music, which all seemed to be in G major, only slightly less so. After about an hour, he banged down the lid of the piano and turned to me in breathless anticipation. 'Well, what do you think?' he demanded; and then, before I had time to express an opinion, 'If you ask me, it's a real goer. I'm going to send it to Shirley Bassey.'

Chapter Seventeen

I had only been contracted to take charge of the one season at Billingham, but with an option to repeat the idea in the autumn if it was judged to be a success. It was, but by that time I had had a very attractive offer to play King Edward VII in an expensive 13-part serial about his life, for ATV. This would take almost exactly a year, so having set up the skeleton of an autumn season and appointed a director to take my place, I said farewell to Billingham, not without a certain regret.

Before starting on *Edward*, I fitted in another play at the Open Space. For Charles Marowitz I always seemed to play homosexuals, and this was another one; Nicholas Selby and I were partners running a very small private hotel in South Kensington. The play was *The Houseboy*, by the then *Times* drama critic Irving Wardle, a witty and well-written study of mild sexual corruption. Critics find it hard to write about other critics' work – Frank Marcus, Herbert Kretzmer and Jeremy Kingston, to name but a few, have all written good things that have been treated rather condescendingly by their colleagues – as was Wardle's play. He's never written another, so far as I know, and I think that's a pity.

The schedule for recording *Edward VII* would be unthinkable today: each episode was given two weeks of rehearsal, with a full week allowed for recording because some of the palace sets (there was for instance always a ballroom) were so huge that they couldn't all fit into the studio at one time. Consequently, some of the sets were erected on Sunday, and those scenes were rehearsed on Monday and shot on Tuesday. On Wednesday there was a changeover, on Thursday we rehearsed the scenes in the new sets, and recorded them on Friday. The cast had Saturday and Sunday off. Interspersed with this routine were batches of outside filming, according to season. The genius who made this sensible schedule possible, so that everything was carefully planned ahead and no-one got overtired, was Cecil Clarke, one of the all-time great TV producers. Senior management threw up their hands in despair at what it was all costing – in the event, the quality of the programme earned back at least four times its initial cost in immediate foreign sales.

We rehearsed in a handsome church hall in St John's Wood. During the first week, two separate people stopped me in the street and asked what I was working on. I said that I was rehearsing as King Edward VII. One of them commented, 'Oh, I don't like Shakespeare', and the other asked, 'Who's playing Mrs Simpson?' Those who still recollect our serial are usually convinced that it was about Henry VIII. 'Saw you as Henry VIII', they say firmly. I suppose there are superficial similarities between the two characters, but you'd think they'd notice that over the 400 years the royal barge had been superseded by the motor-car.

As a matter of fact, I did play Henry VIII once, in a TV commercial. The product was a bar of chocolate called Cadbury's Plain Six, and the commercials showed a series of Shakespearean characters – Hamlet, Richard III, Henry VIII, extolling the virtues of this confection.

As Bluff King Hal, I was discovered sporting on a couch with a comely damsel; during my eight lines of iambic pentameter however, I tired of her charms and reached beneath the cushions to retrieve a bar of Cadbury's Plain Six. It was quite a funny idea, and the director, Richard Lester, was quite happy with progress when we broke for coffee.

Less so was the worried-looking gentleman in the canvas chair marked 'Client'. He asked if he could have a word, so I pulled up a another chair. He drew a long breath.

'Look. What we're trying to sell here is plain chocolate. Right?'

I agreed.

'In fact, this is a *plain chocolate campaign*, right?'

'Right,' I said, less certainly.

'What you are doing would be fine if we were selling *milk* chocolate. Do you see what I mean?'

I tried to get in touch with my brain, but it was shut.

'No,' I said.

He folded his fingers in his lap and sighed. This was going to be a long business. 'At the end of the war,' he began, 'when chocolate reappeared in the shops, it was almost all milk chocolate – it was easier to produce. Our parents bought us milk chocolate, and we in turn passed the milk chocolate habit on to our own children. Consequently, the only indigenous plain chocolate consumers tend now to be in their sixties or seventies, and it's our business to try and enlarge that market.' He looked at me very earnestly.

'You may have seen the advertisement for After Eight Mints?' he went on. 'Grand dinner parties, black tie, women in expensive dresses, candelabra, fine linen, lots of silver. *That's* the impression we're trying to create – the world of plain chocolate is something you need to *aspire* to.'

'You mean – ' I said shrewdly, ' – you want a *soft sell*?' I had only just heard the phrase, and was very proud of it.

He beamed. 'Exactly,' he said.

When we came to shoot it, I just said it all a bit more quietly, and kept my thumb over the label. He seemed delighted.

The product never did sell, alas, and was presently withdrawn from the shops. It was perfectly nice chocolate, six pieces in the bar all of different flavours, and I felt rather offended at its failure to appeal. Years later, on a long train journey, I got into conversation with a Market Research Consultant, and I thought I'd ask him about it. He'd never heard of the product, and as I told him about it his face grew solemn and he shook his head in disapproval.

'Six,' he said. 'That's the trouble. If the buyer wants to share it with someone, how does he break it? With eight pieces, or twelve, or sixteen, he could break it in half. With six, he can't. This gives him a problem. Either he can give his friend two pieces and keep four for himself, which looks greedy, or he can keep only two and give four away, in which case he'll feel cheated. He doesn't want that kind of problem. So he buys a different bar of chocolate.'

TV commercials, however irritating they may sometimes be to watch, have provided an economic lifeline for hundreds of actors, directors and technicians. When I was running the Old Vic, it suddenly became necessary to replace our lighting board. We couldn't afford it. Fortuitously, I was offered a sherry commercial, and I put my fee towards the purchase. For four hours' work on a Saturday morning, I was paid exactly the equivalent of my annual salary as Artistic Director of the Old Vic. This, I hasten to say, was not a princely sum, but it does show the different scale on which these activities are rewarded.

138

Industry is in this way covertly funding the arts. For many actors the occasional commercial, or even a voice-over, can make it possible to accept regional or touring theatre work which they feel it important to do, but which would otherwise result in their being badly out of pocket. The high level of unemployment in our profession is so well known as to have become a cliché, but what is not so generally understood is the number of existing jobs that people actually cannot afford to do. Much of the work produced by Arts Council revenue-funded companies is so poorly paid that actors who have dependants, mortgages or other financial commitments are actually better off waitressing or driving mini-cabs.

This creates huge problems for the producers concerned. A well-established actor can often be prevailed upon to play a leading classical part, because he or she can subsidise it from other earnings. A young actor just starting out, not having too much in the way of financial responsibilities, will probably be glad of the experience. It is in the area between the two, the backbone of the company, that the difficulty arises.

I am one of the lucky ones, of course. Lucky not only that I have on the whole been able to balance my work so that some of it pays for the rest, but in that I have a wife in the same situation; one of us often can manage to subsidise the other, and as long as this doesn't become too one-sided for too long, our *amour-propre* is not endangered. The fact that I was doing *Edward* made it possible for Pru to accept a very small pay packet for going up to Nottingham and playing Katherine in *The Taming of the Shrew* for the director of the Playhouse, Richard Eyre. Repeat fees of *Fawlty Towers*, on the other hand, have allowed me to do a new play at Southampton.

Edward VII was indeed a sumptuous production. There were 187 speaking parts, and casting was on an exalted scale. Annette Crosbie played Queen Victoria, with Robert Hardy as Prince Albert; and Helen Ryan gave a quite brilliant performance as Queen Alexandra. Felicity Kendall, Cheryl Campbell, Ian Gelder, Jane Lapotaire, Michael Byrne, Kathleen Byron, Charles Dance, Alison Leggatt, John Boswall, Judy Loe, Christopher Neame and Gwyneth Strong played various royal relatives, and among the politicians were John Gielgud, Michael Hordern, Geoffrey Bayldon, John Welsh, Lyndon Brook, Basil Dignam, Edward Hardwicke, Edward Jewesbury, Brewster Mason, André Morell, Joseph O'Conor, Geoffrey Palmer,

Christopher Strauli, Richard Vernon and Noel Willman. The other ladies in Edward's life were Francesca Annis, Sally Home, Rula Lenska, Moira Redmond and Caroline Seymour.

Charles Sturridge, soon to make his name as a director with *Brideshead Revisited*, played Edward in the early pubertal episodes, and I took over when the prince became 23. This, I now feel, was ridiculously too soon. The beautiful Deborah Grant was playing the younger Alexandra; five years ago, in *The Italian Girl*, I was her *father* for God's sake, and now here we were getting married. I must have been pretty embarrassing in the first couple of episodes, but as the king got older I got better, and towards the end I think I may have been quite good.

Seven-year-old Sam and four-year old Joe were in one episode as our two sons, the Princes Albert Victor and George, romping around the terrace at Sandringham in sailor suits, and enduring a lengthy Windsor tea-party scene in the studio where Joe actually had one line of dialogue which it took most of the afternoon to get him to say.

Of course every actor has to *like* the person he or she is playing – it doesn't matter whether it's Hitler, or Beelzebub, or Margaret Thatcher; you have to see things their way, otherwise you're commenting on them rather than playing them – and I felt very warmly towards this somewhat marginalised monarch. He had a pretty awful life, really; an infancy passed in the shadow of his elder sister Vicky; an unhappy childhood leading to a furtive adolescence, a long period of frustration as the ageing heir to the throne, finally to become king at 59, when he had run out of energy. He had qualities and abilities of which his subjects never became aware, and an engaging habit of treating his two nephews, the Kaiser and the Czar, as rather over-excited children who had temporarily overstepped the bounds of decorum. Had he lived a few more years, I think this disconcerting familial approach might possibly have had some beneficial effect on international politics.

In the TV serial we had hoped perhaps to rectify the popular image of him as simply a womanising, racegoing hedonist. But to some people, it seems, he will always be Henry VIII in different trousers.

*

Samuel Johnson, Horatio Bottomley, King Edward VII. To be followed in time by Winston Churchill, John Bodkin Adams, William Morris, Mikhail Gorbachev, Lord Reith, Josef Stalin and Sir Thomas Beecham – I was becoming known as the actor who played Real People.

Depicting those who have actually existed obviously holds special responsibilities for an actor, but there are also certain benefits. He or she has to present to the audience a sufficiently recognisable portrait of the subject to gain their trust, while not actually allowing the disguise to take over the performance. Rory Bremner would never dream of keeping one of his brilliant impersonations going for more than a few minutes; in the end, the actor has only one instrument on which to play the tune, and that is himself.

On the other hand, the chances are that the character you are portraying is well enough known to have been fairly widely documented – so a lot can be learned from biographical material, paintings and, if he or she lived within the last 150 years, photographs. There may be newsreel footage, and existing voice recordings. It may be possible to speak to some of those who knew the subject personally; although this requires caution as personal memories tend to be subjective, and two people's recollections may completely contradict each other.

The most valuable benefit of such research, I find, is that your off-stage life is to a great extent mapped out for you. Knowing where you've been that morning, how you got here, whom you may have met on the way, the general state of your health, what might be weighing on your mind, gives a sense of authority that roots your performance in reality. Whereas if you're playing a fictional character, you have to invent it all yourself.

The research you do on any character or on any period or event very often reveals things that are totally at odds with what the dramatist or screenwriter is saying, and you may easily find that for this reason you have to jettison eighty per cent of what you have discovered. The more research you do, though, the larger the twenty per cent you're left with.

It is odd how many people seem surprised that actors do any prior research at all. A professor from an American University wrote to Pru the other day asking whether she considered it advisable to read a novel by Jane Austen before embarking on its television adaptation. Well *yes*. Did I really think it necessary to learn something about late nineteenth-century Norwegian architectural practice before playing *The Master Builder?* I think so. One of our most intelligent drama critics voiced his special admiration for Sir Laurence Olivier's having taken the trouble to visit Collins' Music Hall when preparing to play Archie Rice in *The Entertainer*. Well of course he would.

Playing all these historical characters eventually became rather a millstone round my neck. Casting directors seemed convinced that a Real Person had a unified character label, like a highwayman, an admiral or a drunk. Short or tall, dark or fair, Scots, Welsh or Russian, as long as they'd had their being on this earth, I seemed to be the person to turn to.

This would have been all very well but for the fact that, in our business, if you become known for doing one particular thing, it is generally assumed that you are incapapable of anything else. Fictional roles on television no longer came my way. No, what I did was Real People.

About this time, Pru started recording the first series of *Fawlty Towers.* It was as everyone knows a landmark in television history, and people still watch it and quote from the twelve episodes (there were only twelve) twenty five years later. Pru loved doing it, and will always remain grateful to John Cleese for wanting her to play Sybil. But in a way, she has become a victim of a similar kind of discriminative thinking: 'Oh, she does Comedy,' they will say dismissively, just as about another actor they will nervously enquire, 'Yes, but does he do Comedy?' as if it were a special skill, like speaking Serbo-Croat or riding a unicycle.

These distinctions make me angry. The basic rules of acting apply, whatever kind of show you're in. If you act the situation truthfully, and the writer's intention is that the audience should laugh, then they will laugh. If the intention is that they should feel sad, they will duly feel sad. If the author wants them to feel frightened, or angry, or reassured, or disgusted, the required effect will be similarly achieved.

What are the qualities necessary to play farce well? Passion, single-mindedness and clarity. What are the requisites for the performance of Jacobean tragedy? Passion, single-mindedness and clarity. Comedy that has no basis in truth is not comedy, it's something else –

burlesque, buffoonery. *Fawlty Towers* is about pride, fear and danger, the essential stuff of tragedy, and that's why it speaks to us and has become a sort of classic in its way.

One of the reasons that in today's classrooms there is a marked antipathy to Shakespearean comedy – if the pupils take to Shakespeare at all, it is to the tragedies – is the understandable difficulty in finding some of the 'comic' characters genuinely amusing. When those pupils go to the live theatre, the situation is not helped by the adult audience's apparent incapacity to judge between what is funny and what is merely Funny.

I had better explain my terms. The Funny performance simply indicates that the character is meant to be funny. We laugh dutifully, to show that we recognise this, and because we are good-natured, and because it might be embarrassing if we didn't. The funny performance – small 'f' – on the other hand, produces that involuntary spasmodic muscular reaction known as genuine laughter.

It can sometimes be difficult to achieve this – when, for instance, did you last see a Launcelot Gobbo who kept you enthralled? But it is foolish to strive for the delighted guffaws that apparently greeted Will Kempe and his Elizabethan colleagues; audiences are rather different nowadays, and the important thing is for the audience to get to know enough about you as a 'comic' character to understand your *attitude* to things and to be sufficiently entertained by this to enjoy whatever you then say or do.

When we did *Much Ado About Nothing* for Prospect, Dogberry, the Constable of the Watch (a character that is so often Funny without being funny), was played by Bryan Pringle as a sort of Graham Greene expatriot minor Government official in a soiled white suit. Not only did his effortful expression of self-importance get all the right laughs, but when he came to describe himself as 'a rich fellow enough, go to, and one that hath had *losses*', he gave us a glimpse of a whole past life touched with tragedy. Shakespeare often provides these hidden clues to a minor character's history, and it is up to the actor to find them and make use of them.

Chapter Eighteen

One of the great things about Toby Robertson was that he was *older* than me. When you are rehearsing a play, your director needs to be an authority figure, and as you yourself grow older this can become a problem. Your directors will, in the nature of things, seem to get younger and younger until you find that, whilst certainly no more talented or resourceful than they are, you have unquestionably been around a lot longer. Quite often during a troublesome rehearsal you will be tempted to put your oar in and suggest a solution that worked when you were confronted with a similar difficulty twenty years ago. It is important to know whether such a suggestion would in fact be helpful or whether you will just be being a bloody nuisance. Crucially, it is important to judge when your director might feel you are attempting to undermine his or her authority.

The age range among a single cast may be very wide: a director told me the other day that in the play he was rehearsing his eldest actor was over eighty, and the youngest in her early twenties. 'They all have different agendas,' he sighed. 'The old ones just want to know where to move, and on which line to pick up the decanter. The middle range want to talk a lot about the background and history of their characters. The young ones need to be told how to say the lines.'

He was generalising wildly, of course, but nonetheless pointing up one of the areas of difficulty for a director. Actors, during their professional lives, work with hundreds of different directors, but few of those directors have ever had the opportunity to watch any of their fellows at work. It follows that while actors get used to adapting themselves to the methods of different directors, it is a very unusual director who will be flexible to each actor's personal vocabulary and way of working.

Toby, in the 1960s and 70s, had enormous flair as a director, and we worked together very well. Our families were very close – I was godfather to his son Joshua, and Toby to our own son Joe. Rehearsing for Toby was quite hard work, as he always wanted everything done at performance pitch. He would be delighted with a rehearsal that had been belted out with white-hot energy by actors who were not yet quite clear what they were doing, would give perceptive and useful notes afterwards, and then suggest that we all went out to dinner. If someone said they were sorry but they now had to go home by themselves and *rehearse*, he would think that was very boring.

Actually, it was by no means a bad way to work. Under these conditions you had thoroughly to commit to an idea; you couldn't hedge, moderate or compromise, the options were closed. You simply had to jump in at the deep end, and if it worked in a general way then you could do the fine tuning later. If it didn't, then it would be back to the drawing board.

The next show I did for Toby wasn't for Prospect at all, but for the Chichester Festival Theatre. In early years, the Chichester Board liked the idea of having an actor-manager at the helm: Laurence Olivier to begin with, then John Clements, and when he retired the baton passed to Keith Michell. This was Keith's first year in the post, and the season had not opened to rapturous acclaim from the local audience. The citizens of Chichester have never been in the van-guard of theatrical experiment, but they know what they like, and when a work by Pirandello with the inauspicious title *Tonight we Improvise* was followed by a new version of *Oedipus Rex* presented on a pink set made to look like a female torso, through which the char-acters (including Diana Dors as a jutting Jocasta) entered between a pair of vaginal labia, there was a distinct feeling of alarm.

Toby's production of Turgenev's *A Month in the Country* did something to redeem the situation. Previously this play had tended to be treated as though Turgenev were just another way of spelling Chekhov, but of course the former pre-dates the latter by some forty years. His formative period was spent in Western Europe – he knew Flaubert, George Sand, Dickens and Thackeray, and in his portrayal of restless ennui among the Russian intelligentsia there is much more of the feeling of the *Comédie Humaine* of Balzac than of the delicate character portraiture of Chekhov.

Dorothy Tutin played Natalya Petrovna, Derek Jacobi was her jaded lover Rakitin, and I played Shpigelsky, the doctor who proposes marriage in a spectacularly unromantic way to Natalya's female companion Lizaveta, brilliantly played by an actress named Carol Gillies.

I had the privilege of working with Carol many times before she tragically died of a brain tumour in 1991. Head girl at Roedean, graduating with honours from Cambridge, a fine Russian scholar with rather mannish looks that disguised her essential warm femininity, for some reason she took to the theatre rather than the halls of academe, and became a remarkably talented actress.

While were in Chichester, the two of us drove down to the nearby coast at West Wittering one day, had a picnic and a swim, and then lay and dozed on the beach. Suddenly I realised Carol was no longer with me, and scanning the horizon I saw a distant figure in a green one-piece bathing costume engraving with a stick a long message in the sand, in huge Cyrillic script. I went over to her, and she explained that some time ago she had fallen romantically in love with the great actor Innokenty Smoktunovsky, who played *Hamlet* in the Russian film. When he visited London with the Moscow Art Theatre a year or two later she had gone round to see him, and he had gently told her that any furtherance of the relationship was out of the question, but that she might write to him from time to time.

Having heard that Smoktunovsky was currently making his way to London to collect an award, she was now penning a love letter for him to read as he looked out of the aeroplane on his way from Moscow (for such a very intelligent person, her sense of European geography was disappointing), and the letter, which was by no means finished yet, already covered most of West Wittering beach.

I like working at Chichester. The hexagonal stage of the Festival Theatre is not the easiest of performance spaces; unless you are a long way upstage it is impossible to hold the entire audience in your eyeline. It is a well-managed theatre, though, with comfortable facilities and, as long as they approve of what you're doing, a faithful and appreciative audience:

> 'The Drama's laws the Drama's Patrons give;
> For we, who live to please, must please to live.'

As a matter of fact, when I returned to Chichester years later in a production of *The Rivals*, some of the older members of the audience wrote to the management asking if in future a synopsis of each act could be included in the programme. This very sensible precaution would ensure that if they suddenly woke up during Act Three, they would be able to tell at a glance who, during the bit they missed, had married whom, and who had died.

I lived (*we* lived, when Pru could get there; theatrical married lives frequently entail keeping two or three homes going at once) in a cottage adjoining an old mill a few miles out of Chichester. It had a beautiful garden, complete with a lake on which our two boys in their rubber dinghy paddled away their hot summer afternoons among the frogs and water lilies.

Towards the end of the season, when the family had gone back to London, there was a party after the show, which went on rather a long time, and I drove my way back down the deserted country lanes in my open MGB Tourer with an exaggerated degree of care. I had a couple of friends staying with me at the cottage, and when I got home I found they were still up, and quite ready for a succession of nightcaps. It must have been about three o'clock when finally we staggered upstairs and fell into our separate beds.

A few hours later I was awakened by torrential rain beating against the windows. As I listened to the downpour, I was dimly aware of a voice in my head trying to tell me of some untoward circumstance that apparently had something to do with this rain. My brain was in no state to be cudgelled, so I let the voice take its time, and finally it made me understand that my car, with the hood down, had been left outside in the road. I spent several moments in intelligent appraisal of the situation. Slowly I got out of bed and made my way to the window. Yes, the rain was indeed falling very hard. I discussed with myself the possibility that the inside of the car might at this moment be in danger of getting wet.

Then I was struck by what seemed to me an unusually perceptive thought. The rain appeared to be coming from the *east*. There would therefore be no risk to my car, which I had parked facing in a *westerly* direction. Congratulating myself on my foresight, I went happily back to sleep.

In the morning, the car was full of water, like a bath. I opened the door to let some of the water out, borrowed a hair-dryer and an extension lead, and spent the day trying to dry out the seats, uselessly. From that day onward, anyone who travelled in the car had to insert beneath themselves a full Sunday newspaper to avoid fundamental inundation.

It will be deduced from this that though for some years I was an MGB owner, I was never a real Sports Car Fan. Soon the boys became too big for the back shelf; and this, combined with wet seats and I suppose the onset of the male menopause, converted me from convertibles, and thereafter we just bought conservative family cars. I'm not at all interested in all the power games associated with car ownership – all I want is a car that gets me about, reliably and if possible fairly quietly. There is also the private consideration that our car must be able to accommodate a Victorian armchair, a property trunk and a large wig-box, these being the essentials for Pru's show *An Evening with Queen Victoria*, which, in company with two musicians, she has been touring round the world for the last twenty years.

Whenever possible, I prefer to travel by train. I've always loved railways – not just nostalgically, although I'm fond of exploring restored old lines, and am actually involved with the upkeep of one or two – but because if we're ever to win the battle against traffic congestion in this country, it's railways that will have to play the key part.

Luckless old Dr Beeching, into whose wax effigy railway enthusiasts still stick pins, was only carrying out predetermined government policy when he dismantled so much of our country's railway network in the sixties, leaving people without their local station or branch line and therefore with the sole option of driving their car thirty miles to their nearest railhead or taking it all the way to their ultimate destination, London or wherever. It's hardly conceivable now that the government should have failed to anticipate that in the years to come most people would own a car and feel the right to use it how and where they wished. Before this had a chance to lead to chaos, our nationalised rail system could have undergone a colossal investment programme, renovating and updating the whole network to provide a viable and attractive alternative to choked motorways and the urban parking nightmare: situations, predictably, worsening daily.

Should not moving people about be considered as a public service, like Health and Education? Why was it ever thought that there could be any commercial incentive to running a national railway? It doesn't happen anywhere else in the world; even in Switzerland, where all other public services are privatised, the railways are run by the State. Of course, the colossal financial outlay that would have been necessary in Beeching's day to recondition all that under-maintained track and rolling stock would have brought howls of complaint from the taxpayer and probably crippled the government. Such long-term thinking doesn't as a rule recommend itself to our parliamentary system. Now we're paying the price.

Ours was the nation, the land of Trevithick, Stephenson and Brunel, that first gave railways to the world, revolutionising and enriching the lives of most of those with whom they came into contact. Now we have a system in which the British public, egged on by the press, declares it has no confidence, and which must be the laughing-stock of most of our European neighbours.

Rail privatisation is now generally accepted as having been a disastrous measure, and people cannot be blamed for believing that safety, punctuality and affordability must surely be measured against shareholders' dividends. But's what's done is done, we cannot go on for ever crying over split rails, and now that these disastrous problems are at last being addressed, I believe we must look positively at the improvements being made, the new incentives being explored, the state-of-the-art rolling stock being designed and the imaginative station architecture being commissioned, not to mention the possibility of some derelict lines being reopened to traffic.

Towards the end of the Chichester season I had to catch the train every morning to Brighton, where I was rehearsing *Macbeth* at the Gardner Centre, and already British Rail were beginning to adopt a form of corporate-speak; a train had become known as a 'service', though passengers had not as yet been designated as 'customers'. Having initially been infuriated by the term 'Customer' (I don't want to *buy* the rolling stock), I've suddenly had an idea about it. Perhaps it's a semantic strategy to avoid prosecution under the Trades Des-criptions Act? To be a Passenger, technically you must actually be in a state of passage, you have to be *moving*; in other words, you must have been provided with the service that you paid for. A Customer, on the other hand, is a speculative being – he can go into a shop to ask for bacon, be told there is no bacon, and leave the shop empty-handed; he can buy a ticket and wait on the station, and if the train doesn't come he can go home again: still he is a customer. A disap-pointed customer, granted, but a customer nonetheless.

I didn't make a success of Macbeth. I've done it twice, failing both times, and draw slight comfort from the fact that although I've seen some good performances in the part, I've never seen an outstanding one. Outstanding Lears, Hamlets, Cleopatras yes, and outstanding *productions* of the play, but your eponymous Thane has in my experience finally eluded capture. The ruthless ambition, the weary acceptance of the consequences, the terrified superstition and the headlong descent into the black night of the soul – all of this is within any decent actor's compass; no, the trouble lies in the pivotal Act I scene 7, where, in twenty-eight lines of emotional argument, his wife turns him from clear-headed recital of the many good reasons for *not* killing Duncan, to immediate and unthinking acquiescence. Whatever through-line you try to draw of Macbeth's character, this scene ruptures it, and thereafter the audience doesn't truly believe in you.

The Gardner Centre season, under the overall direction of John David, continued with *Jumpers,* Tom Stoppard's brilliant comedy about the struggles of a Professor of Moral Philosophy to achieve a definition of good and evil in practical modern terms. The action takes place in two main rooms, the professor's study on one side of the stage, and his wife's bedroom on the other, with a narrow hallway in between.

Dottie, the professor's wife, played here by June Ritchie, has (perhaps) killed a member of the University's athletics team, and in order to conceal the body, has hung him on the back of her bedroom door. The door opens inwards and upstage, so that when I, as her husband, come in and leave the door open, I don't see him. One night the hook supporting the rather weighty dead athlete gave way, and the body slumped heavily to the floor. This happened just a few seconds before I was due to enter and find my wife lying naked on the bed. I already had my hand on the door-handle when June's voice commanded me, 'Stop! You can't come in!'

'Why not?' I asked, quite surprised.

'Well you just can't.'

There was a solid wall between me and the bedroom, so I could only listen to the grunting and heaving coming from the other side of the door, and wonder what on earth was going on. Finally an exhausted voice said, 'All right, you can come in now.'

What greeted my eyes was an enormous mound of bedclothes in the centre of the room. Standing over it was a stark naked, perspiring

June Ritchie. I drew my breath and tried to carry on the scene as though nothing untoward had happened, but in skirting round the pile of bedclothes I knocked against a large goldfish bowl that stood on the dressing table, and sent it crashing to the floor.

Now, it was essential that the globe's occupant (dry the ready tear, animal-lovers, it was but an artificial goldfish, propelled round the bowl by thermal ingenuity) remained, for purposes of the plot, alive until later in the play; so June, with admirable presence of mind, gathered it swiftly from the floor and dropped it into her glass of gin-and-tonic, earning an appreciative round of applause from the fascinated audience. However, if they nurtured any hopes of our shortly returning to the play Tom Stoppard had written, these were dashed by the appearance on stage of our Deputy Stage Manager carrying a dustpan and brush. He raised his hand imperiously for silence.

'Ladies and gentlemen,' he announced. 'I am sorry to interrupt the action, but I'm afraid some broken glass has fallen into the mechanism of the revolving stage. I shall try and get it out as quickly as possible.'

All actors can recall unexpected situations in which they have been placed during a performance, but sitting silently on a bed with a naked lady in front of 500 people, while a small bearded man in a blue flowered apron crawled round our feet with a dustpan, claims a special place in my memory.

*

About this time I did another show at the Open Space – a lunchtime play entitled *Down Red Lane*, by B.S. Johnson, about a man resolutely eating himself to death.

During the play I had to consume two dozen oysters (on the Open Space budget these were crushed tinned lychees in second-hand oyster shells), a huge braised steak (brown bread soaked in gravy), a créme brulée (the composition of which I declined to ask), and cheese (cheese). Simon Callow played the ever-provident waiter, and under the table, hidden beneath the cloth, sat Martin Coveney – brother to the drama critic Michael – as the outraged voice of my stomach. The playwright, in whose several novels he would employ typographical techniques such as blacked-out or diagrammatically-arranged print and pages left blank or with holes cut in them, was an unhappy man who finally achieved his own death by the same deliberate assault on his digestion. He may perhaps be remembered for his short film *Fat Man on a Beach*.

I directed another lunch-time play for the Open Space, but by that time it was nearing the end of its very worthwhile life as an experimental producing theatre. Charles had been battling with the Arts Council for a one-off grant to produce a new play which, he maintained, could not possibly be staged without the provision of a fully practical bathroom suite in flamingo-pink porcelain. The argument went on and on for months, the contentious flamingo-pink facilities featuring in the columns of several national newspapers. Eventually the Council caved in and stumped up the money.

I had left the Open Space Board by this time, so I never found out why the play-with-a-bathroom was never in fact done, or if indeed there ever *was* such a play. All I know is, that at a party in the Hampstead flat that Charles was sharing with his current leggy blonde, I went upstairs to the loo, and there it was: the flamingo-pink bathroom suite, in person. I started back, with a gasp; it was as if I'd suddenly barged in on the Queen.

Charles went back to the USA very soon afterwards. He ran an experimental company in Los Angeles, and didn't reappear in England until several years later, by which time the bathwater, as it were, would have cooled down somewhat.

Chapter Nineteen

Concealing all evidence that I might be linked in any way to the Battle of the Bathroom, I accepted an invitation shortly afterwards to join the Drama Panel of the Arts Council, and remained there for four years before shifting to sit on their Touring Committee. Each of the artistic disciplines in those days – Fine Arts, Music, Literature, Dance, Drama etc. – had a large panel of advisors, made up largely of representatives from the Council's client organisations.

We on the Drama Panel were mainly concerned to provide public access to a sufficient variety of performed work, to plug geographical gaps and expand the capabilities of deserving clients. It was good that these things should be discussed within a forum of experienced – and often mutually competitive – professionals. Even when, later on, the Arts Council's vocabulary changed and we started talking about attendance targets, sensitivity analyses and 3-Year Business Plans, the arguments about who was going to get a slice of the rapidly shrinking cake were at least carried on by the claimants themselves. The meetings were often extremely lively, and I was lost in admiration for the political acumen displayed by members arguing the competitive value of their organisations.

They were a very interesting group of people. Among them was Trevor Nunn, already for some years the Artistic Director of the Royal Shakespeare Company. In 1969, just after I had finished the run of *The Italian Girl,* the RSC had asked me to play Sir Toby Belch in *Twelfth Night;* I had said no, for one thing because the part I had just played was in so many ways like Sir Toby, and for another because I'd already been offered Bolingbroke and Mortimer for Prospect, over the same period. My refusal had apparently made the RSC very cross, and friends who were in the company kept ringing me up to advise me that I had poured a whole bottle of ink over my copy-book. So now I was surprised and delighted when Trevor Nunn offered me the part of Judge Brack in his production of *Hedda Gabler,* to go on a world tour.

I am fascinated by Ibsen. Recent productions have come a long way from the traditional hand-wringing, green-lampshaded torment that for years audiences had been taught to expect, and the improvement has had much to do with new translations. Although all recent English versions of Ibsen must owe something to the scholarship of the late Michael Meyer, occasionally a fresh rendering will throw new light on a scene or a line or a significant moment.

For our production, Trevor did his own translation. Not being a Norwegian speaker, he did this by arming himself with dictionaries, other translations and, importantly, a reading of the whole play on tape recorded by a Norwegian actress whose work he admired. This told him about the tunes, inflections and dynamics that Ibsen would have heard in his mind when he was writing the play.

During this work, Trevor made an interesting decision. English is a much more abundant language than Norwegian; for every Norwegian word there often tend to be about five English synonyms, and where the same word occurs three or four times on Ibsen's page, translators have commonly used this as an opportunity for variation. Trevor took the opposite view; he purposely used the same words and phrases over and over again, the thinking being that Ibsen *intended* them to recur in the banal, predictable language of the parochial world in which Hedda feels she been condemned to suffocate.

Glenda Jackson was Hedda; Peter Eyre played Tesman, Patrick Stewart Lovborg, Jenny Linden Mrs Elvsted and Constance Chapman was the Aunt. John Napier's light and airy art-nouveau set had the right feeling of impersonal *House and Garden* chic. The Lighting Designer was Andy Phillips.

After an initial week in Richmond, we left for a fourteen-week tour of Melbourne, Sydney, Los Angeles, Washington and Toronto.

In Melbourne, we played again at the Princess Theatre, where we had come with Prospect three years before. This time the feeling was very different. Instead of a mixed audience dropping in to see an unknown British company that had had good reviews from Sydney, we were now attended by a glittering band of socialites who had fought tooth and nail for tickets simply to see the legendary Glenda Jackson in the flesh.

Hordes of people thronged the stage door after the show, and our company manager had rather peremptorily told them all to wait ten minutes so that the cast could compose themselves. We spent those ten minutes opening bottles, sending our dressers out for extra glasses, and applying after-shave ready for the invasion. Nothing. They'd all got bored and gone home, or to a reception ('Dress – Casual Elegant') being held in an awful club somewhere, and to which the cast were also invited. Apart from a casually-sequinned lady who hadn't actually seen the show – having spent the evening instead tenderly looking after a bottle of vodka – nobody spoke to me the entire evening.

The next day things got back to normal. The Australian theatre people are a byword for friendliness and hospitality, and in addition we were treated very well throughout our stay by the different elements of the Diplomatic Service.

Here, though, there seemed to be a difficulty for Glenda. I think she felt that as a good socialist it was her duty to show republican disdain for the representatives of Queen and Commonwealth, and this even extended to the British Council. It would have been perfectly legitimate, if slightly ungracious, formally to have declined their various invitations, but Glenda had a way instead of turning up late, unsuitably dressed, or accompanied by people who hadn't actually been invited. I seemed to be the person who always had to go back and apologise the following morning, while Glenda and her chums were off to the beach.

Various articles and at least two books have been written about Glenda Jackson, and her biographers have not on the whole been very fair to her. Aggressive she may have been socially, but on stage I found her conduct selflessly professional, and as leader of the company she showed proper concern for her colleagues' welfare. I think she was fundamentally resentful – or at any rate, suspicious – of authority, so the people in the organisation who fared rather badly at her hands were Trevor (with whom she took every opportunity to quarrel) and our co-producer Paul Elliott, who was, I think, terrified of her, so it probably served him right.

Glenda's later decision to abandon her profession and go into politics seemed to astonish people, but then maybe most of us don't understand why anyone should ever want to become an M.P. Neither, I think, do most people appreciate the career problems confronting an actress of star status when she approaches middle age. The film and TV world fast begins to lose interest. In the classical theatre, the few leading parts that are on offer at any one time will keep only a handful of actresses in work; and if you are not numbered among that fortunate handful, the second pickings are not very rewarding. It is different for men; if you can't play Macbeth, then Macduff or Banquo are still well worth doing; you can make something of Ross and Malcolm, and even Duncan is a worthwhile double with the Scots Doctor. But if you're an actress, and someone gets in ahead of you to play Lady Macbeth, then you're left with Lady Macduff (one scene), the Gentlewoman, or a Witch.

I often wonder how different an actress' life – *all* actors' lives in fact – would be today, had Shakespeare lived some sixty years later, when women were first allowed to perform on stage in England. Would he have written many more parts for women, so that our classical companies would now be composed fairly equally of the two sexes? Almost surely not, I fear. Modern large-cast plays are still heavily loaded in favour of male characters, and while there are roughly the same number of actresses in the UK today as there are actors, there are still about five times as many parts for the men.

Whatever were Glenda's reasons, it must have been a painful wrench to part from the profession she had followed for twenty-odd years, and to which after all she had made such a distinguished contribution.

*

It was good to be back in Sydney, with the ferries converging on Circular Quay from the suburbs across the Harbour – Balmain, Hunter's Hill, Neutral Bay, Cremorne, Mosman and Manly; the Edwardian Marble Bar under the Hilton Hotel, Doyles' open-air fish restaurants at Rose Bay and Watson's Bay, and the newly completed Opera House (for all the argument about the misuse of the different auditoria, nevertheless a breathtaking building). The Harbour itself, with its myriad little bays, inlets and promontories, is so vast that wherever you are in Sydney you are never very far from it; you will be walking along an unfamiliar street between terraced houses with wrought-iron balconies, and suddenly you will feel the light fresh breeze and unaccountable lift to the spirits that tells you that if you walk just a little further, the road will abruptly come to an end, and there will be the water again.

The theatrical scene in Sydney had developed considerably since I was there last. There were exciting new actors, directors and designers around and, most importantly, a crop of very interesting writers – Ron Blair, Peter Kenna, Dorothy Hewett, Louis Nowra, Stephen Sewell, and our friend Nick Enright whom we have known over the years as front-of-house-manager, actor, drama teacher, director, dramatist and screenwriter.

There is always something new going on in Sydney. Each time you go there, someone will point you towards a fresh theatrical venue, where the premiere of an exciting play is being brilliantly performed by a brand new actor of astonishing talent, directed by someone amazing you've never heard of before. So you go, and you're enchanted, and when you return three years later you ask eagerly how that incomparable fusion of talent has fared in the meantime.

Oh. That. Well the theatre is now a drive-in-bottle shop. The writer is teaching English up in Kurrajong. The director's in California and the actor's in *Neighbours*. But while you're here you *must* go and see . . .

On our way across the Pacific we had a two-day break in Honolulu, because in crossing the international date line we had gained an extra Sunday. Years later I was to revisit Hawaii, and see the appalling desecration caused by the eruption of the Kilauea volcano in 1989; miles and miles of solidified lava, covering roads and beaches and the remains of villages, churches and schools. The islanders live on such familiar terms with the daily threat of eruptions that they have adopted practically the shortest word in their language, *aa*, to mean the clinkery, burning lava flow that could at any moment bring horrifying and inescapable death. At their University, I spoke to a Professor of Earth Sciences. 'We exist by geological consent', he asserted gravely.

But for the present, all we saw was tourist Honolulu, with Waikiki Beach decorated with coloured lanterns, people wearing *leis* and tropical shirts, and the smell of fast food everywhere.

And then we got to Los Angeles. We were playing at the Huntington Hartford Theatre (now the Doolittle), which is neither in Downtown L.A. nor in fashionable Beverly Hills; it's in Hollywood. By Hollywood, of course, I don't mean Hollywood. Today, if the great stars of screen, stage, radio and the gramophone were to tread their way along the Walk of Fame – the trail of commemorative brass stars let into the sidewalks of Vine Street and Hollywood Boulevard – it could only be to visit a massage parlour, buy a cheap souvenir mug or pick up a Kentucky Fried Chicken. The Movies – except for Paramount – moved out long ago, further west; up on the hill the famous Hollywood Sign with its 45ft high letters looks like the overgrown name-board on a disused railway station.

Those brass stars are worth studying, though, if it be only to notice who has been thought worthy of inclusion and who not. For instance, although the Beach Boys have a star, the Beatles haven't. There's one for Robert Redford, but not for Paul Newman. Mickey Mouse is there, but not Donald Duck. Of course, the fact that you have to pay the Chamber of Commerce $7,500 for your own star may influence your personal wishes in the matter.

My daughter Juliet brought Sam and Joe out to join me – Pru was doing a season at Greenwich, and so couldn't come – and they enjoyed the Californian sun by the swimming pool (even the tattiest hotel in Southern California of course has a swimming pool). They went to Disneyland and Knott's Berry Farm and every-where else, and were looked after and liberally brunched by hospit-able friends.

We had a self-contained apartment within our hotel, and did our own cooking. There seemed to be enough cutlery, crockery and so on, except that I could nowhere find any egg cups. This being my first time in California, I went along to the supermarket to buy some, not knowing that a soft-boiled egg is a completely unknown concept here; eggs are either easy-over, sunnyside up, or scrambled.

Eventually, tucked dustily away at the back of a distant shelf, I found four green plastic egg cups, and put them in the basket with my groceries.

'Irving!' called the clerk at the check-out; 'How much for these little vases?'

'No, they're not vases,' I told him, 'they're egg cups.'

'Egg – *cups*? What do you mean?'

'You put eggs in them.'

He picked one of them up and studied it keenly.

'*Why?*'

'Well – to eat them.'

'You mean like – *raw?*'

'No, no, you boil them. And then you eat them. With a teaspoon,' I added lamely.

He shook his head.

'Shit', he said finally. 'Okay.' But he wouldn't let me pay for them.

The play was sold out before we opened, and the touts were doing a roaring trade. American as well as British actors agree that in general, audiences in Los Angeles aren't very keen on plays in which there's much *talking*. There is rather a lot of talking in *Hedda Gabler*, but people sat through it patiently because of their adulation for Glenda, because they'd paid so much for their tickets, and because Californians are notoriously polite.

Working in the theatre in Los Angeles is rather like going to Lords' to play football. It's essentially a movie town, and while there are huge theatres for the touring musicals, the number of straight playhouses serving this enormous catchment area is very limited. The 99-seater fringe theatres (provided there are fewer than 100 seats, the management doesn't have to pay Equity rates) do some wonderful work, but their casts have to subsidise this work with earnings from their *real* job: that is, films and TV. I was hotly recommended to see a chamber production of *King Lear* at one of these places; when I got there, there was a notice on the door cancelling the performance – the Lear (who had had amazing notices) had been given two days on the TV Soap *Trapper John*, and couldn't afford not to do it.

From Los Angeles the family flew with us to Washington, DC, where I immediately managed to lose six-year old Joe at Dulles Airport. The trouble was I didn't know we'd lost him until our bus had completed its twenty mile journey to the Sheraton Hotel in town. On the bus I had been sitting with Sam, while Juliet, who had tonsilitis, was lying on the back seat with a rug over herself and, I had assumed, my other son.

Phone calls to Airport Security, the PanAm desk, the Duty Manager, were fruitless – no-one had news of an unclaimed child. The hotel manager's sympathetic wife, sobbing with distress, thrust me into her Oldsmobile and drove back down the freeway at breakneck speed, tears cascading from her eyes, while I passed her the tissues and prepared to grab the wheel should it become necessary.

Joe, a thoughtful lad, but one not always ready to share his thoughts with others, had taken a leisurely tour round Dulles

Airport before mentioning to somebody that he had been abandoned by his father. However, by the time we got there he was already in the custody of the police department, having a wonderful time handcuffing all the officers together. When we returned to the Sheraton, it was to the considerable relief of Peter Eyre and Patrick Stewart, who had generously undertaken to sit with me while I made what might have been quite a tricky telephone call to my wife back in England. 'Darling, you know how irritated we get with the two boys when they quarrel and won't share things? Well, I think I may have found a solution . . . '

Washington yielded a number of delights; the Folger Library, the magnificent National Gallery and the different Smithsonian Collections. We went to Georgetown, and heard some very good jazz, and we visited the Capitol.

This was a rather surprising experience. The young Senator who had invited us was giving a speech about the dramatic build-up in Russian submarine strength, and I should have expected the floor to have been packed with incandescent Republicans baying for blood. In fact, there were only two other people in the chamber. One was the day's Chairman-by-rotation, a very small man in a very big armchair, and the other was an elderly Senator who apparently had retired that morning and was now clearing out his desk, carefully examining pieces of string, broken pencils and old cough sweets before consigning them to the waste paper basket.

I asked our Senator what he felt about playing to such a lamentably poor house, but he seemed quite unabashed by the experience, saying that things usually hotted up a bit after lunch.

From Washington we went on to Toronto, where we played at Ed Mirvish's Royal Alexandra Theatre and stayed in a very sombre hotel, the walls of which were lined with suits of armour, and the bars full of solemn men in tartan dinner jackets. I escaped to Stratford (Ontario) on a couple of occasions, and to Niagara Falls, had a weekend in Montreal and a fishing trip on a very cold lake somewhere north of the city. I found Toronto dispiriting, I don't know why; perhaps I was just restless, bored now with the tour (this was the last leg), and homesick like everyone else. Also, discontent was simmering among the company about a proposal that we should film the production on our return to the UK, but with somebody other than Trevor (who had never yet worked with the film camera) directing it. With the modest remuneration and absurdly tight schedule that was being talked about, there would be no time, or indeed inclination, to adapt to any new ideas that a fresh director might want to bring to the project.

Patrick Stewart, a pillar of the RSC, and strongly loyal to his director, led a campaign to make our participation conditional on Trevor remaining at the helm, and correspondence flew back and forth between ourselves, our agents and the producer-elect, Bob Enders for Brut-Fabergé Productions. Glenda's involvement in all this was not solicited, partly because her attitude to Trevor was known to be equivocal, and partly because she was in the throes of a precipitate marital crisis.

It must have been a very traumatic time for her, but she was far too professional to let it affect her performance in any way. Here, even more than Los Angeles, it was her name alone that sold the tickets. Subscription Booking was the new theatrical orthodoxy, and Ed Mirvish had embraced it to the extent of billing us simply as 'May 5th-24th, GLENDA JACKSON'. Stand-up Comedy, perhaps?

We got back to London, and we did indeed make the film. Trevor directed it perfectly well, and the eminent Douglas Slocombe did the photography. We did a one-day shoot on Loch Katrine, a bit of stuff in a garden somewhere, and the rest at the ABC Studios at Elstree. By the end of our fourth week we had, incredibly, got nearly the whole thing in the can – there were just two short scenes left to do.

As we were setting up the last shot of the day, we noticed a number of people tiptoeing into the studio with plates of sandwiches and bottles of wine. A celebration, we thought. But why? Somebody's birthday?

We got the shot in, the First Assistant announced the 'wrap', and a smiling Bob Enders strode on to the set and began thanking everybody. 'It's been a great four weeks,' he said, 'and you've all worked wonderfully. Well done!'

'But – Bob,' ventured Trevor, 'you do know we haven't *finished*. There are just a couple of scenes to do on Monday.'

Bob's tone was avuncular but firm. 'Well no, I'm afraid not, Trevor. This is it, I'm afraid. We just have to do without those bits.'

'But – we *can't!* It's impossible. The film won't make any sense without those scenes – '

'Well, I'm sure that's how it seems to you now, Trevor, but you're new in this business; you'll see, when it's all cut together it'll be just fine.'

'Listen, this is – '

'It'll be JUST FINE, Trevor.'

The upshot was that we did come back on Monday to finish the picture, but with a new crew, Enders having paid the others off. Trevor had to foot the whole bill for the extra day.

On the following Friday we re-rehearsed the play for the stage, opening at the Aldwych a week later. It ran its allotted four weeks to full houses, and then *Hedda* was finally laid to rest.

Chapter Twenty

The only other occupant of the bar of the Western Isles Hotel got up from his stool, came over and extended his hand. I turned from the window, where I was watching a trawler in the little harbour unloading its morning catch.

'Hello,' he murmured casually, 'we've never met, but I'm your cousin Rupert.'

I was dimly aware that my father had a distant cousin called Rupert Elwes. Certainly I had never seen him before, nor did I know that he lived – as turned out to be the case – in Tobermory on the Isle of Mull. Planning to spend three days entirely on my own, trying to clear my head before the next job, I had taken the overnight train to Scotland, and had just crossed over on the boat from Oban. Now here was this cousin Rupert, inviting me to dinner that evening as if we were still in WC2.

Gwendolen, in *The Importance of Being Earnest*, remarks: 'Now that I think of it, I have never heard any man mention his brother. The subject seems distasteful to most men.' To Rupert Elwes, as we sat in his cottage by a dying peat fire, that distaste seemed to have extended to cover the whole family, for he avoided all mention of our mutual relatives, and by the time we finally parted and I walked back down the lane to the pub where I had a bed, I still had no real idea who he was. We never saw each other again, and as he was at least twenty-five years my senior, I dare say he's no longer with us. This reticence is characteristic of our family, and though there is a fairly successful attempt once a year to gather the proliferating West dynasty under one roof, or upon one lawn, members of the clan still tend to circle each other warily, not being quite sure which wife, husband or child belongs to whom.

My mother's family tree is of smaller dimension. My maternal grandfather, who came from County Wicklow in Ireland, graduated in medicine, but threw it over to become an actor, starting up a small touring company with the money his family had put aside for him to buy a practice. I never knew my grandmother, who in the one or two studio portraits that survive seems to be struggling to control her amusement at the serious deliberations of the photographer. She did a bit of acting herself, and under her wing my mother began her stage career at the age of eight, on tour in the American comedy *Mrs Wiggs of the Cabbage Patch*. Grandfather, who professionally styled himself C.W. Carleton Crowe, never quite achieved the career that the grandiloquence of his name seemed to demand, though he can still be seen for a few seconds as Robert Donat's servant in the original film of *Goodbye Mr Chips*.

With my paternal grandparents I was better acquainted. Grandfather West was in marine insurance, for Lloyds'. Of Teutonic appearance, sporting in his early days a von Hindenburg moustache, and making repeated journeys to Hamburg on business, he was arrested in 1914 on suspicion of being an enemy agent. Eventually the authorities decided that such a double-bluff non-disguise was beyond the ingenuity of German military intelligence, and he was released, settling in Doncaster next door to the home of Sir Nigel Gresley, chief locomotive engineer for the Great Northern Railway. Grandfather liked dogs, read me ghost stories, and was firmly convinced that he was the rightful King of Denmark.

My father was his third child, and the youngest of three brothers, of whom the senior was a partner in a publishing firm and lived in a large thatched house near Farnham in Surrey.

As a child, going to stay at The Thatched House was an exciting and often alarming experience. My uncle Douglas had an ungovernable temper, and his fury was habitually aroused by the failure of household objects to function effectively. Table lighters that didn't light, carving knives that were too blunt, telephone directories that had failed to provide information – these would be savagely hurled across the room or, more often, out of the window into the shrubbery. My uncle's preliminary yell of rage would give the gardener just time to protect his head from hazardous missiles.

Douglas' wife Kitty was a remarkable woman, not only on account of her very necessary patience, but of her intellect. The daughter of the classical scholar Walter Leaf and a relative of the Strachey family, with her flat 1920's figure and slight scholarly stoop, her round tortoiseshell glasses and Eton crop, she might have stepped straight from the pages of *A Boy at the Hogarth Press*. Aunt Kitty was a convinced atheist, and Pru and I were apprehensive about asking her to join us for our son Sam's christening. Did she totally disapprove, we asked?

'Not at all,' she replied hotly, 'if they're not brought up C. of E., they'll never understand Eng. Lit.'

There is no inherited attitude to religion in my family. My mother was an Irish Protestant, my father vaguely Church of England, my sister liberal Anglo-Catholic. I have a Born Again Christian cousin, and others with Evangelical leanings. Both our sons profess atheism, though one arranges sacred music for weddings and the other rings the bells and sings in the choir at his local church.

As for me, I know where I stand in the matter of liturgy, if not necessarily of faith. Religious Fundamentalism, of any kind, alarms and depresses me. Firmly what John Betjeman used to call Middle Stump, I love good church music, and value Cranmer and the King James Bible for allowing us to hold hands with the generations that have been saying those same words in that same church for more than three hundred years.

I take issue with a great deal of the current modernisation of scriptural text. The policy of ironing out possible ambiguities that appear in the Authorised Version is, I maintain, culpably simplistic. Ambiguities make you re-examine the subject, they make you *think*. Anyway, the whole exercise is distinctly patronising. A while ago at Guildford Cathedral I was doing some readings which are traditionally required to separate Haydn's *Seven Last Words from the Cross*, each movement of which is announced by Christ's own words. The Precentor handed me what I think must have been called The New English Modified, Attenuated and Emasculated Bible, which required me to say, instead of the well-known 1666 'Father, forgive them, for they know not what they do', the modern improvement 'Father, forgive them, *they do not know what they are doing.*' This completely unnecessary readjustment makes Christ's plea for divine amnesty sound like a complaint about a gang of incompetent builders. I spoke my preferred version; I was in the pulpit at the time, and there was nothing they could do to stop me.

Years ago I remember having a delightful conversation with a West Country rector on a train going to Plymouth. He was talking about the dilemma of the Commuter Christian, who has no time to attend a weekday service in the metropolis, but who, having been so divorced from his or her local community during the week, then feels inhibited about joining the parish congregation on Sunday.

Over a bottle of wine we decided that the answer to the problem lay in the provision of special carriages on commuter trains, devoted to the celebration of Matins, Evensong or the Eucharist, according to the time of day. If the idea caught on, supplementary coaches could be provided for Bible classes, preparation for marriage and Confirmation, and choir practice. I suggested that entire special trains could be put on for the major religious festivals: *The Advent Express*, *The Epiphany Limited* or *The Pentecost Flyer*. Dedicated locomotives would be renamed after different saints, *Thomas Aquinas* and *Ignatius of Loyola*.

By the time we got to Exeter we had accepted the need for an entirely new ecclesiastical structure: sections of each line would assume parish status, with their own clergy, supervised by an archdeacon at every major junction. Each principal London terminus would be regarded as a diocese; there would be Bishops of King's Cross, Euston, Paddington, Waterloo etc., with perhaps Suffragan Bishops of Marylebone, Blackfriars and Fenchurch Street.

Reluctantly, we would have to leave the Roman Catholics to make their own arrangements.

*

I stood on the foredeck of *P.S. Waverley*, as she gently eased her way through the shallow channel into the Kyles of Bute to call at the pretty village of Tignabruaich.

In 1973, by then the only sea-going paddle steamer in the world, *Waverley* had been withdrawn from her service on the Clyde for Caledonian MacBrayne, and would have been broken up like most of her predecessors had it not been for a sympathetic businessman named Douglas McGowan, who purchased her for the sum of £1 for the newly-formed Paddle Steamer Preservation Society, of which I was – and am – an enthusiastic member. In 1975, after a few maintenance repairs, and having been repainted in the LNER colours she wore when she originally went into service in 1947, we had her at sea again, not only in Western Scotland but, as time went on, in the Bristol Channel, Thames Estuary, Solent, South Coast and East

Anglia. She is still providing the unique experience of the day excursion by sea, so beloved in the days when not everyone had a motor car, and still giving delight to hundreds of thousands of people all over the country.

My love of paddle steamers was inherited from my father. Not a man of many expressed enthusiasms, this was perhaps the chief one. In 1940, these ships had been pressed into war service (their comparatively shallow draught recommended them for use as minesweepers), and many were active in rescuing troops at Dunkirk. Several were sunk. After the war, I watched as one by one the survivors of the Bristol-based P&A Campbell fleet limped, grey and battered, back up the River Avon and tied up at Hotwells to await the marine surveyors' sentence of life or death.

On an April afternoon in 1946, my father took me down to Cumberland Basin to await, with several hundred other Bristolians, the reappearance of *P.S.Ravenswood*, to take us on the first passenger excursion a steamer had made from the city in seven years. We heard her siren, and round the bend in the river she came, her white funnel and polished brasses shining in the sun and the gentle beat of her paddle wheels reaching us now as she steamed beneath the Suspension Bridge. The grey filter of austerity that had shrouded half of my young life was lifted away in that moment. Now the war was *really* over.

Over the next few years, *Ravenswood* was joined in the Bristol Channel by others of the fleet, including two newly-built steamers, the *Bristol Queen* and *Cardiff Queen*. I spent many blissful hours aboard, sailing down to Ilfracombe and from Weston-super-Mare over to South Wales. To my father, the officers, engineers and seamen of these ships were as gods. Though he could usually talk without restraint or diffidence to the powers of the Church, Law or the theatrical profession, when Captain Brander of the *Glen Usk* wished him good morning, he blushed, stammered and inclined his head respectfully as the Captain climbed his steps to the bridge.

I often sailed with Syd (my father, when asked what he would like to be called now that we were too old to say 'Daddy', replied, 'oh, anything you want – "Syd" if you like') down the Thames to Margate aboard that Rolls-Royce of paddle steamers, the *Royal Eagle*; but he never managed the journey up here to Scotland, where *Waverley* was now making her way back up the Clyde followed by the reddening

167

evening sun. It had been a perfect day, and I asked myself petulantly, 'Why do I have to catch the sleeper back to London to rehearse in the morning? What am I doing it *for*? Who *cares*? A play is rehearsed, opens, runs, closes and is forgotten, then you start the same thing over again. What is there to show for it?'

My sister at this time was a Psychiatric Social Worker in a particularly troublesome part of Sheffield, doing a very valuable job compared with which we both believed (though I was slow to admit) my own was essentially frivolous. As a matter of fact, it's not the *frivolousness* that bothers me. No, it's the *ephemeral* nature of what we do in the theatre that is so frustrating – we have no means of assessing whether any impression made on the audience will have survived their journey home. We don't know whether our own contribution has served the play properly that evening.

John Gielgud wrote in his book *Early Stages*:

'I have often wished that I were able to rise in the middle of the night, switch on the light, and examine some previous performance of mine as I saw it standing on the mantelpiece . . . '

Nevertheless I did catch the sleeper back to Euston, and began rehearsals for a revival of Toby's Chichester production of *A Month in the Country*, which we were now presenting under the Prospect banner at the Albery Theatre in London. We were also re-mounting Richard Cottrell's *A Room with a View*, and attempting to run the two shows in repertoire.

Actors like repertoire. It gives them a more interesting time, they don't mind playing a small part in one play if they can do a much bigger part in another, and it helps to keep each play fresh if they're not doing it every night. But the British public don't like it. They're used to it at the National or the RSC, but in the West End they just find it confusing. So *A Room with a View*, though it was a charming show, suffered by comparison with its stable-mate, and was scratched.

This was one of the difficulties of bringing the work of subsidised companies into the Commercial West End, a situation which Prospect were now having to cope with more and more frequently. We were a touring company without a London base, but actors like Ian McKellen, Dorothy Tutin and Derek Jacobi had a right to a brief spell in London after ten weeks on the road; London audiences, too, should be permitted the same opportunities to see the company's work as those in Newcastle, Leeds or Birmingham. Up to now, though, we had always had to come in to whatever London theatre was available (if indeed there was one), in partnership with a West End Producer, who would naturally want to present and publicise the play in his own way, and whose expenses would leave very little in the kitty for Prospect at the end of the day.

If we were going to continue producing such large-scale work, with such distinguished casts, we needed to find a London theatre with production and rehearsal facilities which would be our home, and provide a turnover of productions that ensured that while we discharged our touring obligations around the country with one set of shows, our home base would never be left unoccupied.

A year later, we hit on a solution which we thought would solve this situation brilliantly and permanently.

We turned out to be quite wrong.

Chapter Twenty-One

A Month in the Country ran until the end of March 1976 at the Albery, and meanwhile we had been defaulting on our touring quota. We needed something cheap, quick and easy to send out on the road, and we came up with Charles Dyer's two-handed play about the two gay hairdressers, *Staircase.* Derek Jacobi and I played the couple, and enjoyed it hugely – more, I suspect, than did most of the audience.

We opened at the King's Theatre Glasgow, the Tuesday after we had packed up at the Albery. A number of Glaswegian patrons left during the second act, wearing those specially heavy boots that are favoured by people who make a practice of walking out of theatres. From Glasgow we went on to Basingstoke, then up again to Inverness for the first part of the next week, flying back to Luton on the Friday in a small propellor-and-biscuits aircraft in order to perform that evening at the tiny Cricklade Theatre in Andover. Earlier planning might have resulted in a more conventional, and certainly more convenient, tour.

After the final week, at the Gardner Centre, Brighton, I travelled to Bath for a small part in Tony Richardson's film of Fielding's *Joseph Andrews,* some of which we shot in the courtyard of the ancient George Inn at Norton St. Philip.

The weather was boiling hot, and Tony had made the whole place look like a Rowlandson cartoon. Pigs, cows, geese, goats, dogs, chickens and farmers' small children were sliding about and falling in the accumulated stinking mess. Flies swarmed everywhere. Michael Hordern, ploughing through the mire on horseback, had to have a real sheep's liver thrown in his face. In a break between shots, out of the saloon bar came John Gielgud, dressed as an 18th-century doctor and holding a glass of dry sherry, quite oblivious to all the mayhem. He told me a long story about Irene Vanbrugh, while a goat urinated slowly but copiously down his gaiters.

I had to expose my bottom in one scene (for reasons which I am not at liberty to divulge), and Tony Richardson thought it would be a splendid idea if I looked as though I had recently sat in a cow-pat. The make-up department, two middle-aged ladies, began to discuss the composition of an artificial cow-pat mixture that would adhere to the subject, and got quite excited about it. I said, look here, why don't I just go out and sit in a cow-pat, after all there are plenty of them around. They were quite offended by the idea, and proceeded to mix up some oatmeal, molasses and green dye in a large basin. I slipped my trousers down, and the sticky substance was applied over a large area, with artistic deliberation.

'Do you think perhaps a few pieces of straw?' one asked the other.

'Yes. And maybe a feather.'

'Good idea. Here?'

'No – further over. *Yes.*'

It was a work of art. They got a mirror and showed me. Unfortunately, when the scene was over, it proved extremely difficult to get off; the two of them were hard at work with scrubbing brushes for ten minutes before I was able to resume my trousers and what remained of my dignity.

The picture, for all that, was not a success.

Now that I had one or two evenings off – the first at home for many months, I should have been going out to see what was happening in the London theatre. But did I? No.

Why does it often seem such an effort to go out and see a play? I'll go like a shot to the opera, or a symphony concert, I'll visit a jazz club or watch snooker on the television – yes, it's what I *can't do at all* that excites me.

I don't think I'm alone in this. For instance, I'm sure the reason why there are so many cookery programmes on television, though people are *actually cooking less*, is because people like seeing someone else do things they can't do themselves. Logically then, to get the fullest enjoyment from watching an expert at work, it's best to be entirely incompetent. I try to follow that rule as far as possible.

A little while ago I asked a cellist friend whether he was going to the Festival Hall the following evening to hear a mutual acquaintance, also a cellist, play the Dvořák concerto.

'No, of course not,' he said, surprised. 'I don't want to spend an evening listening to some poor sod grappling with the same problems I have to cope with. No, I'm going to the theatre.' That, of course, was just the reason I was going to the Festival Hall.

I am not a musician, having had no formal musical training and playing no instrument. My parents couldn't afford a piano. I learned to read music at school, in order to sing in local choirs. However, I do love music, and get very unhappy if denied access to it for any length of time.

Pop culture missed me by a couple of years; when I was of impressionable age there were no Walkmans, no means of listening to music while I was cycling or on a bus; there were no pop videos or special magazines with intimate pictures of David Whitfield, or articles on the secret love-life of Donald Peers. Buddy Holly, Chuck Berry and The Everley Brothers were coming up on the outside, but I was just too old to start an affair with them. In my sad ignorance I am the despair of the MTV generation, but there's nothing to be done about it. When they ask me what music I like, I have to pretend I've just seen an unusual aeroplane, or been stung by a wasp.

When an opportunity occurs to work alongside musicians I grab it. Actors can learn a lot from musicians, not only in terms of application and teamwork, but because an actor who has acquired some musical sensibility will instinctively know how to phrase text. It really is useful to be able to imagine a line of speech as if it were on a musical stave, to think where the bar-lines come, what the time-signature is, and perhaps even the metronome marking.

As it happened, immediately after *Staircase* Pru and I went straight into a job with a couple of musicians, going on a recital tour for the British Council, to Milan, Pisa, Rome, Athens, Thessaloniki, Amsterdam and Groningen; one of those black tie and black folder affairs that have rather gone out of fashion, which is a pity. I have compiled lots of recitals on different subjects over the years, collating the words of many different people on a specific character, period or situation. They are easy-to-stage Festival fare, and Pru and I still do one or two such programmes together (though we have generally eschewed the black tie and have even boldly experimented with different coloured folders.)

In July I was back again in Italy, to be in a film called *The Devil's Advocate*. It sank so completely without trace that when a few years later Al Pacino starred in a film by the same title no-one was in any danger of being confused. It was what is termed a Europudding: that is, the cast was drawn from any country which might for that reason make a contribution to the investment. The stars were John Mills (British), Stéphane Audran (French), Raf Vallone and Paola Pittagora (Italian), Curt Jurgens (German) and Jason Miller who, as an Irish-American Catholic was naturally playing the Austrian-Jewish Doctor. Daniel Massey was also in it, and there was a young Afrikaaner, and an elderly Spaniard.

I had been cast by mistake. When I got to the location, a mountainous and inaccessible village called Scontrone in the Abruzzi, the director, Guy Green, took one look at me and blanched.

'I – I thought you were much older . . . ' he stammered.

I apologised. The part I was meant to play was of a drunken old priest, and I had presumed that perhaps he didn't have to be quite as old as all that. But I now suspected that Guy must have seen me in *Abelard and Heloise* – one of my cornflour performances – and assumed that was what I really looked like.

We stared at each other for a few moments; there didn't seem to be anything to say. Then a very small bespectacled German make-up artist stepped forward and announced, 'Is all right I make wig.'

He did. He worked solidly for twenty four hours, and when it was finished it looked like a very new but not terribly expensive dish-mop. I was unphotographable in anything closer than long shot, except at night. Most of my part was cut. I didn't mind really, because it was already apparent that it wasn't going to be a very good film. I had enormous respect for John Mills, who not only gave a very good performance in a rather dully-written part, but stayed up every evening with Morris West, the screenwriter, trying to get him to make some swingeing cuts, which the writer (the screenplay being an adaptation of his own novel) was very unwilling to do.

Not being allowed to appear in a number of scenes in which it would have been reasonable to find the parish priest (in church, for instance), I had rather a lot of time on my hands, and had we been almost anywhere else in Italy this would have been delightful. However Roccaraso, the local town where we were billeted, is a minor ski resort – very popular in the winter months no doubt, but this was July. The morose proprietors of the empty hotels sat around in the cheerless town bar drinking with a few local ski instructors who had not been quite good enough to get jobs in Switzerland. I hired a car and drove the 225km to Rome once a week, to furnish the film unit with proper wine, cigars, newspapers and books in English. It rained, heavily, a good deal of the time.

We eventually moved on to a much more congenial location at Frascati, before finishing up in Munich to do the studio work. Dan Massey and I had become friends, and we found that we were to be together in Richard Eyre's production of *Othello* at the Nottingham Playhouse immediately upon our return to England. He was to play the Moor, while I was cast as Iago.

This famous dramatic partnership can strain the firmest of friendships, and the fact that with us it didn't quite reach breaking point, and resolved itself perfectly afterwards, was to a great extent due to Dan, who had by far the more difficult part of the two. Shakespeare does not allow his protagonist, who must engage the sympathy and partiality of the audience, to speak to them directly until the middle of Act III; then, apart from another four lines in Act IV, he doesn't get another chance until his soliloquy beginning 'It is the cause', in the very last scene of the play. Iago, by contrast, chats to the audience continually, taking them into his confidence, telling them of the appalling things he intends to do, doing them, and then discussing the effect with them afterwards.

The actor playing Iago has to justify everyone's description of him as 'honest Iago'. The audience must initially warm to him, and gradually be repelled, not by what he seems to be, but what he does. This does make it especially hard for the Othello to establish a crucial rapport with the audience early in the play. Olivier achieved this in Act I by delightfully giving the Senators the impression that as a black man he might seriously consider eating any one of them who opposed his marriage to Desdemona.

Opinions are divided, but I personally feel there is very little justification for having a white actor play Othello these days, when there are so many fine black actors around. Dan Massey, when he was rolling on the floor in a very disturbing and well-acted fit of jealousy, did elicit a few unsympathetic laughs from the younger element of the Nottingham audience (and blamed me for it – 'What are you *doing* when I'm having my fit?' he demanded; 'Go on, show me, I know you're doing *something*'), and I don't believe they would have laughed like that had a genuine black actor been playing the part.

When he finally came off stage Dan was further disadvantaged by having to spend valuable time in the shower while I was comfortably installed in the pub, and then, despite all his ablutionary care, often had to endure harsh words from his landlady the following morning over the state of the pillows.

Chapter Twenty-Two

When Patrick Allen and I entered the premises of the oldest established wine merchants in Preston and asked to see their list, the elderly clerk at the high Victorian desk seemed unfazed by the appearance of two bewhiskered figures in frock coats and stovepipe hats, probably considering us the only decently-dressed gentlemen who had passed through that door in the last ninety years. As Mr Gradgrind and Mr Bounderby, we were filming the Granada TV version of *Hard Times*, and had stolen five minutes of our lunch-hour to walk down the alleyway to this rather special establishment, whose blackened oak panels might indeed have furnished the walls of Mr Bounderby's office in Coketown.

John Ruskin thought Dickens' smouldering critique of industrial life to be his highest achievement. Shaw hailed it as a work of genius. Even F.R. Leavis, who despised Dickens, allowed the writer to be 'for once possessed by comprehensive vision'.

Though there have more recently been some very good television dramatisations of Dickens, John Irvin's production of *Hard Times* seemed to me the first attempt to get completely away from the tried formula of jolly rattling stagecoaches and melodramatic East End stews. In Manchester, our designer Roy Stonehouse had built the dark lanes of his Acherontic township on the low-lying land behind Water Street, the site of the original terminus of the Liverpool and Manchester Railway, where the unfortunate M.P. James Huskisson had failed to move swiftly enough out of the path of Stephenson's *Rocket*.

Ours was no romantic view of Dickens' satanic mills. As the cast trudged through the black mud and tried to avoid the open sewers, the unacceptable face of the Industrial Revolution glowered down all too credibly from the unseen factory chimneys. Smoke was everywhere, griming our faces and collars, making eyes and noses run, throats sore, and filling our mouths with ashes and grit. The sun never penetrated the sooty pall above us; when evening came on, it hardly became noticeably darker.

Dickens' readers will remember that into the midst of this cheerless community, to the disapproval of the sober Gradgrind and Bounderby, comes Mr Sleery's Circus, the catalyst that admits a sliver of light and imagination into the sombre lives of the Gradgrind family.

Priscilla John, our casting director, had to set about finding suitable acts to go into the circus ring. Now Sleery's Circus historically would not have been a very *good* circus, which meant that Priscilla's job was that much harder. There are not many circuses around these days, and those that there are keep their performers very busy. It must be difficult to locate even competent freelance acts, but how would one ever find out about the *in*competent ones?

In the end, though, Priscilla found an equestrian family act, the members of which didn't mind habitually falling off their horses, a dancing bear who slept all the time, and a man who had a number of performing doves which, when their hamper was opened, flew off to commune with the less refined Manchester pigeons, and failed to come back. Best of all was a fire-eater who hadn't worked for so long that he had grown a full moustache and beard. What happened as he busked outside the circus tent, with a light crosswind blowing, just avoided capture by the camera but may be left to the reader's imagination.

Gradgrind's injunction to the Coketown schoolteacher, 'Teach these boys and girls nothing but Facts. Facts alone are wanted in life. Plant nothing else, and root out everything else', rang in my ears as I returned to London to discuss with Pru our elder son's schooling, as he was just approaching his eleventh birthday.

Trying to be good socialists, we had determined that Sam should go to a state school, of which there were two within reasonable distance of home. However, at that time the Department of Education required primary schools to divide their leaving pupils, on the strength of their examination results, into three categories. These, for convenience, could be labelled Bright, Average and Dull. Each Comprehensive school had then to fill twenty-five percent of its quota of entrants from the Bright sector, another twenty-five per cent from the Dull candidates, and the remaining fifty per cent of their capacity from those in between.

That meant effectively that quite clever or quite stupid children only stood half the chance their Average colleagues had of getting into the school they wanted. Alas, we didn't know about this in time to warn Sam before he sat his exam, and unfortunately he came out with rather good marks.

One of the two possible schools – the one we liked best – consequently had no room for him, and so we went to look at the other.

Wandsworth Comprehensive, once famed for its excellent Boys' Choir (it had gone by then, and so has the school itself now), educated nearly 2000 boys, and had, when we visited it, a sixth form of just sixteen pupils. The playground had seen three stabbings, one of which was fatal, in the previous term. The prefects, I noted, all wore knuckledusters.

So we thought perhaps not. Pru and I were thoroughly behind the theory of comprehensive education, a policy that had been urged for years by the vast majority of local authorities, and had been endorsed even by Mrs Thatcher in 1970. When the argument about non-selective education was finally laid to rest, though, the quarrel shifted to teachers' abilities and methods. Suddenly everyone knew best about education. I suppose going to school is humanity's most commonly shared experience, next only to being born; but that doesn't make us experts on education any more than it makes us experts on obstetrics.

The sad fact is that in any public service operating a two-tier system – whether it be health, education or public transport – there is an economic necessity for the lower tier to be faulty or inefficient in some way. If the fault is not inherent, then it has to be created artificially.

The most imaginative example I've come across was at a laundry I used to go to. It offered two levels of service: Standard, and the more expensive De Luxe.

My shirts were ironed equally well whichever service I chose. The only difference was that the Standard service cracked all the buttons, while the De Luxe did not. Furthermore, the buttons were cracked in a special way – as you removed the shirt from its cellophane bag, every button appeared to be in place; it was only after you had put the shirt on and started to do them up that each button would collapse neatly into two halves. It must certainly have taken time and trouble, nay it must have needed actual skill, to do this so carefully to every shirt. The extra process must have added considerably to labour costs; but clearly it was worth it to the laundry if it drove customers to use the De Luxe service (35% extra) instead.

So in the event Sam, and later his brother Joe, attended Alleyn's School at Dulwich, a co-educational independent establishment where they were very happy. The music at the school was very good, but the drama, in spite of its Founder having been the Elizabethan actor-manager Edward Alleyn, was at that time unremarkable. The school play was traditionally performed with everyone facing out front wearing far too much make-up, and shouting. Sam felt it incumbent upon him to actuate an improvement.

He had, rather ambitiously, decided to direct Max Frisch's *The Fire Raisers*. One evening after school, Sam was rehearsing his cast when the Headmaster walked through the school hall, talking very loudly to one of the other masters who, when they got outside, intimated gently to the Head that he might have interrupted a rehearsal.

Immediately the Headmaster went back to apologise. 'I'm sorry, Sam,' he said. 'I didn't realise you were rehearsing. I thought your friends were just talking to each other.'

'Well, sir,' explained Sam, 'that's what it's *supposed* to sound like.'

That was the moment at which Pru and I began to feel that, should Sam ever consider the idea of going into the business, he might be in with a chance. At that time, though, I think his plans were to become an astronomer.

*

On 28 February 1976, the National Theatre Company had given their last performance at the Old Vic Theatre, and moved into their own new premises on the South Bank. Prospect, still a homeless peripatetic company, put their name forward as a candidate for the tenancy of the Old Vic. It would suit our purposes well, we were already up-and-running as an organisation, and we presented the kind of work with which the theatre had traditionally been associated.

As different alternative schemes were suggested and rejected, Prospect gradually moved into the position of favoured candidate. There were grave difficulties, however. The idea would require additional funding, and we asked the Arts Council whether in the event they would provide sufficient subsidy to run the theatre building in addition to our production and touring costs. They said no. They believed – and went on believing in their hearts, whatever the evidence to the contrary – that once we moved into the building we would scale down or totally abandon the touring operation for which they funded us, and settle down to become a third metropolitan classical company, which they were quite right not to want.

The Old Vic Governors, realising they were not going to have the support of the Arts Council for the Prospect scenario, put off making a final decision by engaging a stop-gap commercial company to present a season of plays, commencing with Glenda Jackson in *The White Devil*. It was a perfectly respectable production, but it wasn't quite the National Theatre, and patrons were disappointed. It failed to finish its run, and the Governors desperately searched around for something else, settling at last on a compendium show called *The Frontiers of Farce* and, for Christmas, *The Ghost Train*. Both lost heavily at the box office, and their producer was declared bankrupt.

The Governors were now left with no other option – Prospect were allowed in, initially for a three-month season. We had three productions already on tour, one company doing *Saint Joan* with Eileen Atkins, and another touring Germany and the UK with *Hamlet* (Derek Jacobi) and a verse/music/dance staging of Christopher Logue's translation of the *Iliad*, known to the public as *War Music* (and to the company as *Bums and Drums*). We brought all these productions into the Vic, adding two more productions in July, *Antony and Cleopatra* and Dryden's version of the same story, *All for Love*.

The Dryden starred Barbara Jefford and John Turner, was directed by Frank Hauser, and designed appropriately like a baroque chamber opera. An interesting contrast, therefore, might have been achieved by dressing the Shakespeare play ethnically Roman/Egyptian, but Toby, who directed it, had engaged Nicolas Giorgiadis, one of the most extravagant designers in the business, to create something that looked like Veronese's *Marriage at Cana*. It was sumptuous and dignified, although Dorothy Tutin as Cleopatra refused to wear the heavy finery Giorgiadis had designed for her, and went out and bought instead some curtain material from John Lewis.

Derek was a fine Hamlet, fast, intelligent and humorous; the production worked well and was extremely successful, but unfortunately the wild expenditure on *Antony* ran away with any profit we might otherwise have made on the season, and we finished up just breaking even.

Leaving the theatre to fend for itself until we returned in November, we set out on a tour of the Middle East taking *Hamlet*, *Antony* and *War Music* – a big company. Besides playing Claudius, Enobarbus and the Storyteller in *War Music*, I was given the job of Staff Director – that is, seeing the productions into the various venues and adapting them to the different conditions we found in each place.

We opened in Istanbul, in the open courtyard of Rumelarhissar Castle, from whence the audience could see the moonlit Bosporus. I used this in *War Music*, bringing the entire company up from the shore carrying flaming torches, which looked rather splendid; but the staging for *Hamlet*, the following night, was fairly straightforward. None of us, though, had quite reckoned on the proximity of a muezzin calling the faithful to prayer just as Marcellus had observed that something was rotten in the state of Denmark.

Our next date was Lubljana, which meant flying in the evening from Istanbul to Bucharest, waiting several hours there for a plane to Belgrade, then in the early morning accomplishing the final stage of the journey; so it was no surprise when we finally reached Lubljana to discover that a number of our wardrobe skips had been lost in transit. Maybe our swords and shields had been impounded at Belgrade on the suspicion of some planned Peasants' Revolt, and the Customs officers were gaily trying on our wigs. Everything did arrive two days later, in time for *Hamlet*, but meanwhile the forces of Rome and Egypt had to go to war unarmed and unwigged.

Lubljana was the one place on the tour where we were not made to feel very welcome. There was a dourness about the Slovenians which we found quite uncharacteristic of the people of Jugoslavia generally. In 1977 it was still one Jugoslavia, and the impression we received during our brief visit was of a community united in its determination, as an efficient Communist state, to maintain political and economic independence from the USSR.

We moved on to Dubrovnik, where we were doing the three shows in three different locations. An arena was built in the square outside the Ducal Palace – a handsome 17th-century building in front of which Giorgiadis' polished breastplates and gold-threaded tunics gleamed magically in the simulated candlelight. We could not begin the performance until well after dark, when the nearby cafés had closed. But we had not bargained for the thousand or so starlings who had gone to bed for the night and who, seeing our stage lights come on, assumed it was morning and started to sing lustily, drowning out every word that was spoken on stage. Not many people stayed after the interval.

The next night we were doing *War Music* in the vaults below Fort Revelin, in the middle of the town, and here we had a different kind of sound problem. Gary Kittel, the virtuoso percussionist who provided the bulk of the war music as such, had an enormous battery of drums, blocks, bells and gongs that all had to be housed somewhere, but no place could be found within these subterranean chambers that did not reflect a thunderous echo when even the least of these instruments was struck by the vigorous Gary. Nothing spoken over the music stood the least chance of being heard, so in my invented character of a modern war correspondent narrating the history, I just opened a can of beer and sat there till Gary had finished.

Our favourite venue in the city was Fort Lovrjenac, a castle perched on the top of a cliff overlooking the Adriatic. Here we were to do two performances of *Hamlet.* The keep accommodated an audience of about two hundred, leaving us with a playing area provided with pillars, archways and flights of steps. We had a full day's rehearsal to explore their possibilities, as well as those of a high castle wall way above the heads of the audience, where brave John Turner as the Ghost stood at the topmost point, isolated with light as though his spectral being were actually suspended in the sky.

I had been to Dubrovnik before, on holiday, and loved the place. Years later it was heartbreaking to see how many of its noble Venetian buildings had been destroyed or irreparably damaged in the tragic conflict of the 90s. While we were playing there, we made friends with the leading Serbian actor Rade Serbedzija, himself an acclaimed Hamlet. He and his wife left Dubrovnik while it was being shelled, and came to London. They have never gone back.

Our last two performances in Jugoslavia were at the Roman port of Split, and here we performed on the forecourt and steps of the magnificent Palace of Diocletian. Here, there was a new worry. To make an exit on one side of the stage, and subsequently to re-enter from the other, an actor had to go down some steps to a courtyard and along a narrow public alleyway into a side street, thence to regain the palace by a side entrance. Sometimes this had to be done very rapidly. On the *Antony* night one of Cleopatra's court, wearing a very bulky robe, had got as far as the alleyway when he found his path blocked by a very fat local citizen coming in the opposite direction. 'Back up, back up!' shouted our actor, but the man, muttering his rights, still refused to give way. The resourceful actor drew his heavy sword and brandished it above his head, and at that his opponent turned and ran, screaming.

Pru and the two boys flew out to join me in Jordan, where we were to play in the Palace of Culture in Amman, actually a 6,000 seat basketball stadium. It contained a thrust stage, so that about a thousand of the audience would be looking at the action from the left side, and another thousand from the right.

This worried me very much, because lights were only capable of being rigged at the front of the stage, so that for a possible two thousand people, the performance would be lit entirely in profile. Even were we to put up scaffolding and build extra gantries, there were no more lamps anywhere in Amman to hang on them. I didn't know what to do if more than 4,000 people turned up.

I needn't have worried. About 350 persons attended the first performance of *Hamlet*, including King Hussein and his retinue. The royal presence occasioned the most exhaustive security search: sets, properties and personal belongings underwent intimate examination. Legs of furniture were drilled through to see if they contained telescopic rifles, even the Leichner sticks of make-up still used by some of the older actors were probed with sharp knives, lest concealed cartridges should be cunningly embedded within. During the performance, heavily armed soldiers were stationed backstage, one of whom delighted the entire audience when the arras was drawn to reveal him poised inquisitively over the dead Polonius.

The company became generally very ill in Amman, with all sorts of gastric disorders. Our family thankfully escaped, but at one time we had committed to hospital eight actors and two musicians, a couple of whom dragged themselves out each night for the performance, and quickly returned to their hospital beds afterwards. Everybody had to understudy someone else, we combined parts, cut scenes and just about managed to make sense of the plot.

Those of us who were still ambulant got up very early one morning and made our pilgrimage to Petra, riding our ponies down the steep gorge before the sun had reached its burning zenith, and suddenly finding ourselves in the Rose-red City, gazing in wonder at the Roman Treasury carved into the rock. Suddenly all the trials and tribulations of the tour seemed worth it . . .

Finally we went on to Egypt, where we were to play three nights at the Theatre of the Sphinx in Cairo. There had been some little negotiation about which of the plays we should perform there; *Antony* was the obvious choice, and the proprietors of the *son-et-lumiere* presentation which preceded our own performance each evening had generously and excitingly offered to illuminate the actual Pyramids for us during the Alexandria scenes. The British Embassy, however, found itself in a quandary. There had apparently been a recent production of *Antony and Cleopatra* (in Arabic and in prose) at Cairo's National Theatre, and the professional cast had been augmented by some of the Cairo notability. It might be more tactful, an Embassy spokesman said, if we were to perform *Hamlet* instead. Of course, should we so wish, we were still welcome to illuminate the pyramids . . .

The stage of the Theatre of the Sphinx is a long platform raised four feet above the desert sand. At each unlit end of the stage is a short flight of steps down to the dressing-tents. On the last night, someone had moved these steps just as I was about to use them, and I fell the four feet – not a long fall indeed, but an unexpected one – and tore my Achilles tendon. In fact I had not quite severed it, it was still hanging by a thread, but I did not know this, and neither did the Egyptian doctor I went to see next morning who bound up my leg with a Viscopaste bandage and advised me to buy a walking-stick.

We flew home to London, and opened in Edinburgh the following week. I couldn't manage Claudius in my present condition, but I could play Enobarbus with a stick as a war veteran, and all went well until the moment when I had to fall drunkenly down into the hold on Pompey's barge.

It was just a six-foot drop onto a thick mattress, and I had managed it all right dozens of times, but on this occasion as I landed I heard a sharp crack like a pistol shot, and found I could no longer walk at all. The last remaining strand of my tendon had given way.

Toby was concerned and full of sympathy, adding: 'You know, I'd been meaning for some time to say don't bother with that fall – there's a lot of action going on in front of you, and you're not very well lit, so nobody could actually see you doing it.'

Chapter Twenty-Three

I went to see an Edinburgh doctor, who told me I would need an operation to have the retracted ends of my tendon sewn together again. In the meantime, I could still walk with the aid of a stick, and fortunately that would allow me to perform everything I had been contracted to do at the Edinburgh Festival, with the sole exception of *Hamlet*. Gordon Honeycombe had adapted a dramatised reading of *Paradise Lost* at the Usher Hall, and I was also playing the Rev. Sydney Smith in a devised programme about this congenial cleric, at St. Cecilia's. After that, I set about booking myself into hospital.

My injury was classed as an industrial accident, so an insurance company was to foot the bill. As it were. I could therefore avail myself of the De Luxe Service and get it done quickly, at a very smart private hospital in Marylebone. I was there for nine days, and on the morning of the tenth went down in the lift on crutches, my leg in plaster, to wait for my friend Bob McBain to drive me to Paddington, to board a train for Exeter and thence to Boscastle to play Thomas Hardy's conveniently gout-ridden father in a BBC film.

Coming out of the lift, I was met by a bronzed, muscular man in a blue suit, who smelled expensively of after-shave. He led me to a chair and sat me down firmly. 'Mrs Schafer from Accounts', he purred, 'would just like a word with you.'

After taking my crutches from me and placing them some little way beyond my reach in case I should be tempted to make a limp for it, he went away to intimidate someone else, and presently a lady in a neat grey two-piece and diamanté spectacles, carrying a long envelope, glided over and introduced herself. She handed me the envelope and, lowering her voice to avoid embarrassing me in front of the oil sheikhs sitting around, informed me: 'As you know, our terms here are strictly *settlement on departure*.' I had opened the envelope and was now looking at what appeared to be the bill for a month-long world cruise for four on the QE2, First Class, with champagne at every meal.

'But – ' I croaked, 'This is all to be paid for by the insurance company – this was an industrial injury – '

'I'm sorry, we do not appear to have any communication from an insurance company. Perhaps the easiest thing would be for you to settle with us now, and contact your insurers as soon as you can.'

Her tone did not seem to admit of argument, so I weakly gestured towards my suitcase which had also carefully been deposited just beyond my reach. I retrieved from it my cheque book, wrote a perfectly useless cheque for the preposterous sum, and she carried it away to her lair. I sat there listening to the second hand of the electric clock thudding out what must surely be my last moments of freedom before being hauled off to a debtors' prison. Bob McBain finally appeared and as he loaded me into his Mini Minor I whispered hoarsely, 'Stop at the next phone box'. I got out, rang the insurers, shouted at them, heard a gasp as I read them the figures, banged the phone down and much to my surprise never heard another word about it.

This was not, however, the end of the Achilles Tendon Saga. While still in a plastered condition, I did two further films; one an enjoyable small budget movie about William Morris, the other a rather confused feature about the mysterious temporary disappearance of Agatha Christie in the late nineteen-twenties. Whilst shooting one or the other of these, I had contrived to tear open the surgeon's stitches, and the wound, inside its plaster casing, had gone septic. I will not disgust the reader with a description of how I was alerted to this by my own nostrils while sitting at dinner in Blackpool's Clifton Hotel next to the Mayoress, of how I managed to excuse myself, rush up to my bedroom, pour a bottle of TCP into the plaster cast and slosh my way downstairs again to join her for the pudding; I will simply admit that the thing would have taken considerably less time to heal if I had treated it with more respect and patiently allowed it to pull itself together.

A couple of months after finally emerging from the plaster, I got a message to ring an unfamiliar number in Los Angeles, and a voice answered that I had not heard for some time. It was Charles Marowitz, asking if I'd like to be in a comedy he was coming over to direct at the Royal Court, and play two parts, Ivan the Terrible and a Nazi fanatic in charge of supplying the ovens at Auschwitz.

'Erm – a comedy, you said . . . ?'

'Yeah, a comedy. It's by Peter Barnes.'

That explained it, and also explains a little why I did the play, having always been excited by Barnes' anarchic writing, risky and challenging even when in some cases it was not entirely successful.

This play was called *Laughter,* and the author's intention was to illustrate the fallacy of laughing away the horrors of human history. 'Laughter cures nothing but our consciences, and so makes the nightmare worse', a character points out at the beginning of the play. 'It softens our hatred.' There were indeed some very funny lines and funny situations in the piece, which but for this admonitory introduction might have had the desired effect on the audience of making them laugh in spite of the horrendous context, and then feel guilty about having done so.

Even so, the most consistently and surprisingly funny play ever written would have had a tough job wringing genuine laughter out of the barbarism of the Tsar or the nightmare of the gas chambers. As it was, the audience merely felt manipulated and rather resentful.

It was powerfully written, though, and certainly physically lively. As Tsar Ivan I had to dance a vigorous gopak with David Suchet, then go straight into a heated battle with him, kill him, and immediately sing *Chiamo il mio ben cosi* from Gluck's *Orfeo ed Euridice*.

'It's a bit hard getting my breath back in time to sing,' I complained to Peter. 'We've been going at it quite hard for about five minutes.'

'Oh.' He looked rather dashed. 'I thought actors *liked* having a lot to do,' he said plaintively.

After the horrifying atrocities described in *Laughter*, the ordinarily vicious domestic strife of Harold Pinter's *The Homecoming*, which was my next engagement, came almost as light relief.

We opened at the Richmond Theatre, and the local press reminded us that when the original production had played there ten years earlier, the performance had been stopped in the middle of the third act by protests from the National Front. I hadn't realised that members of the Front were that much given to theatregoing; they didn't reappear in Richmond for our revival, which perhaps reflected some sort of failure on our part. What we did get, though – and I encountered the same thing years later when Pru and I were on tour with *The Birthday Party* – was people stopping us in the street and demanding, 'What was all that *about*?'

Somebody, I think it was Verlaine, once asked Chekhov the same question about *The Cherry Orchard*, and was told that it was about a cherry orchard. 'Well yes, but what *happens* in the play?' he persisted. Chekhov replied: 'Act One, the cherry orchard is in danger of being sold. Act Two, the cherry orchard is going to be sold. Act Three, the cherry orchard is sold. Act Four, the cherry orchard has been sold.'

I can't do any better than that with most of Pinter's plays, nor do I think more should be expected. A gigantic amount of erudition, more, possibly, than on the work of any other living playwright, has been expounded on the hidden significance of practically every moment in every play Harold Pinter has ever written, but it seems to me that his particular way of letting us absorb information is in fact much akin to our own personal experience.

Normally, when we watch a scene between two or more people, the dramatist has already told us – or will tell us in the course of the scene – who these people are and what they are actually talking about. Pinter, however, treats us as eavesdroppers, listening in on conversations and witnessing behaviour the background to which we can only guess – just as we would if we walked in on an animated discussion between two people we didn't know at all. Are they really arguing? About what? And why? How did it start? Who is in the right? Is one of them lying? Are they both? Is each quite sure of the other's identity? The ordinary playwright makes sure you know more about the characters than they know about themselves: Pinter wants you to know less.

His plays disturb us, because the unknown is always unnerving; and if we can't place positive constructions on what we see and hear we become keenly aware of the tension and danger lying beneath the most apparently commonplace situations.

Though the audience may be unsure about the people they're watching on the stage, of course the actors have to know exactly who they are and what they want, just as they would in any play. On the evidence of what the character says and does (and always bearing in mind that we don't necessarily say what we mean or mean what we say, and that we are most of us given to telling untruths, particularly about ourselves), the actor will find a history and a being that makes sense.

The director of *The Homecoming*, Kevin Billington, was invited immediately afterwards to direct one of the plays, *Henry VIII*, making up the marathon BBC TV Shakespeare canon, and asked me to join the cast. This account of all thirty-seven plays – impossible to imagine as TV entertainment these days – deliberately conformed to no house style, editorial concept, or technical regimen. Some of the plays were shot on multi-camera video, others were filmed, in various locations. There were three different Executive Producers, and many different directors. Sometimes the casting relied rather heavily on the profession's classical repertory resources, sometimes unconventional ideas paid off – as for instance with John Cleese, a definitive Petruchio in *The Taming of the Shrew*.

Some results were better than others. *Henry VIII* is one of Shakespeare's least popular works, and its first line 'I come no more to make you laugh' was perhaps bound to provoke the response, 'Right, let's see what's on ITV, Mother', but in fact it came out rather well – rather better, in fact, than it often does on stage. We filmed it in and around Leeds Castle, Hever Castle and Penshurst Place (12th, 13th and 14th centuries respectively). In each building the private rooms are very small and, apart from Penshurst, even the banqueting halls are comparatively modest in size, heating of course having been a major consideration in their construction. *Henry VIII* is a political play, with sensitive information constantly being covertly passed between allies under the noses of others who must not see or hear. This is very difficult to do convincingly on a large stage; but between the close thick walls of Hever Castle, where indeed some of those very conversations may in truth have taken place, it was entirely believable that X could whisper to Y while smiling at Z, a few feet away, in spurious amity.

John Stride played the King, with Claire Bloom a very moving Catherine of Aragon, and I was Wolsey. The fine cast included Jeremy Kemp, Julian Glover and Ronald Pickup. Altogether I think it was one of the major successes of the series.

*

Every actor who looks even remotely like him is sooner or later asked to play Winston Churchill. In 1979 it was my turn. I stress 'remotely', because when the American co-producers of the BBC's three-and-a-half-hour television epic *Churchill and the Generals* looked at my photograph, they insisted on make-up changes that each day would hail me from my bed in the very smallest hours of the morning. My hair was bleached white, and a matching piece added on top. I had a prosthetic nose added, and prosthetic *ears* – an extravagance I had never encountered before, but then Churchill's ears did extend further down his face than most people's.

My eyes were wrong, too. Winston's eyes were a watery blue, mine are brown. I had worn cosmetic contact-lenses before, as Horatio Bottomley, but had had rather longer to become adjusted to them than would be the case this time.

'Wear them just for an hour at a time to begin with,' the practitioner advised me at the final fitting, 'and try to avoid strong lights and cigarette smoke.'

'Ah,' I said. 'Fine. I shall be filming in them for probably ten hours a day, in studio lighting, mostly smoking a cigar.'

If you have naturally blue eyes, and want to change them to brown, contact-lenses do the job very well. The reverse is more difficult; in order to avoid a tell-tale thin brown ring round the pupil of your eye, the lens' own pupil has to be made smaller than the real thing, giving you the impression of peering through a tunnel. Watching myself in close-up afterwards, I felt my face was obliterated by a mask.

I tried not to let the same thing happen to my voice. The orotund delivery we have on record is all very well for public rhetoric, but I had to find some distillation of it for everyday conversation. The tones that we know so well were, after all, studiously practised for effect. (Although apparently he never quite understood the microphone; he had an idea that the nearer he got to it, and shouted, the more powerful would be his message to the people of Britain. To avoid the BBC engineers at Evesham collapsing with burst eardrums, Michel St Denis, who produced some of his wartime broadcasts to France, sometimes had to sit on the Prime Minister's knee to anchor him to his seat. Michel was a man of much the same build as Churchill, and I wonder if someone somewhere has a pictorial record of the conditions under which some of those soul-stirring speeches must have been delivered.)

Churchill and the Generals explored Winston's relationship with each of the war-time Allied Commanders: Alanbrooke, Wavell,

Auchinleck, Alexander, Montgomery, Ismay, as well as Eisenhower, Marshall and de Gaulle. Ian Curteis in his screenplay examined Churchill's tendency finally to rely on his own instinct rather than the advice of his expert commanders; a tendency that became almost a principle, that probably led him to make terrible mistakes like the monstrously ill-advised invasion of the Dardanelles, but that nevertheless finally won the war.

Originally, the schedule had provided for us to spend a couple of days in North Africa to shoot an important sequence during the campaign in the Western Desert. As so frequently happens in filming, budgetary readjustment took us instead to Camber Sands in Kent.

It was May, but one of the coldest Mays in recent memory, and the bronzed soldiers going about in uniform singlets had to be kept far enough from the camera for the goose-pimples not to be visible beneath the glistening artificial sweat. Patrick Allen as Auchinleck and I had a breakfast scene in a tent, and the Director, Alan Gibson, had asked that there should be flies buzzing about us as we ate our bacon and eggs.

The Property Master explained that, the outside temperature being about two degrees centigrade, flies were not at the present moment an option. But the Director was insistent.

I think I would rather not know where they actually found some flies, but a hundred or so were eventually brought back in a small tin. Most of them died as soon as the tin was opened, but a dozen or so still fluttered weakly. 'Warm them up,' said Alan, 'and we'll shoot the scene.'

Alas, the few survivors expired even in the time it took to set up the first shot. Alan, however, was not to be turned from his purpose by considerations of muscatory inadequacy.

'Get a fan, and blow them about,' he ordered.

Patrick and I settled to our breakfast, edging the wind-driven corpses aside as they plopped into our fried eggs. Where, we asked ourselves, was the glamour . . . ?

With Pru in California. The anniversary of something somewhere.

'Real People': (1) Mikhail Gorbachev.

(2) Josef Stalin.

(3) Winston Churchill.

(4) King Edward VII.

(5) Horatio Bottomley.

(6) Making up as Sir Thomas Beecham.

(7) Dr John Bodkin Adams.

(8) Lord Reith.

Two Granada TV essays on the Unacceptable Face of Capitalism:
(1) Hard Times, *1976. With Patrick Allen (L) and Harry Markham.*

(2) Brass, 1982-3. With Robert Reynolds.

With Joe and Pru.

Joe with some of his class, Zongoro, Zimbabwe.

Filming an HTV Documentary on the Talyllyn Railway, Abergynolwyn, Gwynedd, 1989.

The Talyllyn Railway. Driver Maurice Wilson takes on water at Dolgoch Station.

P.S. and T.W. with Waverley; Brodick, Arran, 1997.

Sailing at Fishbourne, Isle of Wight, 1978. Sam at the tiller, with Joe.

Aboard our Narrow Boat. 'Pottering along the canals ... I will always find things to delight in.'

With Sam in Henry IV, Parts 1 & 2, *English Touring Theatre, 1997.*

'*If I had a thousand sons ...*'
Sir John Falstaff in conversation with his grandson Clément.

Chapter Twenty-Four

*F*rom flies to bees. One of the most popular television shows of the seventies and eighties was the 30-minute series *Tales of the Unexpected*: the original stories written by Roald Dahl, but with later scripts by several other people, including Robin Chapman who wrote one about a beekeeper who spikes his baby's milk with Royal Jelly, turning it into a bee pupa, before finally developing signs of becoming a bee himself.

The series was made by Anglia Television, shot in their Norwich studios and, for our own story, at a large apiary nearby. I played the beekeeper, and Susan George was my understandably apprehensive wife.

The unusual rapport that I was supposed to enjoy with my bees required me to remove a populated frame from one of the hives, examine and replace it, without the benefit of any protective suit, veil or gloves. I was a little nervous about this, and the day before we were to do the scene, I asked the professional beekeeper, among whose hives we were filming, whether he thought this would be all right.

'I think so,' he said, after a moment. 'There are one or two things you should bear in mind.'

I was anxious to know what they were.

'Don't wear blue,' he advised, 'or anything fluffy. Don't wear any after-shave, eat any onions beforehand, or drink any beer. But above all,' he continued, '*talk* to them; quietly, of course, and sensibly – don't patronise them.'

'Treat them as equals, you mean?'

'Exactly. And not as a group; I like to talk to them *individually*.'

'Individually.'

'Yes.'

'How many are there on a frame?'

'About four hundred.'

The next morning, as I stepped out of my caravan, I was confronted by the unnerving spectacle of about twenty people, including Susan George, the director Herbert Wise, the entire film crew and a doctor who had been summoned from Norwich, just in case; all clad in brand new white protective suits, hats, veils and gloves.

I did the scene, taking out the frame, wishing the bees good morning and murmuring a few things from the Home News pages of the *Guardian* that I thought might be of interest, and in due course replacing them in the hive. There was no problem at all, and the doctor, already irritated about having his surgery time wasted in such frivolity, briskly removed his hat and veil. A stray bee promptly stung him on the ear.

*

Since the move into the Vic in 1977, the Prospect Theatre Company had been advertised as 'Prospect at the Old Vic'. and had now started to style themselves simply 'The Old Vic Company'. I saw nothing wrong with this – we were after all the resident company at the Old Vic, and no-one was as yet trying to evict us – but it seemed to increase the tension between the company and the Arts Council, who had very strongly questioned the suitability of some of our recent offerings: a one-act opera by Garrick and Dibdin, a new play *The 88* about Irish Republicanism, and Joe Orton's *What the Butler Saw*, with Pru playing Mrs Prentice.

Furthermore, the Council were worried about our financial situation. We had really only had one sure-fire moneymaker, Derek Jacobi's *Hamlet*, and this production was coming to the end of its long life. With Barbara Jefford still playing Gertrude and with Julian Glover having taken over as Claudius, the company was now in China.

While they were away, our Administrator Andrew Leigh received a rather strange phone call from the Arts Council offices at 105 Piccadilly. Senior representatives of their organisation, they said, required an urgent meeting with our Chairman, our Administrator, and one additional member of our Board. The meeting, to be held on our premises, was officially secret, we were told – it would not appear in anybody's diary, and were it ever referred to outside these walls, the Council would deny all knowledge of it.

Toby was in China with the company, as they knew, so as a hands-on Board Member I was telephoned to join Andrew and our Chairman David Russell in a carefully chosen eyrie at the top of the Old Vic, away from human habitation. There we awaited with curiosity the arrival of our visitors from Piccadilly.

What they had to say was very simple. They would be prepared to continue their £350,000 annual grant-in-aid to the company only on three conditions: one, that Toby be required to step down as Artistic Director and take a sabbatical of unspecified length; two, that the company's substantial accumulated deficit be recovered within the coming year; and three, that we continue to provide sixteen weeks of suitable touring product within the UK. Were we to default on any of these conditions, our entire grant would be summarily withdrawn. Think it over, they said, and went away.

We did think it over, very thoroughly. The last two stipulations presented no problem; Andrew had already been trimming the sails and was some way towards clearing the deficit, which had come about through the kind of overspending we were determined to avoid in future. As far as the touring commitment was concerned, we had been faithfully fulfilling our 16-week obligation and would continue to do so with careful attention to what the Council considered 'suitable'.

No, the difficulty was what to do about Toby. He had been involved with Prospect practically since its inception, and had been its Artistic Director since 1964. We knew that he would be mortally offended by the suggestion that he should take an unlimited (and unpaid) sabbatical away from the job to which he had devoted the greater part of his energies for the last sixteen years, and would probably react by separating himself permanently and irrevocably from the company. We knew that personal relationships would be incurably damaged, and that we who had been Toby's friends would now be regarded as perfidious snakes-in-the-grass.

Our most pressing concern, though, was to find someone to take charge while we looked for a new Artistic Director – which might prove a very lengthy process. The Board, who of course had needed to be told the substance of the clandestine meeting, asked if I would step into the breach, and, after probably insufficient thought, I agreed. It seemed to me that the company had a record of which it should be proud, that the move to the Old Vic had been right and proper, and that our continued existence as the major classical touring company of our time was more important than what might be conceived as personal loyalty. I knew how much I personally owed to Toby, but also knew that nothing could be gained by blowing the Arts Council's gaff and making a public demonstration of support. On the contrary, I felt that we really owed it to Toby to keep the flag flying.

David Russell went to Beijing to break the news. The shock waves reached us hours later in the Waterloo Road: How could this happen; Toby *was* Prospect. Incredulous telegrams from Derek and Julian and other members of the company demanded to know exactly what was going on, but of course we could only say that the Prospect Board, on advice from the Arts Council, were instructing Toby to step down for an unspecified period. Toby was indeed very wounded and, as we had feared, washed his hands of the whole business.

We knew that the profession, and the media, would delight in portraying all this as a palace revolution, and inevitably things would be said which, though inaccurate, we would be powerless to correct without breaking faith with the Arts Council. (That is exactly what I'm doing now, but it doesn't matter any more; twenty years of blood under the bridge has dwindled now to a thin trickle.) In these circumstances, it was naturally hard to persuade anyone to take on the Artistic Directorship until the storms had died down. I approached a number of possible candidates – Robin Phillips, Anthony Quayle, Michael Blakemore and half a dozen others – without success. It was clear that, for a year at least, I was going to have to do the job myself.

In many ways it was exciting and fulfilling; our Piccadilly paymasters had given us a defined goal towards which to work, Andrew and I got on very well together and had the same sort of ideas for the company, and indeed I was surrounded by brilliant and supportive people in the office. We already had one production committed for the autumn: Toby had, before his departure, signed a contract with Peter O'Toole to appear in a production of *Macbeth*, but had planned nothing else in the interim, so we had to fill the theatre with bought-in product of variable quality.

I was also professionally busy on my own account. I'd recently done a show at Salisbury about the conductor Sir Thomas Beecham, compiled by Ned Sherrin and Caryl Brahms, and we were now about to bring it to London for a short season. While we were waiting for this to happen, I was offered a few days on a film in California, *Masada*, to play the Roman Emperor Vespasian.

The story of *Masada* is that of the gallant Israelites encamped on the top of the mountain of that name, holding out in their apparently impregnable fortress against the mechanical mountaineering of the invading Romans.

The time-honoured Hollywood tradition was observed whereby the good guys (the Israelites) were all played by Americans, and the bad guys (the Romans) by us Brits. That would have been all right had it not been for a contractual obligation to allow equal screen time to the two factions. The Zealots' conduct was heroic and inspiring, and their situation tragic, but in terms of dramatic development it all boiled down to one simple decision: do we surrender, do we stick it out, or do we jump? The Romans, on the other hand, were faced with complex political issues, fascinating engineering problems and the difficulties of maintaining military discipline while campaigning in a foreign desert. So the Romans had a lot of stuff to talk about, while the Israelites, to justify their time on the screen, had to resort to parenthetic Jewish soap-opera dialogue: should resentful old Chaim bury the age-old family hatchet and turn up, after all, at grandson Moishe's barmitzvah? And will little Rachel's broken wrist ever be strong enough to play violin for the Israel Philharmonic? That sort of thing.

Starring as the Roman general was Peter O'Toole, and having heard that I had taken over at the Old Vic, he told me his ideas about *Macbeth*, and about the discussions he had had with Jack Gold, who was to direct it. There was quite a time to go before we would need to start planning seriously, so we didn't go into things very deeply, but he was obviously full of enthusiasm for the project, and so indeed was I. I had perfect confidence in Jack Gold, and I left California a few days afterwards, feeling quite happy about the immediate future.

Chapter Twenty-Five

On my return, Andrew brought me the *Macbeth* contract, which had only just been returned by Peter's lawyers (his decision to employ a lawyer rather than an agent tended to slow things up rather). In this contract, I was astounded to see, Toby had given O'Toole total artistic control over the production. Now, whoever the personalities involved, this arrangement is a sure recipe for dissent if not disaster, and I said so to my Board. Among the members at that time was a healthy sprinkling of seasoned practitioners, Tony Quayle to name but one, and they all shared my feelings of alarm. The situation was referred to our solicitor Laurence Harbottle, to see if there were any way round it. Laurence felt that our change of Artistic Director might constitute grounds for questioning the validity of the contract, but Peter's lawyers would undoubtedly come on strong if we tried to back out, and sue us for every penny we patently hadn't got.

So there we were. I went in to the Apollo Theatre with *Beecham*, spending my evenings after the show happily entertaining the many people who had played or sung under Beecham's baton (but not *danced*, I noticed; latterly he had not shown much patience with the law of gravity), and who would come round and tell me new stories about the man. So many of these stories deserved a place in the script that we had to keep taking other things out to make room for them.

My daylight hours were less happily spent. The first note of doom was struck when Jack Gold came to see me, pleading to be released from his obligation as he had been offered a major film to direct. What can one say in such a situation? To hold someone to their contract when they give you reasonable notice, knowing that all the time they were working they would be wishing they were somewhere else, can only be unproductive, so I agreed to let him go, and set about looking for a replacement. Not surprisingly, nobody jumped at the idea of directing a play over which they were effectively to have no control. Various people got as far as talking to Peter about it, but always either they or he came away feeling that it wouldn't work out.

Also, we had to find a designer. I immediately thought of Bob Crowley, whose work was always imaginative but could well be adapted to the simplified dictates of touring. He produced a model, and came to show it to us. Now, Peter O'Toole had not done any Shakespeare since his Hamlet for the National in 1963, and had not taken into account the way in which Shakespearean stage design had become less descriptive and geared more towards flow and continuity of action.

'If it's a castle, where are the bloody crenellations?' he would ask. 'If this is Lady Macbeth's bedroom, where is the bed?'

So Bob Crowley was turned down, and no other name seemed to meet with Peter's approval. He told us that his original conception of the play had involved the use of inflatable scenery.

I looked blankly at Mick Wicks, our Production Manager, and Mick looked at the ceiling. 'Inflatable scenery?' I ventured.

'Oh yes,' Peter assured me. 'I am a director of an Irish concern called La Botta Ltd., so named because an entire set, when deflated, can be packed into the boot of a car. I suggest I bring our designer over at my own expense, set him up in a rehearsal room for two weeks to build the set, and after that time we'll have a demonstration on stage. We have also designed a lighting rig using very small but very powerful lamps made of Campbell's Soup tins, which can be operated from a transistorised panel on someone's lap, sitting in the stalls.'

If he was having us on, he was keeping an admirably straight face. But he might not be. It would certainly be *different*, the experiment wasn't going to cost us anything, and at the same time we'd quietly continue to pursue more conventional channels. So we said we'd give it a try.

The Irish designer arrived, and installed himself in Rehearsal Room B with an enormous pack of black dustbin bags and some tins of adhesive, saying he required nothing from us except a bottle of Power's Whiskey to be left outside his door every morning.

The promised demonstration was put off and put off, but finally the genius announced that all was ready. The one or two people who had not as yet positively said no to the idea of directing *Macbeth* had been invited to watch. I sat with my colleagues, and in front of us sat Peter with two fellow directors of La Botta Ltd., who had flown over from Dublin that morning.

The curtain was down as we came in. Before it rose, our ears were suddenly assailed by a noise as if of a gigantic vacuum cleaner operating at full tilt. I leant over to Peter. 'What's that noise?' I asked.

'Air compressor,' he said shortly. 'We can deal with that.'

The curtain rose to reveal a dimly lit collection of black plastic phalluses swaying in the wind. There had been a half-hearted and wholly fruitless attempt to apply different coloured scene-paint to some of them, but the general effect was of a blustery day during a refuse collection strike. Into the gloom, from behind one of these erections, emerged a young actor in a black cloak, shouting above the noise of the compressor: 'Thou Nature art my goddess . . . '

We were just beginning to be aware of the smell of burning oxtail soup, when I stood up and stopped the proceedings. I suggested to Peter that we all meet in my office, and without the bin-bag artist.

We all sat down in silence; were there going to be excuses, explanation, justification? Not at all. Peter at once began shaking with merriment. 'No, no, it was terrible,' he gasped, and in relief that, for once, something had happened that we could agree on, we all collapsed into helpless laughter, crying with delight each time anybody remembered some fresh detail of the afternoon's disaster.

It was the last happy occasion I shared with Peter. I was not the right partner for him. What he thought he wanted was a complaisant business associate who could laugh with him, make rude jokes about subsidised theatre, join him in a barnstorming assault on an Old Vic audience that hadn't really existed since the time of Lilian Baylis, and miraculously meet all the bills out of the box-office.

It would be wrong to dismiss these ideas as essentially anachronistic and impractical. There is a lot to be said for the seasoned troupe going round the town halls, schools and local theatres, as the great Anew McMaster (I suspect an idol of Peter's) used to do in Ireland, delighting the populace with their vigorous accounts of the classics. If that was what Peter really wanted to do, I could have provided him, I think, with a framework in which to do it, and would have welcomed his company back into the Vic when they had finished their tour. But I had a shock when he told me the casting he proposed for such an enterprise.

'Meryl Streep is who I want for Lady Lauder,' (he pandered to the old theatrical superstition that it was bad luck – ho ho – to quote from this play, and always referred to it as 'Harry Lauder'), 'and John Gielgud as Duncan.' When I remonstrated, he said that if it had been a film, those would be the first people he would approach for the parts. I had to point out that there was a world of difference between appearing in a feature film which would involve either of them for only a week or two for a very considerable fee, and appearing night after night, not only in London but in Liverpool, Bristol, Leeds and Coventry, for a relative pittance.

'Well, they wouldn't have to do the tour,' he replied.

'But they *would*, Peter.' A cold sweat crept over me as I finally realised he had absolutely no idea of how the company, of which he had insisted on being named as an Associate Director, worked. 'That's what we're funded for, and what's more the play will be in repertoire with *The Merchant of Venice*, and obviously I want as many people as possible to be in both plays.'

'You must fight for your production, I'll fight for mine' was his reply, and he stalked off.

In the end we came up with a more sensible list of possible Lady Macbeths, and he showed enthusiasm for Jane Lapotaire, a choice I applauded warmly. I duly agreed to offer the part to Jane, and Peter went back to California to finish *Masada*.

Jane and I had lunch, she liked the idea, and we rang her agent Jeremy Conway with the offer. On his return from the States, I told Peter the news. 'Jane Lapotaire?' he retorted. 'Oh, no. I want Frances Tomelty.'

An Artistic Director who has to explain to an agent that he offered his client something by mistake and doesn't really mean it, does little for his own professional credibility. I don't know why Jane and Jeremy were so extraordinarily generous about it, but I shall always be grateful to them both.

Frances Tomelty was duly engaged, and so were the witches. Gradually we began to assemble a cast.

Over the weeks Peter had allowed himself to become convinced that I and the rest of the organisation were out to sabotage his show. Why he thought we should be so anxious to shoot ourselves in the foot with the first production of the season I don't quite know, but he firmly believed that we were there not to help but to hinder him at every turn. He refused to set foot in our office building, referring to it as The Gas Light and Coke Company, and would have nothing to do with us, apart from handing over various invoices for payment.

We were still without a director or designer. In desperation, I suggested to Peter that the logical step would be for him to direct it himself, since he was essentially making all the decisions, but he declined. Instead, he came up with the unusual suggestion of Bryan Forbes, the film producer, director, sometime actor and head of British Lion Films. I didn't know when Bryan had last directed a play on the stage, but by now such considerations had become largely irrelevant. The main thing was that Peter actually got on with him; costume designers, assistant directors and stage management had one by one been sent packing as suspected agents of The Gas Light and Coke Company and of its supremo, Miss Piggy (me).

A set dresser from a film Peter had worked on was finally engaged to design the scenery, and a clutch of supernumerary actors dressed as soldiers had been recruited to stand around filling the gaps.

I was forbidden the theatre during the rehearsal period, but insisted on my right to witness the first dress rehearsal, which was in fact postponed twice and then held on a Sunday, occasioning a large bill for overtime.

My assistants, before they were banished, had warned me not to expect too much, but even so I was shocked by what I saw. Peter looked as though he could give a perfectly good account of the part, if only he could surrender his own personality to Macbeth's. His verse speaking was quirky but intelligent and often exciting. Brian Blessed roared with laughter and radiated loyal good humour as Banquo, and Frances Tomelty wived her Thane with attractive fierceness, but there was no evidence of any *thought* having been given to the play, and most of the other characters just stood around looking lost.

I took pages of notes during the dress rehearsal, and listed a number of specific problems which it wouldn't take long to sort out, and which, if sorted out, would substantially improve things before the show opened on Thursday night. I gave the list to Bryan Forbes the following morning, but while he agreed with a lot of what I'd suggested, he said he would have to discuss it with Peter. I tried one last time to talk to Peter, but he wouldn't see me. I knew it was hopeless, and went back to the office to think what we should now do.

Some form of self-protection was necessary for the company. There was the rest of the season to think of, and the autonomous identity of this one production had to be made clear to the funding bodies, to the touring theatre managers, and to patrons themselves. Andrew and I therefore put together a brief statement, to be slipped into the theatre programme, saying that this one production was under the direct artistic control of Mr O'Toole, and that further productions in the season, by the Old Vic Company, would include *The Merchant of Venice, Trelawny of the Wells*, and the rest of the list. The text was circulated to our Board, and to Peter's lawyer Bill Fournier, and was approved.

Thursday night came. The evening sun shone upon an eager public crowding into the auditorium; the great, the good, the knockers, the wellwishers, the ordinary public, God help them, the paparazzi, and all the other people who for some unaccountable reason seem to like going to first nights. There was an air of real excitement: the opening of the new season, with a new and untried Artistic Director at the helm, and the first time Peter O'Toole had been on the London stage for fifteen years.

As I stood dinner jacketed and suicidal in the foyer, old friends passed me, smiling encouragingly. Irving Wardle gave me the thumbs up, colleagues clapped me on the shoulder. I managed a sickly return smile and watched, powerless to save the passengers as they pushed their way determinedly up the gangways of the *Titanic*.

The last person to go in happened to drop his programme on the floor, and out came the slip with our prepared statement. He looked at it for a moment, and then came over to me.

'Does this mean what I think it means?' he asked.

'It means what it says,' I told him.

'I see,' he said thoughtfully, and went into the auditorium.

The lights went down, and the performance began. I made my way with leaden feet up to the back of the gallery; intending, I suppose, to get as far away from the stage as possible.

The audience were at first bewildered by what they saw, then there were some giggles, and when Peter appeared after the murder drenched in blood from head to foot, there was a burst of laughter. Peter, expert comedian that he is, waited at the top of the stairs for the laughter to subside before exclaiming, 'I have done the deed', which brought the house down. From then on, right up to the final moment of the play when a nervous Dudley Sutton, as the victorious Macduff, retreated in terror before the superior swordplay of a Macbeth in modern baseball boots, not much could be taken seriously.

I left before the curtain call, went round briefly to thank everyone as they came off stage – I didn't see Peter – and went home in despair.

The following morning I was woken at seven o'clock by a phone call from Michael Owen of the London *Evening Standard*. The man who had questioned me in the foyer had apparently also been a journalist, and had rung Owen, who now wanted to know was I actually *disowning* the production? I was still half asleep, but had to think quickly, and I told him there had never been any question of my being asked to own it; that it had been understood from the outset to be Peter O'Toole's own production. He rang off.

At lunchtime, out came the evening papers (two in those days) with the big headline WEST DISOWNS MACBETH on the front page of both.

I suppose it was natural that a lot of people would assume I had read the notices (which were indeed terrible), panicked and tried to distance myself from the debacle. It would have been both tedious and impractical to try and explain the true circumstances, so I let it ride, and concentrated on *The Merchant of Venice*, which was due to open in a couple of weeks and in which I was playing Shylock.

The Merchant opened without fuss; an intelligent and attractive, fairly traditional production by Michael Meacham, set in the 18th-century Venice of Canaletto, whose drawings show us an upwardly mobile city being everywhere rebuilt, renovated or temporarily held up by wooden scaffolding. Maureen O'Brien was a sensitive, witty and dignified Portia, and there was a nice cohesion of acting, decor and music. The public reception on the first night smacked more of relief than exuberance, but the show did well at the box office and after a few weeks the two plays went out on tour together. I never saw *Macbeth* again, although I should have liked to, because I gather Peter did quite a lot of work on it; but I was directing the next play in the season, *Trelawny of the Wells*, and so had to spend all my time in London except when dashing up to Coventry, Bristol etc. for the evening to do Shylock.

One night in Leeds, I had only just made it. Because of a meeting of our Heads of Department first thing in the morning, I had let the afternoon's rehearsal run on half an hour longer than I should have done, and then, thanks to a traffic jam, missed my train at King's Cross. The next one got me in to Leeds only ten minutes before the curtain went up, but luckily, not being in the first two scenes, I was on stage just in time. When I made my last exit after the trial scene I heaved a sigh of relief, and there being a little while before I was needed for the curtain call, I went along to the backstage bar (not many theatres have this old-fashioned facility; the Leeds Grand is one of the very few left) and asked for a whisky. I had no money on me, being in costume, so I asked the lady behind the bar if she would put it on a slate.

She looked at me in my 18th-century gaberdine coat and breeches, my yarmulke, curls and false nose, and asked dubiously, 'Are you in the play, love?'

Chapter Twenty-Six

'*R*ight, one two three PULL . . . ' The Old Vic team gave a gigantic tug, and finally uprooted the concrete signpost round which the rope had been secured. Jim Champion nodded in comparative satisfaction.

One of the suggested attractions at the forthcoming Lambeth Fete in Brockwell Park had been a tug-of-war contest between the National Theatre and the Old Vic. We hadn't quite known how to respond to the idea until Jim had offered to coach us, with instructions to turn up for training on a piece of waste ground behind the theatre for a quarter of an hour every morning.

Jim Champion with his son John, who married our Wardrobe Mistress, ran the Royal Victoria pub, which used to stand next to our original stage door in the Waterloo Road, and which as a consequence became our second home. As well as their theatrical clientele, they had connections with some of the established families of South London villains, and they both knew how to look after themselves physically. As a tug-of-war coach, Jim was a hard taskmaster; but he knew what he was about, and by the end of a week's practice our four-man team, consisting of Andrew Leigh, Mick Wicks, Alan our maintenance engineer and myself, felt ready to meet our opponents.

On the Saturday afternoon we arrived at Brockwell Park to find four heavily-built stage hands in track suits bearing the NT logo. One of them was wheeling a supermarket trolley full of cans of beer. 'For the winners,' he said shortly, and casting one look at Andrew, bespectacled in a three-piece suit with silver watch chain, wheeled the trolley back to their end of the pitch.

Jim had come along as starter and referee. We grasped the rope, positioned our feet and distributed our weight in the way he'd taught us, and the contest began. A look of incomprehension, disbelief and finally anger crept over the faces of our adversaries as the first, the second, the third and at last the fourth of them was dragged over the central line.

'Best of three,' snapped their leader.

We set to again, and the same thing happened. The spectators cheered. Flushed with success, we challenged all the children we could see, and allowed a long line of them to pull us all the way round the park. When we got back to our starting place, the National Theatre team had vanished, and so had the beer.

This was just one of the local events in which the Old Vic got involved. The spirit of Lilian Baylis, the founder, still hung about the place (she had actually appeared to one or two of the staff in the downstairs bar, apparently), and the theatre continued to enjoy a close relationship with the surrounding tradespeople. The Old Vic, or 'Royal Victoria Coffee Tavern and Temperance Music Hall' as it once was, stands on the corner of Waterloo Road and The Cut, a friendly street of useful non-touristy shops with a market at one end, street parking, another theatre (The Young Vic) across the road, a couple of pubs and some very good restaurants.

A stone's throw from the Waterloo main-line and underground stations, and on a number of bus routes, the Old Vic is nevertheless generally regarded by the public as being off the beaten track. They don't mind trudging their labyrinthine way from Waterloo Station through urine-pervaded tunnels populated by the sleeping homeless to emerge at last, with ankles bruised by marauding skateboarders, into the desolate purlieus of MOMI, the National Theatre or the Queen Elizabeth Hall; but in no other wise will the public venture across that apparently insuperable barrier, the River Thames.

So the Vic has ever had to struggle for its audience, which has always responded best to a resident company producing the classical repertoire: an expensive proposition, and one that demands not only public subsidy but reliably high attendance figures. Much more distinguished producers than myself – Jonathan Miller and Peter Hall for instance – have put on consistently excellent work with their companies, and still come unstuck.

Our *Trelawny of the Wells* opened in Nottingham. There was praise for a fine performance by Robert Lindsay as Tom Wrench, and a splendidly crusty Sir William Gower by the wonderful Bill Fraser. I gave the part of the elderly and outdated actor-manager James Telfer to my old employer Lionel Hamilton, and he would have been fine if he hadn't thought it necessary to give a character performance instead of just being himself. Never mind, he and the rest of the company had a good time when we took the play, together with *The Merchant*, to Hong Kong and Perth in Western Australia for their Arts Festivals.

In Perth, we played at the beautiful Edwardian Her Majesty's (originally His Majesty's) Theatre. I had been to the city once before, during the recital tour of 1979, and was delighted to be back. In the whole vast area of Western Australia there live not many more than a million souls, nearly all of them in Perth itself. It is technically the most isolated city on earth, being 2,500 miles from its nearest neighbour Adelaide, and the very expensive internal air fares could well make the inhabitants feel the outside world to be totally inaccessible. Ironically, though, because it's practically as cheap to fly to Rome or Athens or San Francisco as it is to visit Auntie Maud in Woollara, NSW, one constantly comes across people in Perth who have done the annual round of International Festivals – Bayreuth, Aix, Edinburgh, Salzburg – and whom poor Auntie Maud consequently hasn't seen for twenty years.

Perth numbers among its citizens a good many people who have become especially eminent in their field – surgeons, judges, newspaper editors, professors of biochemistry – who, because they stand so high in their profession, can choose to live anywhere in the world and be visited by those who need their services, instead of having to do the visiting themselves. The climate, the sailing, the wine make Perth a good place for such mandarins to settle and eventually retire, and they themselves made for very entertaining and generous company.

On our return to London, Andrew and I went along to 105 Piccadilly to attend a meeting of the Arts Council Touring Committee, of which we had both been members for some time.

The feeling round the table at the afternoon's meeting was uncomfortable. Rumours of severe cuts were in the air, and the representatives of one or two of the client companies, Glyndebourne Touring Opera, for instance, looked distinctly nervous. After a little general discussion, some of us were asked to leave the room, while our organisations were discussed among those who remained. Andrew and I sat out in the corridor for half an hour before Jack Phipps, the Director of Touring, came out to tell us that as the meeting was just about drawing to a close, there was no point in going back in.

We didn't go back in that afternoon, or, as things turned out, ever. Just before Christmas, Andrew received a phone call from someone at the *Daily Telegraph*.

'Well?' asked the caller immediately. 'What are you going to do?'

'About what?' said Andrew.

'*You* know.'

'No, I don't.'

'Well, if you don't know, I can't tell you. It's embargoed until tomorrow.'

We sat down to puzzle the meaning of this disturbing piece of non-information. If we were facing some unknown peril, who was there who could point out from what direction it was to come? Immediately, Joan Bakewell sprang to mind; she was married to Jack Emery, who was in charge of our marketing, and she always had wind before anyone else of whatever was happening in the world of politics or the arts.

We rang her, and she simply asked if we had known that there had been an emergency meeting of the Arts Council the day before.

After about an hour we managed to get to speak to one of the Council's senior officers, who said, 'Yes, well, haven't you had a letter from us?'

No. We pointed out that during the two weeks prior to Christmas, postal delays were by no means uncommon, and that if they had bad news for us it might have been considerate to make sure we knew about it before the *Daily Telegraph* did. What was *in* the letter? No, they couldn't tell us that over the telephone. The letter would arrive, eventually.

It took another two days to do so, but in fact we had known the score immediately we put the phone down. They were withdrawing our whole grant. Forty-one arts organisations, both big and small, lost their grants in 1981, for a total saving of £1.4 million – about as much as one average-sized regional German theatre receives in a year.

So what, indeed, were we going to do? We still had some Local Authority money, and a little private sponsorship. By dint of hard work and good housekeeping we had very nearly recovered our inherited deficit. *Macbeth* had made some £20,000 over budget (the press would insist that this was due to the awful notices, and that people just wanted to see if it was really that bad; but of course this is nonsense: Peter O'Toole in a popular Shakespearean tragedy was always bound to attract huge audiences), though unfortunately the £20,000 was cancelled out, almost to the penny, by the rehearsal overspend on delays, wastage and unnecessary overtime.

Without our Arts Council grant we were very soon going to be liable for debts to the service industries – scenery builders, lighting contractors, costumiers, wigmakers – that we would be unable to discharge. We hoped that perhaps our creditors would agree to a 'composition', whereby in order to let us remain trading (and therefore be given a chance of eventually paying them what was owed) they would accept part payment on trust. The drawback to this scheme being that creditors had to agree to it unanimously. We had to wait and see whether they would do so.

Our next play in the season, *The Relapse* (an unfortunate title in the circumstances) by Sir John Vanbrugh, was given a good production by Michael Simpson, with John Nettles an excellent, masculine Lord Foppington. Bad luck, though, dogged us even here; a young actor playing one of the two juvenile leads suddenly decided he owed it to himself to leave the production on the morning of the dress rehearsal, and flew off to Madrid. His place was taken by another actor, Richard Kay, who courageously stepped into the breach (we couldn't afford understudies) and learned the part in twenty-four hours. We opened, a day late, with Richard giving a brilliant performance. The delay, of course, was made full use of by a Press who now turned straight to the Old Vic whenever they were short of bad news to print.

While Andrew and his staff were coping courageously with the dismal situation in Waterloo, I was off round the UK and Europe with a remarkably successful tour of our *Merchant*, playing in Eastbourne, Blackpool, Nottingham, Milan, Brussels, Eindhoven, Ludwigshaven, The Hague, Rotterdam, Arnhem, Wiesbaden, Luxembourg, Strasbourg, Copenhagen, Stuttgart, Zurich and Rome.

It was in the stalls of la Scala, Milan, while we were watching a dress rehearsal of *The Marriage of Figaro,* that I was handed a tele-gram telling me that our creditors had refused a composition, and that the Old Vic Company was, consequently, bankrupt.

My chief sensation was of guilt. It felt as if I had been given this china ornament to look after; a piece not of immense quality or beauty, but an heirloom of some sentimental value; and had dropped it. And yet how long could I, or anyone for that matter, have held on to it? The Arts Council's blow had been unexpected, carelessly delivered and perhaps unfair in view of their earlier promises, but I could quite see that, faced with Thatcher's swingeing cuts, we were among the logical first victims. The Royal Shakespeare Company was now doing some regular touring, and the National were being pressured to do so. If we were only able to keep going by running productions like *The Merchant* into the ground until the costumes were frayed and patched, the scenery chipped and the actors bored with their parts, what actually was the point?

The Company's last performance took place at the Teatro Valle, Rome, on 13 June 1981. Ironically, Rome was the least successful date on the tour. Nearly everybody gets out of the city in summer, down to the south or elsewhere, and among those who stayed, nobody seemed to know when we were on or indeed where the theatre was. Nobody came round after the show, not even the theatre manager. Some of our company went out on the town for a farewell party, but all I wanted to do was eat a quiet supper and go to bed. The next morning we all got on the plane, and at Heathrow we said goodbye. Some of us had been together in the company for five years. I didn't even go back to my office at the Gas Light and Coke Company, where the fearsome representative of the Official Receiver was busily impounding our furniture, stationery, the pictures off the walls, the Australian Chardonnay out of the refrigerator, and I suppose the refrigerator itself.

My father invited me to lunch at the Green Room Club. While I was waiting for him, a friend of his commiserated with me over the demise of the company, and then said, 'Mind you, your father will be very relieved.'

'Oh? Why's that?' I asked.

'He hated your going into management,' I was told. 'He said to me, 'Why has he thrown up a perfectly good acting career, and gone over to the other side?''

The other side? I had never seen it quite in those terms, thinking we were all in the same business really; but of course as a potential employer, every time I turned down an actor for a part, passed over a director or rejected the work of a designer, I was distancing myself from the congenial fraternity of the theatrical market place, and perhaps losing a friend. Possibly making an enemy, one never knows.

Feeling a bit worn out, I decided to book myself in to a Health Farm near Newbury for a week's rest. I thought I could just about stand it for a week, but it was a strain. The place stood in beautiful grounds, there was a swimming pool, and bicycles were available for roaming the countryside. The diet of lettuce-leaves, however, left me with no energy to enjoy any of these facilities. I did suggest a game of tennis to a fellow inmate, a young conductor, but after we had conceded to each other a whole series of love games in which we had each served exhausted double faults into the net, we decided to call it a day.

There was a bevy of young female media executives, who having eaten their lettuce dinner went down to the village pub and drank champagne for the remainder of the evening, bringing back brief-cases full of pork pies to see them through the night. One morning crumbs were found in their beds, and they were formally reported to a dramatically disappointed Matron.

When I returned to the spiritual and bodily sustenance of my own home, it was to find an invitation from the University of Western Australia to go out there for a semester as Director in Residence with their English Department, to assist them in their study of Jacobean Drama.

Well, if at first you don't succeed, do something entirely different. I'd already visited the very attractive campus in Nedlands. I'd also met one or two of the Faculty, and liked them. So it seemed to me a very good idea.

This was not for a couple of months though, and in the interim I did a couple of films for television: one, a version of *Oliver Twist*, in which I gave my Mr Bumble and George C. Scott surprised us by playing Fagin as a wholesome and compassionate Dr Barnado, and the other an Agatha Christie murder mystery, in which I was supposed to have been engaged, many years before, to Olivia de Havilland.

For some reason that I have forgotten, a photograph had to be produced in evidence showing the two of us together at the time of our engagement, and this presented something of a challenge to the property department. Theoretically, all they had to do was find a picture of Miss de Havilland taken when she was in her twenties, and a picture of me at about the same age, and fuse them together over an unfocused background. The trouble was that the star of *Gone With the Wind* came up with a gorgeously-posed Hollywood Studio portrait of her youthful self, whereas the only picture that I could lay my hands on showing me at the same age was the one that had been stuck up outside the theatre in Salisbury, taken by the local wedding photographer. The styles were as different as chalk and cheese, but somehow they managed to make us look as though we could at least have inhabited the same universe.

Pru joined me in Australia, as did the boys during their Easter holidays, and after I finished at the UWA we were invited to do *Uncle Vanya* for the National Theatre of Western Australia, with Pru directing and myself as Vanya.

Though Perth's wealthier citizens may have used their isolation as an excuse to broaden their global horizons, the theatre community had become very self-contained. It was considered impracticable to bring actors over from the Eastern states, partly because of transport costs but partly I'm afraid because most Australian actors don't want to spend that amount of time away from Sydney or Melbourne. It also makes the Perth actors very competitive for what opportunities there are, and quite jealous of each other.

The 'cultural cringe', as it was termed, has to all intents and purposes long vanished from the shores of the Antipodes, but in 1982 there was still a ridiculous lack of confidence in much that was being produced in Australian literature, music, drama and the fine arts, and it led some people to question why British practitioners would want to travel twelve thousand miles to get involved. Broadly speaking, they felt that the first time you came over, it must have been because of the climate. If you came back a second time, clearly things were not going too well for you back home. A third visit could only mean you were after their jobs.

Well, this was my third time in Perth, and I was digging myself in for quite a few months, so it was hardly surprising that Pru and I found ourselves suffering a little at the hands of a small coterie of malcontents. In the main, though, our colleagues could not have been more welcoming and supportive, both at the University and at the Playhouse, where we were doing Pru's excellent production of *Vanya*. It must be confessed that there were already two Britishers in Perth in key positions within the arts establishment, both now permanent Australian residents; one, the actor and artistic director of the Playhouse, Edgar Metcalfe, and the other David Blenkinsop, supremo of the biennial Perth Festival.

David, a Yorkshireman like Edgar, had been General Manager of the Bournemouth Symphony Orchestra before coming to Australia to take over the Festival, which over the years he had built into a world-class artistic event. Apart from music and the theatre, his main passion was cricket, and a highlight of the Festival was always a match between teams drawn from the city and from the Festival participants and staff, captained by David himself. He always put himself in to bat at no.5, and it was tacitly understood by all not only that the Festival side should win, but that he was to emerge as Man of the Match. I played for him once, and was out for a duck in the first over, to a ridiculously easy catch. David, a very nice man, eventually forgave me. I love cricket, but was never any good at it (nor, for that matter, at any other sport).

One weekend we took the train across to Kalgoorlie to explore the Goldfields. It was an extraordinary experience. I have often gazed at fragments of Roman tessellated pavement and tried to picture the house as it once was, the owners sitting about in their togas, servants going to and fro with dishes and flasks of wine, and thought it wonderful that these tiles have survived the millennia to tell us their story. But the little piles of rubble, the overgrown pathways and the occasional gravestone which mark out the Australian prospectors' townships of Kunanalling, Carbine, Broad Arrow, Gem Stones and Siberia are all that is left of what were still vibrant, bustling communities within the memories of many people who are alive today.

In the early years of the last century, 12,000 optimistic speculators lived in the town of Kanowna, which had, in addition to its shops, banks, churches and schools, a fine Town Hall, a hospital, sixteen hotels, two breweries, an hourly train service and its own daily newspaper. Of the silent ghost town, nothing remains. Gold was first discovered here in 1893, bringing thousands, with their families, to try their luck against the odds of chance, drought, scurvy, dysentery, typhoid and the miners' most prevalent killer, dust in the lungs.

Death and disappointment exacted a steady toll on the population figures of the whole area. The gold is still there, and is being mined commercially around Kalgoorlie, but the few last individual speculators gave up in the 1940s, dismantled their clapboard homes, and faded from history.

One building – the only one for several miles – still stands on the dirt road in what used to be the little town of Ora Banda. It is a pub, run by a Scots couple, and we stopped for a beer. We were the only people they'd seen that day, and as we looked out across the porch at the endless silent landscape, I asked what had brought them to this desolate spot. The man turned to his wife, and placed a huge affectionate hand on her shoulder.

'It was getting awful noisy in Glasgow,' he said.

Chapter Twenty-Seven

A script arrived from Granada Television for a series called *Brass*. It was a send-up of everything that has ever been written, painted or filmed about the North of England. Nothing was sacred: D.H. Lawrence, J.B. Priestley, L.S. Lowry, *Love on the Dole*, *Hindle Wakes, Hobson's Choice*, even *Coronation Street* itself. I thought it wonderfully funny, and brilliantly written by two men who could hardly have been less alike; the acerbic Mancunian John Stevenson and the extravagant Shropshire landowner Julian Roache used to meet once a week in an abandoned British Waterways office equidistant from their homes, and put together the next adventure of super-capitalist mill-owner Bradley Hardacre, his dipsomaniac wife, his four children, his mistress, and his downtrodden but faithfully cap-doffing foreman and his family.

I was offered the part of the terrible mill-owner, and was very keen to do it, but only on the understanding that the recordings would take place without a studio audience. A spoof, which is essentially what it was, must look and sound very authentic. If half your studio is filled up with tiered seating for the audience, it severely limits what your designer, cameras and lighting department can do. Also the dialogue must be spoken realistically fast, and if everything had to stop while 200 people laughed at any of the very funny lines, the show would be on the floor.

The director, Gareth Jones, and producer Bill Podmore thought exactly as I did, but I believe they had quite a battle with the Granada management. Comedy shows always had a studio audience, that was the law. If you didn't have an audience, then the project had to be lifted right out of its Light Entertainment framework, and dumped down in Drama. What Bill and Gareth were suggesting would virtually demand the creation of an entirely new production ethos.

The bosses saw the point, though, and in the end agreed that we should do without that unseen mass of laughers (where are they supposed to *be*, these people? sometimes in a sit-com you hear two hundred and fifty people laughing in a *phone box*); and this incidentally freed us to do several takes of each scene without fear of boring the audience. Alas, though the series was a big hit in the North, the Home Counties generally didn't care for it so much. This, it was explained to me, was principally because we had decided against a studio audience. I really cannot believe that viewers need to hear that laughter as a sanction to laugh themselves – surely they know when it's funny? Do they need to hear people crying in the background to tell them when it's meant to be sad?

Altogether we made 32 episodes of *Brass*, and it was one of the most enjoyable things I've done in my life; the result of perfect teamwork, not only by the regular cast – Caroline Blakiston, Barbara Ewing, Geoffrey Hinsliffe and the others – but by all the visiting actors, the brilliant crowd artists, and the entire crew, who entered into the spirit of the thing and were amazingly inventive.

Even God seemed to contribute to the joke. The rows of small terraced houses in Ramsbottom have today been renovated to look rather smart, but at this time they served well for the humble dwellings of my underprivileged workforce. Up on a nearby hill, standing amid spacious lawns and sumptuous flower beds, was Holcombe House, the graceful domain of the Hardacre family with their butler, footmen and a bevy of impregnated parlourmaids. Every time we filmed in the Ramsbottom streets, it poured appropriately with rain. As we climbed the mere mile or so to Holcombe, the sun came out. It was the same thing in reverse; we would begin the day at my house, and the perfect sunshine would persist until we had finished. Then as we went down the hill the skies would cloud over, and just as we set up the first scene outside a tenant's hovel, down would come the rain.

After the first block of recordings of *Brass*, Pru and I had a short break in Venice, where practically the first person we saw was Ronnie Barker, on holiday in a restaurant. Every actor has their own 'I know your face, but . . . ' story, but Ronnie's was one of the best I'd heard. The day before he had been stopped by a woman who clutched at his arm and declared 'I know you, don't I.' Ronnie made an appropriate noise of embarrassed deprecation, but she pressed on. 'Wait a minute – don't tell me . . . ' Ronnie duly waited a minute, and then she got it. '*I* know. You've been on the two Corbetts.'

Pru had to fly back to record *The Merry Wives of Windsor* for BBC-TV, and I went home on the Orient Express – something I'd wanted to do for some time.

Of course, if you're intending to travel only one way on this train, you really ought to go from London. Leaving Venice in the evening, it's dark by the time you reach the Simplon Pass, so you miss all the majestic scenery. The actual train, though, has a beauty of its own; the furnishings, the marquetry in the woodwork, the lighting are all superb. There were, however, a couple of teething problems from which the operation was suffering in 1982, but which may well have been solved by now. The main one was that the train, running as it does on tracks that belong to other railway authorities, had occasionally to retire to a siding to allow the national companies' expresses to pass. Our schedule provided for this, but if we were in the siding for any length of time our batteries would run down, and lights, refrigerators and cooking stoves would gently fail all along the train.

I settled into my private compartment, and as we pulled out of Venice there was a knock at my door and a beautiful blond young man in lavishly gold-braided uniform came in, carrying a clip-board.

'I am your boy,' he announced.

I was a little taken aback.

'Oh, yes?' I said.

He was Swiss French, like most of the staff. 'I want to know,' he announced briskly, 'what time you would like your breakfast in the morning.'

'Well – any time,' I replied cautiously. 'I mean – I'm on this train, I'm not actually going out anywhere.'

'No – I have to *know*,' he demanded, tapping his pen on the clipboard.

'Well; between what times may I have my breakfast?' I enquired.

'Any time between seven o'clock and nine thirty.'

'Oh – all right, then. Eight o'clock.'

'No.'

'What?'

'No!'

'What do you mean, no?'

'*No!* At eight o'clock we shall be at Paris Austerlitz. I must buy croissants – I must buy brioches – I *cannot* give you your breakfast – '

'Yes – yes – all right – I see that. Very well, eight thirty then.'

'Eight thirty.' He wrote it down. 'Merci, et bonne soirée.'

I dutifully changed into my dinner jacket and walked along the train to fight for a drink (twelve coaches having disgorged their passengers at the same moment into the single Club Car), and went on to enjoy an excellent dinner, and a brandy back in the now less populous Bar.

Next morning, though, I was quite ready for breakfast, and at 8.30 duly cleared away my books and papers to make a place for it on the table. It didn't come. It hadn't come by 8.45., nor yet by 9.00 At 9.15, I got up and strode down the corridor until I found another uniformed Adonis, leaning exquisitely against the window and regarding the passing meadows of Picardie with world-weary disdain,

'Do you know what's happened to my breakfast?' I ventured to ask.

He seemed surprised at the question, and looked at me suspiciously from beneath half-closed lids. 'Which is your coach?' he demanded.

I knew that one. 'Coach G'.

He took a surprised pace backwards. 'You must find your own boy,' he told me indignantly. 'I am the boy for Coach F.' His voice rose. 'Go back to your own coach – I cannot attend to you – I have other passengers – '

I never did get any breakfast. Nonetheless, all in all it was a very worth-while experience, though, as it turned out, rather more expensive than I expected. All charges for drinks and so on were made out in Swiss Francs. Now of course if you're journeying, as I did, from Venice, your wallet is full of Lire that you are probably anxious to dispose of; if you're coming the other way, what you have in your pocket is Sterling. The exchange mechanism seemed to get more approximate as the evening wore on – when I finally got off the train at Victoria I found I had a pocket full of Deutschmarks.

*

We were still asked to do itinerant performances of *Beecham* from time to time, and we were booked to play a Sunday night at the Belfast Opera House. The stage management had taken an earlier flight than Terry Wale (my partner in the show) and me, but when we got to the theatre they had still not arrived.

At that time the Belfast Airport security was particularly vigilant, and as soon as our stage management team had retrieved the costume and property cases from the carousel, they were asked to open them up for inspection. The first thing they found was a packet of twenty boxes of Swan Vestas – as Beecham I smoked a lot of cigars during the show, so I had boxes of matches all over the set, and in each of my costumes.

This immediately started, in the minds of the security officers, ideas of intended arson, probably for terrorist purposes.

In the same case they found a heavy 1950s-style telephone, with a long lead attached to a bell-push. Whether the apparatus contained an explosive, or whether it was simply a paramilitary field telephone, the evidence was mounting up.

The pointed end of my conductor's baton was gingerly tested on the palm of an officer's hand. Then they opened the second case, in which were my wig, nose, moustache, goatee beard and the make-up materials necessary for my disguise. This seemed to clinch matters, and the poor stage management were subjected to intensive grilling before being allowed to pack up and get post-haste to the Opera House.

Apart from *Beecham*, which couldn't technically be described as an actual play, I hadn't for some time done any *new* work for the theatre. The only trouble with a course of classical revivals is that you become more concerned with the How than with the What. So when my agent rang me about a play at the Leicester Haymarket by the prolific and admirable writer David Pownall, I was very anxious to read it.

The plot of *Master Class* – not the later play of the same name which was all about Maria Callas, and which curiously enough was played in a similar setting of a semi-circular room with a grand piano in the middle – is an imaginary (though possible) meeting between Josef Stalin, his Cultural Minister Andre Zhdanov and the two principal Russian composers of their time, Prokofiev and Shostakovich.

The date is 1947, the place the Kremlin, and the occasion the notorious Musicians' Union Conference at which delegates were told that for the amount of money the State was spending on music, the

people had a right to something that made them happier, more pro-
ductive and more ready to toe the party line than the compositions
that had recently been available to play through the factory loudspeakers.

It is a play that makes you laugh delightedly, and then suddenly
turns round and bites you, hard. I played Stalin, and at one point,
having flattered the sickly and frightened Prokofiev by showing him
the entire output of his composition on 78 rpm records, I deliberately
smashed the lot, one by one. It is one of the most painful things I
have ever had to do on the stage – made worse by the fact that the
records were all real – it would have been easy enough to manu-
facture artificial ones that looked right, but the crucial breaking
sound could only be achieved by the original shellac. Consequently,
I would pick a record at random, glance quickly at the label, and
perhaps find Alfred Cortot playing the Schumann A Minor Concerto
– but I couldn't put it back, so, *smash* . . .

Stalin – statesman, philosopher, murderer, clown – decides that
contemporary Russian music needs to recover touch with its
national roots. As a Georgian himself, that means Georgian roots,
and by the exercise of emotional appeal and chilling coercion, he gets
the two composers to agree to compose, with the participation of
Zhdanov and himself, a Folk Cantata based on the Georgian poet
Rustaveli's epic *The Knight in the Tiger's Skin*. The resulting compo-
sition-by-committee, with the four men sitting at the piano in turn
and proffering suggestions, is one of the funniest scenes I can ever
remember. But at the end of the play, the audience is left with two
uncomfortable questions to ponder. First, has the State the right to
interfere with the artist's freedom to compose as he wishes, when he
is only permitted to compose at all by the generosity of the State?
Secondly, is a tyranny that takes art seriously necessarily worse than
a free society that treats it as a harmless irrelevance? Is the true
power of music finally measured by the early-morning knock at the
door so dreaded by Dmitri Shostakovich?

David Bamber played Shostakovich, Peter Kelly Prokofiev and
Jonathan Adams Zhdanov – all of them accomplished pianists. I had
to play a bit, but only with one hand, as Stalin had lost the use of his
left arm through childhood polio. The piano was the fifth character
in the action; when the play received its first production in the
United States, four excellent actors were cast who, however, could

not play at all, so the piano was turned round with the keyboard upstage, and they mimed to recordings. The play lost immeasurably by this, and was not accounted a success.

A few years later, Vanessa Redgrave brought over a regional theatre company from the USSR to play their own production of *Master Class* for a Sunday afternoon at the Queen's Theatre in Shaftesbury Avenue, and I was asked to relay the instantaneous translation over the audience's headphones. Not knowing more than a couple of words of Russian, I sat at a table beneath the stage with a microphone and a copy of the play in English, and a brilliant lady interpreter beside me who pointed to the words of the English text as they were spoken in Russian.

At least, that was the theory. Just before the curtain went up, the Russian director warned us that they had made a number of changes to the text, principally because this was the first time the figure of Stalin had been permitted to appear on stage, so to lessen the shock for the home audience all the political dialectic had been cut, and Stalin was portrayed simply as a drunken buffoon. The director also mentioned that the actor playing Prokofiev was a last-minute replacement and had had very little rehearsal, the Zhdanov had never known his lines properly, and the Stalin was famous for improvising round the text – even the text that he had rewritten himself.

We prepared ourselves for a stimulating afternoon. There was, in the event, very little text left to translate, most of the afternoon being filled up with the four characters drinking vodka, singing and falling about. Every so often my companion would hear a line she recognised, and quickly stab a finger at the appropriate place in my script. Sometimes minutes would go by while she turned pages backwards and forwards in a fruitless attempt to discover where they'd got to. Occasionally I would say a line – though whether it had any connection with what was being spoken on stage I have no idea – and friends that had been in the audience told me that some of the author's lines still managed to get their laughs.

I met David Pownall in the pub afterwards. 'You know, I once wrote a play something like that,' he said, cheerfully downing a pint.

Chapter Twenty-Eight

Master Class was well received by the National Press, and it was decided to try bringing it in to London. I was committed to a second series of *Brass*, however, so it couldn't happen for another twelve months. When it did, the theatre we were offered was none other than the Old Vic.

Any fears that I might have had that the old place would stir unhappy memories were instantly dispelled as soon as I set foot in the newly renovated building. After the departure in 1982 of the Royal Shakespeare Company, who had been shooting their nine-hour television version of *Nicholas Nickleby* on the stage, the Governors had put the theatre up for sale. Three days before the bidding closed, an offer of £550,000 came in from a totally unexpected source – the proprietor of the Royal Alexandra Theatre in Toronto, Mr Ed Mirvish.

£550,000 may not seem much for the freehold of a working theatre in London, but to speak the truth the place had already been showing considerable signs of dilapidation when Prospect took it over in 1977; dilapidation we never had the resources to fix properly. New seating in the auditorium was well overdue, the electrical wiring was in a parlous state, and the Fire Inspectors couldn't have extended their leniency for very much longer.

Mirvish's bid topped Andrew Lloyd Webber's nearest offer of half a million, and on 23 June the theatre became his.

Ed, whose Toronto empire embraced restaurants, bars and an antiques market as well as the Royal Alexandra, and was soon to include an additional, larger theatre, was a man of unusual energy. He immediately sought advice from the leading theatrical historians and the best people in theatre building design, and determined to restore the Old Vic to its mid-Victorian identity. The consultants Renton, Howard, Wood and Levin, working from drawings in the 1870 numbers of *The Illustrated London News* and other periodicals,

223

restored the boxes, which had been removed in 1950, and lovingly recreated the decorative motifs that adorned the auditorium of the Royal Victoria Palace Theatre, as it then was. The stage area was widened, and the orchestra pit enlarged, but the most noticeable innovation was the fine staircase, with an authentic cast iron balustrade, leading from the now spacious and inviting foyer up to matching spaces (equipped with bars) on the Circle and Gallery levels. Before, Gallery patrons had not been allowed to mingle with their superiors, being sent round the corner to a separate entrance in Webber Street, thence to climb never-ending stone steps. This entrance now became the Stage Door, while the old stage entrance in Waterloo Road was closed up. With it, I'm afraid, went the Old Vic pub and our friends the Champions, père et fils.

Ed Mirvish had as yet no plans actually to *produce* shows at the Vic; the theatre was to be a receiving house. It reopened with the musical *Blondel*, which was not an enormous success. We followed with *Master Class*. Ed was a keen advocate of Subscription Booking, whereby patrons would be offered the opportunity to book for a whole season of plays, each of which ran for six weeks. *Master Class* did very good business, so of course we were caught in the old trap; we had to turn audiences away and couldn't extend the run because of the next play in the season.

At this time, there were a lot of shows on the road waiting to come in, and a serious shortage of West End Theatres. We were very lucky in that Wyndham's had a play that was coming off earlier than expected, and we could go in there just for another six weeks, after which time we'd have to clear out because *that* theatre had been booked then for something else.

We continued to play to full houses, and again had to turn people away.

At a Writers' Conference held in London at this time, two tall, vigorous, bespectacled men stood chatting. One was our own writer David Pownall. The other man said he wished he could get to see *Master Class*. David told him it just wasn't possible; the run at Wyndham's was just coming to an end, they'd been looking around for a third theatre, but 'Bloody Timothy West is going off to do some damned thing in Australia.'

'I know,' said the other man. 'I wrote it.'

David Williamson's television film *The Last Bastion*, which I had agreed to do because I didn't see how we could possibly go on trailing round with the play indefinitely, knocking on doors to see if anyone would take us in, was the story of the fall of Singapore in World War II, told from the Australian point of view. In this light, Winston Churchill (me, thankfully brown-eyed this time; nobody seemed to complain) emerged less as the saviour of Europe than as the autocrat who shipped Australian troops off to fight overseas, leaving a few sheep farmers to guard the Queensland coast against possible invasion by the Japanese, and who had failed to notice that the guns of Singapore were all pointing in the wrong direction.

The central figure in the story was the Australian Prime Minister of the day, John Curtin, played by Michael Blakemore, known better over here as a major director. There were fine performances from native stalwarts like Ray Barrett, Bill Hunter, Peter Whitford and Rhys McConnachie, and the only problem was with the intransigence of Australian Equity.

There must have been about two hundred and fifty speaking parts in the film, but Equity had allotted work permits to only four non-Australians: Robert Vaughan, playing General Macarthur, Warren Mitchell (who was about to take Australian Citizenship anyway) as Roosevelt, a Japanese actor playing the leader of their forces, and myself. There was, however, an important sub-plot concerning the appeasement-seeking cartel of Menzies, Beaverbrook and Lloyd George. On the books of the Sydney theatrical agents there are not many small Welsh sixty-year olds looking like Lloyd George, and the producers wanted someone to be brought over from Britain.

Australian Equity said no. You've had your four, and that's it. The result was that a young fairly short Sydney actor was pressed into service, wearing an absurd wig and moustache and speaking in a curious half Scots, half Mid-West American accent. For this and a few isolated similar reasons, the film failed to find buyers among the major overseas networks.

While I was there, there was an enquiry from the Sydney Festival whether I'd like to do *Beecham* for them. I'd have loved to, but they wouldn't allow Terry Wale – who played Beecham's musical secretary, and indeed everything else – to come over, saying they would find me a very good Australian actor instead. I had to say no – not that there weren't a number of excellent Australians I knew who would fit the bill, but the stage relationship that Terry and I had

225

worked to achieve over five years of occasional performances was something that could not be re-learned overnight. It would not be the same show, I told them; it would not be the show they deserved.

The union wouldn't budge. It didn't happen. Instead, Terry and I found ourselves invited to New Zealand, where they weren't so fussy.

We opened in Christchurch, on the South Island, then moved up to Wellington, New Plymouth, Tauronga, and finally Auckland. We found it an exciting country physically: snow-capped mountains in the south, with tropical palms and date trees only 400 miles to the north; and in between, Yorkshire moorland, Cornish cliffs, German forests and the grotesque sulphurous bubbling wastes of Rotorua. We were struck by the paucity of audiences and the plenitude of sheep.

As we drove from the airport, past red pillar-boxes, neat bungalows with trim herbaceous borders, gnomes and little concrete rabbits, Terry turned to me and said, 'I can't understand why we've just flown thirteen thousand miles, and we're still in Thames Ditton.'

*

Pru and I were back again at the Old Vic a few months later, in a farce by Bamber Gascoigne called *Big in Brazil*. It was set at the turn of the century; the story of a Halifax industrialist whose lady friend is a keen amateur actress. To please her he rents a theatre a safe distance from Halifax – up the Amazon in fact – and advertises her as Mrs Patrick Campbell in a series of Feydeau farces. Unfortunately Feydeau himself, who has always harboured a secret desire to sleep with Mrs Pat, finds out about the season, and arrives in Manaos to seek her out. The rest of the play did not entirely live up to this promising beginning, although there was a nice idea in Act Three where all the cast, one by one, catch psittacosis from a tame parrot: Bamber decided that the way the disease affected humans was to make them behave like parrots.

Mel Smith directed it. We all thought it very funny, which is usually fatal. The public, on the whole, didn't. We only just about lasted to the end of our six-week slot in Mirvish's not, overall, spectacularly successful season. Andrew Leigh, who had stayed on to manage the theatre, was cynical about the whole idea of Subscription

Booking in London. 'The real advantage of being offered six shows for the price of four,' he observed, 'is that you can stay at home for one, and still save money.'

In the autumn I found myself back in a place that really did harbour unhappy memories: Holloway Sanatorium. The mental hospital had been closed down a few years back, and for some time the enormous building had remained unoccupied. Weeds sprouted up between the broken tiles, rain seeped in through the sagging roof, windows were smashed and balustrades falling away. The only evidence of its former identity were the names of the wards, TUKE, CLOUSTON, MARIE CURIE, still faintly visible above the doorways.

An Anglo-American TV film was being shot here, about Florence Nightingale. The eponymous lamp-bearer was played by Jaclyn Smith, of *Charlie's Angels*. The title was *The Nightingale Saga*. It was the kind of film where, in a long corridor stacked with tiers of bunks, wounded British and Turkish soldiers lay restlessly groaning until – suddenly – lamplight illuminates the wall at the end of the corridor, and we see the silhouette of a head and a nineteenth-century nurse's cap.

'Ah – 'tis the Lady with the Lamp!' croaks one; and then, as she passes down the corridor, they all reach out to touch her garments, then sink back and die, happy.

In appearance of course the real Florence Nightingale was nothing like Jaclyn Smith; she was as tough as old boots, and looked it. But Miss Smith did work very hard at being English, and would indeed have got on better without the assistance of her Dialogue Coach, a very tall American in a Stetson hat. We were doing a scene in the hospital at Scutari, where relief nurses were just arriving from England. One of them was a woman Florence had known in Harley Street, and she had to improvise a greeting. I happened to be standing next to her, and she whispered anxiously, 'What shall I say to her?'

'Just say, 'How nice to see you again,' I suggested.

'Can I really say that?' she asked doubtfully.

'Well certainly you can.'

We rehearsed the scene, and set up for a take; but the man in the Stetson hat raised an imperious arm to stop the proceedings, and strode heavily over to his pupil.

'I don't think that's a very period line there, Jaclyn.'

'Oh – isn't it?'

'No. You should say, 'How happy I am that you are here.'

'Is that right?'

'That is what they would have said. In those days.'

And she said it. It was that kind of film.

The reader may wonder why I got involved in pictures like that – why I said 'yes' to them. The truth is that I had never really cracked the film world – just doing a small part every so often, and sometimes a bigger part in a film that would be shown for a week at The Screen on the Hill, and then on Channel Four at 11.15 on a Tuesday morning. The British actors who made a lot of films all seemed to have looks that went with their personalities, and voices that went with their looks. I grew up with the idea that acting was pretending to be someone else, and so I was at a disadvantage. I felt I had to grab every film offer that came along, even *The Nightingale Saga*, which they had mis-typed on the contract letter as *The Nightingale Sago.*

Just recently, my present agent Gavin Barker said to me: 'Look, you do realise that casting directors are after you all the time for films, but you're never available; you're always off on tour somewhere with a play.'

I felt astonished, flattered, and apologetic. 'I'm sorry,' I told him. 'Very well, I won't do any theatre work at all next year. All right?'

So I didn't, and waited for the phone to ring. Nothing. After a few months Gavin sent me to see an American director, who was indeed quite keen on me, and when I said I'd like to be in his film he went back to his producers at Fox and told them the good news. So they sacked him.

Then Luc Besson offered me the part of Bishop Cauchon in his *Joan of Arc*. I was quite excited about this, because although I hadn't much cared for *The Fifth Element*, his earlier films like *Nikita* and *Léon* were very stylish. I wasn't sent a script of *Joan of Arc*, and nor apparently were John Malkovich, Faye Dunaway, Dustin Hoffman or anyone else. Luc just liked to give you each evening the pages you were going to shoot next day, because he maintained you should know nothing about any scene in which your character was not present.

This is all very well in theory, and it's a technique Mike Leigh uses to great effect, but only after considerable exploration into who you are and what it is you want. In Luc Besson's case I felt patronised by the suggestion that I lacked the intelligence to grasp the overall style and shape of a film by studying the script, or that having that knowledge would somehow be bound to make me act self-consciously. In the event everyone, having never been allowed access to the full story, seemed rather to be acting in a vacuum, and this effect was enhanced by Luc's peculiar method of directing. He operated the camera himself, and directed from that position, constantly throwing out instructions whilst the film was running. I would say the first sentence of a speech, and he would stop me.

'Be more angry with her!'

I'd say the line again, angrily.

'But not too loud.'

Again, but quieter.

'Also you are frightened of her.'

Am I? We didn't discuss this. Oh well.

'And you find her funny.'

The film was still running, and he would 'end-board' all of this. Then he would turn the camera round to face the other person in the scene – usually his then wife Mila Jovovich, playing Joan – and he would do the same with her. Not only that, but he would subject me to similar treatment when I was giving her my 'off-lines' from beside the camera. What his poor editor then had to cut together was a series of arbitrary unrelated close-ups combining to make a scene nothing like the one we'd originally rehearsed.

Filming in the Paris studios had had to be temporarily abandoned a couple of times while Luc went back to Hollywood to raise the money to continue. Luc's mixture of boyish charm and ruthless singlemindedness (I decided he was an amalgam of Joseph Stalin and Peter Pan) seemed to work wonders with the investors; but back in the studio, economies began to be exercised in surprising ways. As Cauchon, I presided over Joan's lengthy trial, assisted by a number of subsidiary bishops and other clerics, all played by quite well-known British actors. When there were still a couple of days to go on this scene, I suddenly discovered that my companions had been sent back to England on the Eurostar, and their places taken by a substitute crew consisting of the studio's office staff, a Vice President of Columbia who had come in for a meeting with Luc and had been sent off to Make-up, and the driver of Dustin Hoffman's Winnebago.

Jeanne d'Arc was a success in France, because Luc Besson is a national icon and because the film depicted the British as inhuman monsters (which they were); but in Britain and the USA the only remarkable thing about it, apart from some very exciting battle scenes, was held to be its unconscionable length.

Shortly afterwards, I was in Luxembourg to shoot a film called *Villa des Roses*; this was as different from the *Joan of Arc* experience as it could possibly be. Although the budget must have been a tiny fraction of that of the French epic, unstinting care and consideration were shown to everybody in the preparation of the film. Far from being kept in the dark about script or style, our Dutch director Frank van Passel furnished us well in advance with documentary videos, cassettes of popular music, photographs and outfitters' catalogues all relating to the place and period (Paris, 1913) in which the story was set. When we went over to Brussels for costume fittings, Frank discussed with us our character backgrounds, showed us sketches of the sets and photographs and short biographies of the other actors (we were an international cast who mostly didn't know each other), and introduced us to his Director of Photography and other key people in the unit. The net result of all this was that on arrival to start work a few days later, I knew exactly who I was and where I lived. I also felt welcome.

Given a good story, which this was, and good people to tell it, which I believe we were, this seemed to me the way to make a good film. It's on a very modest scale, and at time of writing it has yet to be released. I can't imagine what kind of distribution it will find. Modest production budgets imply modest marketing, and I'm afraid it may turn out to be just another of those 'quality' films that get elbowed aside by a lot of indifferent mainstream blockbusters, so that nobody actually gets to see them.

Chapter Twenty-Nine

My wife is a workaholic. An idealistically motivated workaholic. To work, or have the immediate prospect of work, is to her as essential as food or drink. This malady is aggravated by a peculiar kind of occupational agoraphobia: she feels it wrong to stir from the house for recreational purposes, and the idea of packing and unpacking a suitcase is almost enough to negate any pleasure she might derive from a holiday. Her reluctance to go on any journey can be overcome only by the promise of work at the end of it, and I think she looks forward to the time when all acting can be done on the Internet.

I am completely different. Work is not to me the be-all and end-all of my existence; rather it is the related benefits of an actor's life that attract me more than actual performance – the people we meet, places we go to, things we discover, scraps of information that generally remain in the head long after the actual lines are forgotten. We learn, rudimentarily at least, to do practical things we wouldn't otherwise be asked to do: ride a horse, conduct a symphony orchestra, pass oneself off as a transvestite, drive a steam locomotive, print hand-block wallpaper. It has always seemed to me that an actor at a party should be capable of carrying on a conversation on almost any topic, for about thirty seconds. After that, we have to excuse ourselves and get a drink.

Sometimes, we are invited briefly into some esoteric social enclave, as for instance when I was invited to perform in, and help compile, a concert performance about Gerald Berners, the composer, painter, novelist, diarist and rather self-conscious eccentric.

When Lord Berners died in 1950, he left his house, Faringdon in Oxfordshire, to his companion and amanuensis Robert Heber Percy, who maintained it exactly as it had been in Berners' life, complete with messages for the dog pinned to the furniture, and a flock of doves dyed in various pastel colours.

I had always liked Berners' music, particularly the ballet *The Triumph of Neptune*, and his novels were mischievous and fun to read. To talk about the programme, I was asked to lunch at Faringdon by Robert Heber Percy. I arrived a little late, and apologised, asking which road my host would have recommended my taking out of London. 'Well,' he replied, 'that depends on whether you're coming from the Tate Gallery or the Zoo.'

His other guests were a pair of elderly literary ladies, whose names I was never to learn. One of them wore a plaid Inverness cape and was accompanied by a very old Labrador.

After lunch we retired to the graceful sitting room, looking out over the park and lake, and Robert went straight to sleep. The two ladies carried on a loud conversation about the decoration of Harold Acton's house in Florence, while I picked up a book, and the Labrador sat on the hearthrug and masturbated very slowly and elaborately against the fender.

At the concert, a fortnight later, a remarkable audience was assembled; Sitwells, Mitfords, Waughs, people who had known Berners in his heyday and some of whom had travelled a great distance to be at the Wigmore Hall that evening. There was a party afterwards at which I felt an intruder among all the reminiscences of extravagant practical jokes shared on summer evenings at Faringdon long ago, and I slipped away before the Daimlers arrived to take their distinguished passengers back through a world that they must have felt no longer quite understood them.

The other day while searching for razor blades in the bathroom I came across nine complementary sponge-bags bearing the insignia of airlines that went out of business long ago. Though Pru, of course, hates travelling, I love it. Exploring new territory, revisiting old haunts, adventuring far afield or just pottering along the canals in our narrow-boat, I will always find things to delight me.

We do go out together sometimes. I have even once or twice managed to haul my protesting bride off on a sea cruise. Our friends Sydney and Doris Samuelson – Sydney was the man responsible for setting up the British Film Commission – invited us to sing, or at least hum, for our supper aboard the QE2 on a winter voyage to the Canary Islands. While other passengers were playing with the fruit machines, my beloved and I walked round and round the gigantic deck in the howling Atlantic winds to remind ourselves that we really were on a ship at sea. It gave us an appetite for the enormous dinners that were served in the elegant dining room lit by the shimmering bugle-beading of a hundred and twenty ladies' jackets.

The previous Christmas we had enjoyed a memorable and very different kind of trip up the Nile Valley, with a really first-class academic guide and a very bossy tour manager. Finding ourselves moored in Luxor on Christmas Eve, we had challenged this lady to find us a Midnight Service we could attend. Incredibly she did, in the chapel adjoining a small Benedictine monastery in the town.

The place was packed, and the doors were left open to allow three hundred other people in the street to hear what was going on. The whole service was gone through in Arabic, Latin and English, and took three hours. The Gospel was read in English by a minor official from the British Consulate wearing an appalling toupée. The lamentable sounds coming from the small electric organ were mercifully silenced by an explosion from the fuse box – all the lights, which were simply screwed to the wall, went out; but an electrician in blue overalls, who seemed to be part of the clerical team, calmly went round with a cardboard box full of bulbs replacing them. Our fellow passengers from the ship, who had initially been bored by the whole idea and resented being dragged along, were in the end deeply moved by their experience.

The next cruise we undertook was on the Canal du Midi, on a hotel boat; exploring from the Mediterranean end of the canal up to Carcasonne, wondering whether we might hire a boat of our own to travel along it at some future date. The scenery offered an authentic Corot at every turn; the food and wine were delectable, and altogether it was a great success. One cannot, however, guarantee what one's fellow passengers are going to be like on this kind of holiday. There were only seven of us on board; all, apart from ourselves, American. There was a very nice publisher and his wife from Connecticut, but there was also a man of about sixty-five who opened the conversation at dinner on the first night with the words:

'I consider it the inalienable right of every American citizen to carry arms.'

We decided that on the whole it might be as well to deflect the conversation towards some other topic, at which point he brought out a pack of visiting cards, and passed them round the table.

'I need to solicit support for the Primaries', he told us urgently, pressing a card into my hand.

Good God, I thought, can this man be a Senator? A Congressman? A surprise Presidential candidate? It finally transpired that he was actually lobbying for election to the San Diego Water Board, but personally I wouldn't have backed him, even for that. His large forty-year-old daughter, with whom he shared a cabin, trained Girl Scouts in Texas, and was one of those people who was unable to utter the simplest observation without following it with a gay laugh: 'I guess I'll try the grapefruit this morning, aha ha HA!'.

The deck was mercifully capacious, and there were bicycles.

A trip I took on my own, Pru having pleaded some TV play or other to detain her safely within the metropolis, was on one of the two remaining Scottish Puffers, part of a whole fleet of small vessels which once plied their leisurely way around the islands of Western Scotland delivering meat, vegetables, dairy produce, soap, wire, sweets, nails, paraffin, fishing tackle and darning wool. The VIC 32, one of the two survivors – VIC stood for Victualling Inshore Craft – had been converted within to carry twelve passengers in a modest degree of comfort. She was captained by her owner Nick Walker on a programme of six-day cruises throughout the summer months.

During the French hotel boat cruise my masculine pride had been somewhat affronted at the spectacle of the two beautiful bronzed South African girls (the crew) steering, shipping fenders, leaping ashore with ropes, tying up and casting off; *chaps'* work, I thought, and I had insisted on doing a bit of it, probably just getting in the way.

No such embarrassment on the VIC 32. If you were a man, you were expected – well, firmly encouraged – to lend a hand. The vessel cast off from her mooring at the little village of Crinan in Argyll, at the Western end of the canal that cuts across the northern part of the Mull of Kintyre, and sailed into the canal's bottom lock, on the side of which was piled a substantial heap of coal. The male passengers set to with shovels and two wheelbarrows, and tipped four tons of coal into the ship's starboard bunker, after which she backed out of the lock, turned round, came in again forwards, and we repeated the operation on the port side. Then we set off.

Happy, exhausted and covered in coal dust, one or two people went down to the engine room to follow up their ministrations by stoking the furnace; I went to the wheelhouse, where I learned how to navigate the vessel. This was not a complicated art, the only instruments being the ship's wheel, a speaking tube through which to shout at the engineer and, most importantly, the echo-sounder. There was fairly basic radar, a binnacle, and a chart. The wheelhouse was scarcely big enough for two, so I was left in sole charge.

VIC 32 moved very quietly through the water, at a maximum engine speed of six knots; her vertical compound engines beating a lovely gentle rhythm. The tide was against us, but by keeping close to the shore I could manage to achieve the rate of five knots. There were a number of small craft to avoid, and a plethora of almost invisible lobster pots. There were also a considerable number of submerged rocks shown on the chart, and I kept one eye on the echo-sounder, which after fluctuating mildly for twenty minutes or so suddenly began to suggest that the sea-bed was hurtling up to meet us. Having absolutely no idea of the ship's draught, I yelled for the captain.

Nick Walker ambled slowly along the deck and joined me at the wheel. I pointed at the echo-sounder, trying to keep the panic out of my voice. 'Are we all right?' I enquired tremulously.

'Well,' he said slowly, 'that depends how good you are at spot-welding.'

In fact we were in no danger, as I had been confusing feet with fathoms; once I had mastered this I managed pretty well, and it became my chief occupation during the six-day voyage. We were not lucky with the weather; there was a great deal of that very fine but very wet rain that is characteristic of Western Scotland, and it hid from us much of the beauty of Loch Sween, where we dropped anchor on the second night off the village of Tayanvallich. Our hardy passengers were by no means deterred by the weather, though, and in relays we rowed the ship's dinghy over to the village and tramped across the sodden moorland.

They were a very interesting group. Not young, by any means: my first impression had been that I was going to sea with the Garrick Club. They were, however, uniformly energetic. There was a very convivial retired Scots surgeon and his ex-schoolmistress younger wife; an elderly architect who had been a Bletchley codebreaker during the war, with a very smart lady friend; another doctor who was apparently a VIC 32 habitué, courteous, melancholy, unlit pipe clenched permanently between his teeth; a female piano teacher from Winchester; an amply-proportioned butcher from Malton, Yorks.; and a quiet rather secretive man who had been with the British Waterways Board.

There was one other. Wherever you find gatherings of people drawn by the irresistible attraction of steam – whether that steam be used to drive a ship, a railway locomotive, a traction engine or a fairground organ – you will find among their number at least one paralysing bore. I know, because I'm probably one myself. This particular man, who spent a week aboard the VIC 32 each year, had become the bane of Nick Walker's life not only on account of his endless tales of Aveling-Barford steamrollers and the Walschaert's Valve Gear, but of his insatiable masochism, which drove him deliberately to mess up some task he had volunteered to do aboard the ship, just in order to be roundly told off.

The poor weather continued for another couple of days, during which we were confined to the lee shore of the sparsely populated Isle of Jura, where those rare little creatures, ermine, are still occasionally sighted and where George Orwell came for peace and quiet to write *1984*. Peculiar to these islands are the 'raised beaches' – long flat stretches covered with shingle, forty or fifty feet above the present shore line, showing the level reached by the sea at the end of the Great Ice Age.

Then it cleared up, the sun came out and we skirted past the perilous whirlpool of Corryvrecken, slipped into Loch Melford and rowed ashore to the Gardens of Arduaine, where we sat watching the sun go down behind the Paps of Jura with our little ship quietly at anchor in the bay, a thin wisp of smoke from her chimney rising vertically in the still evening air.

We were told an intriguing story. In 1941, two British destroyers sheltering in Loch Fyne lost their bearings outside Inverary, went the wrong side of a light and ran themselves aground. They were stuck there until the next high tide, and in the meantime the incident was discussed by the Campbell family over dinner at Inverary Castle. One of the maids waiting on them was, can you believe, an enemy agent, and having overheard their conversation, secretly radioed her Control.

Two German bombers were immediately dispatched in a surprise attack, bombed the destroyers and disabled them. Suspecting a security leak, the police conducted a house-to-house search, including the castle itself; the girl's radio was found and she was arrested. MI5 officers collected her from Inverary Police Station and drove her to the Tower of London, where she was tried, convicted, and shot.

Now, I don't know another holiday where you could shovel coal, steer the ship, stoke the boiler, row the dinghy, knead bread, help with the washing up and walk in the footsteps of a German spy, all for £450.

Chapter Thirty

Market philosophy has turned head teachers, Vice Chancellors, consultant surgeons and Heads of Chambers into businessmen, and to a certain extent the same is true of those of us who feel concerned for the welfare of our own profession. We sit on committees, become trustees, directors or governors, and of course ninety percent of the time is spent talking about money. As we get older, these responsibilities tend to multiply, and we have to be careful that they don't begin to clog our wheels, sap our energy and perhaps become an excuse for not having done something a bit more creative.

Very important to me is an association with the oldest drama school in Britain: LAMDA, the London Academy of Music and Dramatic Art. (Actually we don't teach so much Music nowadays, but we really can't call ourselves LADA). The reader will perhaps remember that I never went to drama school at all, so it is rather a cheat that, having been invited on to the Board of Governors in the early 80s, I went on to become Vice-Chairman, then Chairman, and am now called President.

There are, of course, too many such establishments spread around the UK, but the present system of assessment by the National Council for Drama Training ensures that only those of the highest standard are granted official Accreditation, and even then only for some of the several courses they offer.

At one time, most Local Authorities would provide grants for drama and dance students. Pru, for instance, had both her fees and maintenance covered by her local County Council when she was at the Old Vic School; but over the years Local Authority input has virtually dried up, while Central Government has traditionally never provided a penny. Very recently, however, the Department of Education decided to commit a certain amount of money to pay the tuition fees of a proportion of each intake of students, though it doesn't cover their considerable maintenance costs. We still essentially have a situation where LAMDA's first choice of students (we accept only 3.5% of our applicants) very often cannot afford to take up the places they have been offered. Were it not for the generosity of a few individuals and Charitable Trusts, and notably a number of senior members of the profession who subsidise students or feed money into bursary funds, we should find ourselves at the beginning of each new year with a class composed entirely of the sons and daughters of well-heeled Home Counties families.

Some schools have found a way out of this by becoming affiliated to a Further Educational College, and offering degree courses; in this way their students qualify for automatic Government grants. I can't help feeling, however, that acting is one of a number of subjects that cannot truly be classed as academic (though that number is rapidly shrinking: I have just read that the University of Surrey is about to offer an M.Sc. in Airline Catering). I'd rather go to see an actor who could play Hamlet well than one who could write a good essay about it. How are future directors, casting *Romeo and Juliet*, supposed to make their selection? 'I want a Double First for each of the title roles, and an Upper Second for Mercutio; Benvolio and Tybalt can be II(ii)s . . . '

Meanwhile, the market demands that we initiate more and more specialised courses, all of which need extra space for tuition and rehearsal which at LAMDA we simply don't have; rehearsal rooms have to be rented in various parts of south-west London, wasting untold time and money – we were recently quoted £900 a week for a Scout hut in Ealing.

Some people ask what is the point of going to drama school at all, when the bulk of available work is in the kind of television drama that seems actually to require no training at all? Well, actors may not want to do that for the rest of their lives. I'm convinced that if you can play Otway you can do *East Enders*. I'm not so sure that the reverse is equally true.

*

My parents' next-door neighbour rang to tell me that quite suddenly, in the middle of the night, my mother had died. It was heart failure, apparently brought about by food poisoning.

A war-time housewife, Mother had a horror of letting food go to waste. Covering the remains of a meal with an upturned soup bowl, she would put it away for future use. 'There's some of that nice fish pie,' she would tell us, or, 'Would you like some of that nice lamb casserole?' By the phrase 'some of that nice', my sister Patsy and I came to understand that the dish described had spent a little more than its recommended life-span in the fridge or, in earlier days, the meat-safe. My poor well-meaning mother – and such a good cook, really – had now fallen a tragic victim to her own lifelong habit of economy.

The most upsetting thing about unexpected death is the threads that are left hanging in the air. Pru was away in Australia, but the boys and I went straight down to the parental cottage in Brighton, where we found half-finished knitting on a chair, a shopping list, a picture postcard marking the place in her library book. It seemed that any minute we should hear her key in the lock as she returned from the grocer's.

Why had I not used the time better whenever I was with her? So many conversations we should have had, so many shared memories we might have mulled over for hours. I never felt any urgency about it; she seemed so resilient that I supposed she would just go on and on.

Wives of the older Wests traditionally had tended to consider themselves as subservient to their husbands, and for quite a long time I think my mother had decided meekly to accept this role. There had been periods of quiet unhappiness in her life, but more recently she had pulled herself together and begun to acquire more and more interests; in people, in books, in ideas, in religion. It was cruel and absurd that this positive phase of her life should have been curtailed so abruptly by a malign pork chop.

My father was never quite the same after her death. He got through the funeral very well, while shrinking from all offers of condolence and affection, but over the next few months seemed somehow to get smaller and certainly less confident.

A few weeks after mother's death Pru and I took him up to Kidderminster, to see Sam who was doing his first professional acting job. Squeezed in between school and university, he was playing the schoolboy Taplow in a Birmingham Rep small-scale tour of *The Browning Version* – he was actually the tallest person on the stage, with the deepest voice, but he played it very well. His grandfather was immensely proud, and the three generations went on to enjoy a celebratory dinner at the Stone Manor.

So Sam didn't go to drama school either. He did an immense amount of acting while at Oxford, but was still determined to take up the place he'd been offered at the Bristol Old Vic School when he came down. In the event, though, just as he was about to sign his acceptance Harold Pinter telephoned, saying he'd written a screenplay from Fred Uhlman's book *Reunion*, about two schoolfriends growing up together in Vienna at the time of the *Anschluss*. Harold wanted to know if Sam would be interested in playing one of the two boys, the son of an aristocratic pro-German diplomat.

That was that, really. Like me, but more quickly because things did move more quickly now, Sam basically learned how to do it by doing it. If Pru and I helped him at all, it was probably by having quite a lot of books and records and playscripts in the house, by taking him to the theatre and concerts a good deal, and subjecting him to our grumbling at the breakfast table about directors, critics and the state of the business generally. At least he went into it without the encumbrance of rose-tinted spectacles.

One other area in which I am involved with drama students, or at least with students doing drama, is as a Trustee of the National Student Drama Festival. Nearly half a century after my pivotal encounter with Harold Hobson in the Gentleman's Lavatory at Bristol, the Festival is still going strong, and remained, until he retired in April 2000, under the directorship of Clive Wolfe, who had played Dr Gibbs in *Our Town* that very first year.

The eight-day-long Festival was held at a different University campus every year until, thanks primarily to the generous assistance of Alan Ayckbourn, we settled permanently for non-academic Scarborough, and every year hundreds of young people, and many not so young, swarm in to perform, take part in workshops, talk, listen, criticise, argue, drink and help to bring out the Festival newspaper. At the same time distinguished writers, directors, producers, performers, designers and technicians turn up to give talks, take part in discussions or direct workshops. The list of alumni over the forty-five years of the festival's existence reads like *Who's Who in the Theatre*, or would if it hadn't ceased publication in 1980.

Occasionally I used to do some teaching for the British American Drama Academy, which runs a summer school every year for students, professionals and theatrical devotees from the United States and elsewhere, in the romantic environment of Balliol College, Oxford. Again, the Faculty each year is composed of experienced people, some of whom have sufficiently high profile to draw students (and their enrolment fees and air fares) from Princeton, UCLA and Baton Rouge.

I did have one significant disaster there with Strindberg's *The Father*, which I had chosen in order to explore with this group of senior students the complex psychological relationship between the Captain and his wife. It was a bad choice. All the women in the class decided the play was anti-feminist and walked out. We had to abandon the project, and I don't think I'll be asked back.

I believe they were being over-simplistic in their judgment of the play, but it did raise the question of whether you should be involved with a play that appears to you to be saying something of which you don't personally approve. First of all, you have to separate the subjective feelings you have about your character from your objective view of the *play*. Secondly, you have to consider the play in its historical, geographical and cultural context. Time and again I have heard actors at rehearsal complain, 'I can't say that – he/she would never say that'. Well, perhaps they wouldn't today, but in seventeenth-century Verona, or eighteenth-century Bath, or nineteenth-century Mayfair or twentieth-century New York, they might have done. An archetypal instance is, of course, Katherine's speech at the end of *The Taming of the Shrew*.

Some girls cannot bring themselves to say it without making it plain they're being heavily ironic, but the play demands that it be delivered with *apparent* sweetness and humility. The clever actress will make sure that the audience knows the reason she's saying it is so that Petruchio will win his bet.

Chapter Thirty-One

*T*he story as I heard it, in the bar of the Penhelig Arms at Aberdovey, on the fortieth anniversary of VE Day, went like this:

A journalist from the *Cambrian News* was recently buying some toothpaste at Medical Hall, the Victorian waterfront chemist's shop in Aberdovey, when he was intrigued to overhear two middle-aged male customers in walking gear, who had previously been conversing together in German, now talking to the girl behind the counter in perfectly good Welsh.

The journalist went up to them. 'Excuse me,' he said. 'I don't wish to be impertinent, but it struck me as very unusual to hear someone of your – pardon me – apparent nationality speaking our language. Do you know our country well?'

'Oh yes,' said the one who'd actually been doing the talking, 'I was here for the while, in the wartime.'

The journalist put on a sympathetic look. 'Ah. I'm sorry. Were you interned nearby? I hope they treated you well?'

'No, no,' the German assured him brightly. 'I was not interned. I was in U-boat in Cardigan Bay. We are waiting for British destroyer, but it is not coming. We are getting very bored, you know. So I am young man, I am coming ashore in rubber dinghy to get fresh eggs for our U-boat. And I was in love with your country, and I am learning your language – Cymru am Byth! – and now I am bringing my friend Albrecht to climb the mountains with me.'

The man who was telling me this story apparently heard it from the journalist himself, who offered it up to his Editor. It was turned down as being too far-fetched, but I want to believe it. West Wales was a very long way from the war, and I can quite see one of the local inhabitants saying quietly to the grocer: 'Hey, I bet that chap's a Jerry, Ieuan – look at his haircut. I should put another threepence on his eggs; we ought to do our bit for the war effort.'

The Penhelig Arms has been a favourite haunt of mine ever since

Pru and I came here just after we were married – partly to enjoy the beautiful scenery of the Dovey Estuary, but partly to inspect the progress of the Talyllyn Railway, the narrow-gauge line built in 1865 to carry slate from the quarries at Bryneglwys to connect with the newly-opened Cambrian Railway at the seaside town of Tywyn.

After an initial period of opulence, the railway's goods and passenger traffic declined slowly until, with the death of the Company's Chairman Sir Haydn Jones in 1950, his widow put the deeds of the now practically defunct operation into the hands of a Preservation Society, the guiding light of which was the remarkable engineer and author, L.T.C. Rolt. The Society (yes, I'm a Life Member of that, too) managed to get the line back on its feet, and it is now run very efficiently as a serious railway still using some of the locomotives and rolling stock dating from 1885.

It is worth recording that Tom Rolt's venture was the first effort of its kind to form a charitable body to take over and manage a railway line which would otherwise have been torn up, the land sold, the stations and buildings pulled down and the vehicles destroyed. When the suggestion was made that the idea be repeated for a *second* abandoned railway, people shook their heads sagely and declared that public enthusiasm would be spread too thin and would exhaust itself. There are now over forty of such projects, and the list is still growing.

In 1985 I was in Merionethshire not just to visit the Talyllyn Railway, but to play the General in Alan Bleasdale's *The Monocled Mutineer*, the story of the youthful con-man and racketeer Percy Toplis, who served as a soldier in the First World War and was centrally involved in the mutiny of British troops behind the lines at Étaples. Not far from Tywyn was the abandoned RAF Station at Tonfannau, and this became for us the notorious training camp at Étaples, the inhuman regime of which sparked off the mutiny and led to the establishment of a self-governing community of well-armed deserters in the surrounding forests.

The Official Secrets Act prevented any news either of the deserters' settlement or the mutiny itself ever reaching the ears of the British public, so that when the facts were finally explained in the book by William Allison and John Fairley, on which Bleasdale's script was based, the Establishment responded with indignation and fury. When the programme was shown, certain newspapers predictably took up the cry. Oddly enough, the hottest manifestations of their rage seemed to be reserved for accusations of bad behaviour by the mutineers in the town of Étaples itself. Drunkenness? Pillage? Rape of the townswomen? Unthinkable by British soldiers, they declared. One national newspaper even went so far as to send a reporter to Étaples, who found an aged retired doctor who was prepared to state that in fact nothing of the kind ever happened – high spirits maybe, perhaps a table overturned in a café, a few rowdy songs, nothing worse.

The doctor's name rang a bell with me, and I looked through the material I had been given to read as background to the events at Étaples. This same doctor, then a young man, had given evidence of behaviour that, while perhaps understandable in the heated circumstances, did actually occasion quite a lot of damage to persons and property. Obviously the sensible old medic had said to himself: 'Ah, ces Anglais; on me paye pour dire ceci, et ensuite on me paye pour dire le contraire . . .'

In the intervals of filming, savouring one of those extreme dramatic contrasts that television still occasionally affords, I went to visit Pru in Rye, Sussex, where they were filming E.F. Benson's *Mapp and Lucia*.

The attractive old town is peopled today by individuals who, in figure and vesture, closely resemble the 1920s characters in Benson's series of novels. One of the main reasons for this phenomenon is the cobbled streets, the negotiation of which requires a distinctive kind of wide-legged gait, fitting the outer edge of the shoe into the cracks between the cobbles.

Benson lived here, in Lamb House, once also the home of Henry James, and there is a flourishing Benson Society in the town. And no, I'm not a member. There was naturally a great deal of critical interest when the LWT film unit arrived. One day they had just begun shooting a scene in the street between Geraldine McEwan and Pru, when a front door opened in the background of the shot, and a woman stepped out.

'I hope you're going to get it *right*,' she said loudly.

'What? I'm sorry? Cut . . . ' said the director.

'I hope you're going to get it *right*. We're very fond of E.F. Benson here,' she announced. 'We *were* hoping that Maggie Smith and Penelope Keith were going to play the parts; however, I'm sure you'll do your best.' She threw one last unconvinced look at the two actresses before reluctantly going inside, shutting the door and peering out through the window.

*

In October I received a rather unusual request. An International Cultural Symposium, to mark the 1000th anniversary of the Martyrdom of St Cyril and St Methodias, was to be held in the Vatican, and they were looking for a British actor to contribute by reading something to the Pope. His Holiness wanted to hear Thomas a Becket's Christmas sermon from T.S. Eliot's *Murder in the Cathedral*. All the Roman Catholic actors, starting I presume with Sir Alec Guinness, must have been busy, and by scraping the barrel they eventually came up with me.

I pictured myself standing in evening dress at an elegant Bernini lectern in an ante-room adorned with exquisite frescoes. Sitting before me attentively would be the Pontiff in immaculate white, flanked by the crimson outlines of perhaps a dozen of his best-loved Cardinals faintly discernible in the golden candle-light.

No. The modern public auditorium in the Vatican holds 8000(seated) or 15,000 if two-thirds of them are prepared to stand. The building is so long that the far ends are shrouded in mist. The stage, across which I am required to process in Archbishop's garb, preceded by four altar boys, is gigantic. At the end I find a lectern, on which lies the great book into which my text has been pasted, and a microphone.

However, the stage management have closed the book before the paste was dry. The pages have stuck together, and the noise of my tearing them apart is hideously amplified over thirty or forty powerful loudspeakers. People leap to their feet, cover their ears, security guards reach for their guns; only the Pope remains bravely impassive. I was very impressed by this.

The day before the performance, I had had a slight brush with the authorities. The director of the event, Monsignor Don Lavagna, had provided me with a thurible containing burning incense, for me to swing as we proceeded ceremoniously towards the lectern, in an attempt to enliven our long trek across the wastes of the stage. I found it very hard to get the hang of the thing, holding the outer chains with two fingers while using the third to agitate the bellows that puff the incense. After my unruly altar-boys had been reduced to fits of laughter at my dismal efforts in rehearsal, Don Lavagna suggested that I take the article back to our Ambassador's house where I was staying, and practise privately.

As my British Council driver paused at the City gate, one of the Swiss Guards discerned a thin trail of smoke issuing from a supermarket bag on my lap. He asked me to get out and come into the guard room. Inside the bag he found this beautiful example of episcopal hardware – for all he knew it could be solid gold and those red glass stones could be rubies. I tried to explain to him how and why I came to be carrying it, but his English was worse than my Italian, which is only good for restaurants or grand opera. I wondered whether, as a Swiss Guard, he spoke French. I explained to him, in halting French, that I was not a burglar, merely an actor, and that this was a prop for a show.

His face lit up. 'Ah! Comédien anglais, vous? ' he asked. 'Connaissez-vous Benny Hill?'

'Mais oui!' I replied. 'C'est mon grand camarade.'

After that we were all right. I have since found that Benny Hill is an extraordinarily good name to drop, almost anywhere in Europe, when you're in difficulty or want something special. I never actually met the man, and don't believe I ever watched one of his shows, but I'm prepared to discourse about him at length, as in this case and in French, if it gets me out of a tight spot.

I was never very good with the thurible, and my domestic efforts to master it must have made His Excellency David Lane and his wife Sara feel that their ambassadorial home had been commandeered for a particularly energetic celebration of High Mass.

Rome was at its very best: not too hot, not too crowded. I wandered the streets, and went to look at the ancient Theatre of Marcellus, begun by Julius Caesar and finished by Augustus – the only theatre of its time still left in Rome. Just down the road are the remains of the Tarpeian Rock, from which traitors were spectacularly hurled to their death. The juxtaposition of these two centres of public entertainment must have been convenient.

The last time I had been in Rome was for the final performance of *The Merchant of Venice*. I wondered now whether the opportunity would ever occur again to go out on one of those British Council tours that, despite all their problems, were one of the chief rewards of the Prospect/Old Vic days.

The tradition of overseas touring for British actors goes back a very long way. In the mid-19th Century, if you were leading a company, visits across the English-speaking world were an integral – and profitable – part of your life. A list of 333 regular British playhouses, prepared at this time, includes Boston and Philadelphia.

Nowadays we can perform in our own tongue in countries where English is not generally spoken. We can supply printed synopses and background material, and in some cases provide electronic instantaneous translation, so audiences know they'll understand pretty well what's going on. Though I have to say that even without these aids, foreign audiences in general seem much better able to cope with English texts than we are with theirs. Your average German, French or Swedish theatregoer will have a good working knowledge of most of the plays of Shakespeare; how many of us could say the same about Schiller, Racine or Strindberg?

The British Council, founded in 1934 to promote a wider knowledge of the UK abroad, is funded by the Foreign Office to provide for a huge variety of mainly educational activities. In 1997 the Council's Arts Programme, developed to stimulate the export success of Britain's creative industries, presented some 2,700 events round the world, concentrating on our more innovative artistic achievements and specifically aiming to correct the image of the UK as a nation of tea-room trios and water-colourists at village fetes.

I'm afraid that the baby of classical drama may have been flung out with the bathwater of the tea-room music. Apart from one or two very high-profile visits to specific areas by the National Theatre and Royal Shakespeare Companies (for which the Council will only be one of a number of funding partners), the current concern is with contemporary small-scale work that says something about the UK today, rather than examples of our 500-year-old dramatic heritage.

Well, they have a point. Up to a point.

By chance, while I was filming *A Shadow on the Sun* in Kenya in 1988, the Council brought over the Oxford University Dramatic Society's production of *Macbeth,* in which Sam was playing Seyton. I caught up with it at a teacher-training college in Nyere. The audience, composed entirely of the college inmates, loved the play and the language. Some lines earned a spontaneous laugh and shout of approval, simply because they were terrific lines. Now if that same audience had been presented with a successful modern British play about juvenile crime in the inner cities, or the spiritual bleakness of the acquisitive society, I doubt if they'd have had such a good evening. They have their own playwrights, who are writing about Kenya's own contemporary problems – they don't really want to know about ours.

The Council's workforce, I understand, is being re-structured. I shall miss that traditional figure, the Representative, in tweed jacket with patched elbows, meeting the company at the airport, often in the small hours of the morning, cheerily leaping over the barrier to offer the tired Immigration officers his assistance, collecting all the passports and looking them over quickly to spot anything politically embarrassing. I remember their man in Nicosia successfully obliterating the evidence of someone's recent visit to Turkey, by sticking a British postage stamp neatly over the word Istanbul.

'It just saved time,' he said afterwards. 'You needed to get to your hotel.'

Chapter Thirty-Two

I first went to Zimbabwe in 1986 to play a minor part in Richard Attenborough's film *Cry Freedom*, the story of the persecution of the Liberal newspaper editor Donald Woods by the South African Government because of his support for Steve Biko. The film, for obvious political reasons, had to be made in Zimbabwe rather than South Africa, and had the full support of President Robert Mugabe. At the time, we all thought Mugabe a fine man; he was spending the money on all the right things – health, education, roads, and agriculture. Land Reform was on the agenda, certainly, but as a matter for calm legal negotiation some time in the future. Even when two years later I returned to visit our son Joe, who was then teaching in Zimbabwe, the President seemed, at any rate by recent African standards, to be behaving fairly admirably.

Joe, during his gap year between school and university, was part of a scheme called Schools Partnership World Wide, organised to supply extra teaching assistance at the new schools that were springing up all over the country. Joe's 'A' levels had been in English, French and Music, so naturally he was teaching Science and Religious Knowledge to a class of Shona pupils some of whom walked five miles every day to St James' School, Zongoro, in the hills above Mutare. He was also, at eighteen, Deputy Headmaster. The Headmaster was nineteen.

Pru and I came out to see him two or three times, together or separately. The first occasion was when I had a break during filming in Kenya, and I flew down to Harare, hired a car, and took nearly thirty-six hours to find the school. Joe in the early weeks of the exercise was very idealistic about the whole thing; if I were ever to visit him, he told me, it must be to Feel The Real Africa – there would be no shirking off to hotels or restaurants, I was to sleep on the concrete floor of his hut, use the pit lavatory, eat sadza and drink Chibuku, the brackish orange-coloured brew in the local beer-shop.

That was all right, really, though the mosquitoes swarming round the lavatory pit were an element of The Real Africa I could happily have done without. When Pru and I returned later in the year, we stayed instead, at my suggestion, in Mutare's hotel, the Manica. While there we discerned among the scheme's young teachers working in different schools in the area a strong feeling in favour of a square meal and a hot bath. We subsequently rounded most of them up and took them back to the hotel. Next morning, the chambermaid was intrigued to find eight different kinds of pubic hair in the bath.

St James' had begun life just as a primary school, but had been so successful that a new building had been constructed for the children to be able to continue their education at secondary level – hence the need to import three extra staff. The children worked eagerly and their parents gave the school every support, but officialdom was very lax both over staff salaries (some of the African teachers hadn't been paid for many months), and in the supply of books and equipment. Joe for his Physics classes had improvised funnels, beakers and measuring jugs out of plastic beer bottles, dug clay from the river-bed and fired it in an oven to make crucibles, and fashioned almost everything else out of wire coat-hangers. All three teachers were desperately short of text books on absolutely every subject. I was told that a requisition form had been sent ages ago to the Government Education Office in Mutare, but nothing had happened. As I was the only person in possession of a car, I said I'd go down and talk to them.

The office building was itself a converted school, and I went upstairs to see the Director in the classroom he had adapted for his use. He looked harassed and overworked, and brusquely directed me down to the basement to see a Mr Mtasa, who, he said, dealt with all school books.

I found Mr Mtasa in what had clearly once been the school's science laboratory, but was now full of books. There were books piled on every available surface, and spilling out of packing cases; the sinks in the benches were full of books, and mountains of books stood in front of the windows, blocking out the daylight. At the far end of the room, behind a table piled with books, sat Mr Mtasa.

'Mr Mtasa,' I began, 'I am from St James' School, Zongoro. We have many new pupils, and I have come to you for some books.'

He gazed at me levelly. 'I have no books', he declared.

I looked around the room. 'Now, that's not quite true, Mr Mtasa,' I said gently. 'I mean, I'm now actually *standing* on a book which – let's see – is a rather old Latin Primer. In German. And here in the sink is a Beacon Reader, gosh, I remember them, just. So there *are* books around, you must admit.'

He shook his head sadly and remained sunk in thought. Then an idea occurred to him. Standing on tiptoe, he peered out over the top of a pile of *Hymns Ancient and Modern* and *Durrell and Fawdry's Elementary Algebra* and caught a glimpse of my car parked beneath the trees.

'You have a car?' he enquired hoarsely. I nodded.

All at once his troubled countenance cleared, as he saw hitherto undreamt-of improvements to his environment suddenly becoming possible. If some of these books were removed, there would be more light, he could see out of the window, and he might clear a convenient path directly from his table to the lavatory.

Without another moment's hesitation, he picked up an armful of books at random, and indicated to me to do the same. We went out and filled the boot of the car with volumes on every academic subject, in different languages, some of them relics from a bygone scholastic age, a few published relatively recently. We came back for more. We put them on the floor, on the back seat, on the passenger seat, right up to the roof.

'You want maps?' asked Mr Mtasa breathlessly.

Rolled-up maps, for Geography. 'Yes, please.' Half a dozen of them were produced from a tea-chest, and we strapped them to the roof rack.

'Clobs?'

'I'm sorry?'

'Clobs? You want clobs?'

I improvised. 'Yes', I said quickly. 'We do indeed want clobs; it's been very difficult doing without them all this time. How many have you got?'

'I can let you have four.'

'Four? Well, we really need eight . . . but all right, I'll take four. Where are they?'

They were globes. Inflatable world globes. We squeezed them in somehow, and with the chassis scraping along the dirt road I slowly drove the thirty miles up to Zongoro.

When Joe saw the car, he turned white and sat down heavily on the grass. 'We'll all be arrested,' he said.

I suggested we tipped the whole lot out on the grass, clobs and all, and he took anything he wanted; then, later, the other schools could come along and pick over what was left.

As we sorted the books out, I began to imagine returning at some future date officially to open the Timothy West Library in one of the school buildings. As things are in that country at present, though, I don't think it's likely. We do happen to know that in spite of everything, St James' School Zongoro is still functioning. I remember so well the laughing faces of Joe's pupils . . .

*

In 1987 Ronald Harwood did a brilliant dramatic reconstruction of the Reykjavik Arms Talks, in which the Canadian actor Robert Beatty, looking incredibly like the President, played Ronald Reagan, and I was Gorbachev. It's fashionable to despise Gorbachev these days, but those talks reveal him as a skilful, patient and diplomatic negotiator, meeting Reagan's waffling — sometimes genuine, sometimes tactical – with a calm, judicious perseverance uncharacteristic of Soviet Presidents before or since.

Breakthrough at Reykjavik was a Granada TV Production, and while we were making it, the finishing touches were being applied to the Granada Tours complex – Manchester's answer to the Universal Studios Tour in California. I wanted to have a look before it officially opened and the coach parties started flooding in to stand at the bar of The Rover's Return, stroll down Sherlock Holmes' Baker Street or sit on the Treasury Bench at the House of Commons. So in my lunch hour I sneaked out of the studio building by a back door, in full costume and make-up complete with Gorbachev birthmark and spectacles, and was stopped by a man in a hard hat.

'Hey. Do you work here?' he demanded.

'No,' I answered. 'I am General Secretary of the Union of Soviet Socialist Republics.'

He considered this for a moment. 'Well,' he said finally, 'you'll have to ask at the main gate.'

Most of the television I was doing at that time, though, was for the BBC. Under the umbrella title *Theatre Night*, works written for the stage but produced as television plays rather than attempting to photograph them as theatre performances. We thought the series worked very well, and introduced a wider television public to some good plays they might not think of going to see in the theatre. I was in a number of them: Joe Orton's *What the Butler Saw* (with Pru), John Galsworthy's *Strife*, and, perhaps my favourite, David Storey's *The Contractor*, known when it was done on the stage as the play about putting up a tent.

The Contractor of the title is Frank Ewbank, who for years has professionally hired out and erected marquees for different functions around West Yorkshire. His daughter is getting married, to a young man who is faintly embarrassed by his in-laws and the family business, and Frank is providing his very best marquee, erected on his lawn and splendidly fitted out for his daughter's wedding. This sensitive and poignant play is divided into three parts: first, the erection of the enormous marquee, during which the various undercurrents among Frank's diverse workforce are finally channelled into the creative effort of getting the tent up, lined and decorated, the dance-floor laid and the gold-painted furniture and floral arrangements brought in; second, the wedding celebration itself; and third, clearing up, collapsing and dismantling the marquee, packing it away and the van driving off leaving Frank and his wife on their empty, discoloured lawn bleakly wondering what is left for them in life, while Frank's aged father wanders about, clutching an old piece of rope and complaining that nobody makes rope like that any more.

Another play in the BBC *Theatre Night* series was *When we are Married*, J.B. Priestley's great comedy about three respectable Edwardian West Yorkshire couples who discover on their joint Silver Wedding Anniversary that due to a technical oversight they are not really married at all. The TV version followed a very successful stage production with virtually the same cast, all of whom had been born or brought up in the north. I was playing the unbearable Councillor Albert Parker, and Pru his long-suffering wife Annie. Pru's family had been in the wool business in Bradford, so she was all right, while I kept very quiet about having left that city at the age of three weeks. It was one of those blissful shows where everyone worked together wonderfully as a team, under the faultless direction of Ronald Eyre, himself a West Yorkshireman who had grown up among all the concerns of nonconformist middle-class propriety which are the bedrock of Priestley's comedy.

The last show that Ron Eyre was able to direct, before losing a courageous battle with cancer, was *The Sneeze*, a compendium of Chekhov's one-act plays, short stories and monologues, translated and put together by Michael Frayn. He asked me to be in it, alongside Rowan Atkinson and Cheryl Campbell. Ron confessed afterwards that he was unsatisfied with his production, but I don't think anything was his fault beyond perhaps in the first place casting three people whose natural styles were so dissimilar. We all had things to offer, but they weren't the same things. Consequently, the show was unsure of its identity: was it vaudeville, intimate revue, Fun Chekhov, or what was it?

We toured and then came to London: the Aldwych. The three of us had quite a lot of lightning quick changes during the show, and a 17-year-old dresser named Helen had been assigned to me for this purpose. She had found life quite comfortable in the modern dressing rooms of the recently-refurbished touring theatres in Newcastle and Bradford, but when we arrived in the beloved tatty room I had occupied in the old Royal Shakespeare days, she complained bitterly about the decor and the rather basic facilities.

'Oh, I don't know, Helen,' I said. 'I'm very fond of this room, and it's nice to have it to myself at last. I used to share it with four others.'

'When was that?' she asked.

'Well – ' I said apologetically, 'that must have been, let me see, 1964.'

'*EEEEEEEEEURGH!*'. Her meaning was clear, and could have been expressed thus: 'In the course of my work it seems I am going to be required actually to touch the flesh of someone who was sitting here in this same room before I was *born* . . . '

She was never quite the same from that moment.

The production was dogged by misfortune. Cheryl Campbell, who had injured her back months earlier while dancing the tarantella in a production of *A Doll's House*, chose to leap over the back of a sofa during one scene in *The Sneeze*, and one night in doing so caused something serious to happen in her lumbar region. In great pain, she was sent home by the company manager in the middle of the performance, and in fact did not reappear for the rest of the run.

Rowan Atkinson, who loved motor racing, shortly afterwards drove into a wall, and was unable to perform for several nights. In having to attend an emergency understudy rehearsal to cope with this latest problem, I had to cancel the visit I had arranged to see my father, who had just been taken ill, and was in a nursing home in Brighton.

I rang him to apologise for not coming down that morning, and told him the reason. Always a true professional, he sympathised and said that naturally he understood; we said we'd see each other at the weekend. But we didn't. Three days later his condition sharply deteriorated, and before I could get to Brighton, he died.

The death of your surviving parent moves you up a generation overnight. While you have a mother or father still living, you feel you are in a sense still growing; that you may yet develop in some unexpected way. With their death, you realise you mustn't entertain any more of those thoughts; you've arrived now, this is how you'll be from now on.

I regret never having sat down with a tape recorder and a bottle of wine and got 'Syd' to talk to me in detail about the many and profound ways in which our business has changed since he threw in his job with Doncaster Collieries and became an actor in 1927. There were all sorts of things I never knew about him; for instance, whenever we visited my parents, he would excuse himself after dinner, go into the other room and remain at his desk for half an hour or so, and I used to assume he was studying a script, perhaps learning his lines for the next day. Sometimes I would see him jotting things down in a small Woolworths' notebook. After his death, when we were clearing out his belongings, I came across about thirty of these little red books, and opening one of them I saw that each evening he had been meticulously noting down every single item of expenditure for that day: Newspaper, 15p; Coffee, 12p; Bus fare, 20p; Torch batteries, 88p. Though he and my mother had for the last forty years lived quite comfortably within their income, Syd apparently liked to imagine himself constantly on the verge of penury. If he had not worked for a month, that signified the end of his career. 'The boycott has started,' he would tell us. 'I am in the gutter.' If I ever complained about some aspect of a job I was doing, I would be stopped with a sharp rebuke: 'Remember you're very lucky to be working.'

He loved arguing with the Inland Revenue, sometimes over tiny sums, and would invent euphonious names for commodities that he considered should be allowed against tax. Incensed at being told toothpaste and mouthwash were not regarded as professional expenses, he resubmitted them under the title 'Unguents and Pomades', and got away with it. This made him really happy.

Chapter Thirty-Three

One way and another, I was quite relieved when *The Sneeze* closed – it was a miracle it had lasted as long as it did, with two of its principals off sick; and when our producer Michael Codron heard of my father's death I think he fully expected me to beg him for time off as well, and was poised to put the notice up there and then.

I wanted to do something entirely different for a while. An organisation with which I was involved, called the International Foundation for Training in the Arts, had principally been concerned with the USSR, inviting a large group of students from the Moscow Art Theatre School to work with our own drama students and perform in workshops with members of the Royal Shakespeare Company. The idea now was that there should be a reciprocal visit by British students to Russia, to go and work for a while with the school in Moscow.

Brian Cox was the driving force behind this idea, but as he was busy I offered to select sixteen students from eight of our top drama schools, rehearse them in scenes from Chekhov and Ostrovsky, take them to Moscow and, together with Caroline Keely the Administrator of IFTA, look after them.

Our first experience of Soviet life, when we arrived at our hotel at eleven o'clock at night in April 1989, was not encouraging. Not enough rooms had been booked, the dining room was closed, there was nowhere open to eat in the area, we couldn't change any money. The following morning there was no breakfast, the buffet had run out of food, someone was supposed to arrive with some roubles for us all, but didn't. Someone else, from one of the TV channels, was meant to come and do an interview, but they didn't show up either.

A bus arrived, eventually, to take us to the Moscow Art Theatre, and on our way to the centre of the city our spirits rose as the monolithic Stalinesque skyscrapers, designed to ram home the message that the individual is less important than the State, gave way to huge gold domes, striped minarets and graceful 18th-century palaces.

For the next few weeks we rehearsed scenes and attended classes. Various people came and gave lectures, the value of which for us depended entirely on which interpreter had been allotted to us that day; these ranged from the brilliantly accurate to the uncomprehendingly inventive. We visited theatres, we went to both opera and ballet at the Bolshoi, to Novodiviche Cemetery, the Turkish Baths, St Basil's Cathedral, Lenin's Tomb and the Gum department store. Finally, on a perfect spring morning, a Monday when the estate is closed to ordinary visitors, we were taken to Chekhov's house at Melikhovo. We had a film unit covering our stay in Moscow, and I was allowed to film a couple of scenes from *Uncle Vanya* with our students inside the house. In these simple rooms, small, unfussy, utilitarian, every movement, every look, every word spoken had a rightness, an authority about it.

What a shame we so seldom have the chance to play Chekhov in rooms that are the right size. The same is true of other naturalistic playwrights such as Ibsen. The trouble is that the two of them wrote famously good parts, parts which appeal to popular actors. Popular actors attract big audiences, big audiences need big theatres, big theatres have big stages, big stages need big sets, and before you know where you are, the first act of *Three Sisters* seems to be happening in the Ballroom at Grosvenor House.

The Professors of the Moscow Art Theatre School (MXAT) are also practising directors, and are, or have been, actors themselves. They were all trained at the School (everyone has to be trained, even drama critics). Accepting that Stanislavski's teaching is just a matter of common sense, the instructors are refreshingly practical and free of cant.

One of our young students was playing Sonya in the second act scene of *Vanya*, where she sits down to an improvised supper with Astrov, the neighbourhood doctor. Professor Bogomolov watched the scene, and then asked her:

'Why? Why you do this? Why you give food, wine Astrov – why you stay up with him in middle of night?'

'Well, because I love him. It's an excuse to sit and talk with him while nobody else is about.'

'*No*. She *fridge-raider*. She very unhappy girl, so she eat for comfort. Every night she wake up feeling sad, she come downstairs, eat bread, cheese, maybe sausage. So she get fat, maybe she get spot on face, so men not look at her. Is sad.'

In British productions of the play, Sonya tends to be played by the prettiest actress in the company with her hair scraped back and no eye make-up, her essential beauty being allowed to peep through at odd moments, as in one of those American films where in the last reel the local librarian takes off her glasses for a moment, and the hero breathes, 'Why – you're beautiful!'. Bogomolov's genuinely tragic perception of the character seems to me to make much more sense.

Over one point of interpretation, though, I did quarrel with the professor. In the last act of *The Seagull*, Nina returns unexpectedly one night to the house at which, two years before, she had performed a play by the young Treplev on an improvised stage in the garden. Exhausted and emotionally disturbed, she has come to say goodbye to him, before she leaves to take up her first job as a professional actress, in a winter season at the provincial town of Yeletz.

To me the scene has always appeared unbearably sad; in saying goodbye to the tattered remains of the old garden theatre, she seems to be unconsciously extinguishing in herself an innocence, a spark of individual promise; and that when she tells the ineffectual but possibly talented Treplev that she is going off to become a provincial actress – a younger Arkadina in fact – we have misgivings about the path she has chosen, feeling that something valuable has been lost for ever.

Bogomolov didn't agree with this. In Russia, he said, an announcement that a person was going to become an actress – an artist – is, or should be, greeted with unalloyed delight. She has been given a mission in life, she is embracing her destiny, she is a privileged human being. It was useless to try to explain to him the kind of conversation that might greet such an announcement in the Home Counties.

A NEIGHBOUR: Tell me, how's Nina? What's she doing just now?

NINA'S MOTHER: Nina? Oh, she's decided she's going to be an actress.

NEIGHBOUR: (politely) An actress? Really? (A pause)Are we going to see her in anything?

MOTHER: Well, she's going to go to Colchester.
NEIGHBOUR: Colchester. Ah.

Of course it has to be remembered that our visit to Russia took place before the red flag was lowered. Attitudes towards art are probably now not so clearly defined – at least, I imagine not; Pru and I have been unable to re-establish contact with the people we knew at MXAT.

While loving Russia and its people, lots of things about Moscow drove me mad. The best interpreters, we found, were in constant fear of losing their work permits and being sent off to live in Yakutsk. Official arrangements about nearly everything were arbitrarily changed at the last minute. Restaurants which were seen to be serving people dinner would claim they were closed, or when practically empty, would declare themselves to be full. Theatres tended not to perform the play they were advertised to perform that night, or if they did, it would be at a quite different time. Taxis would not stop unless we waved a pack of Marlborough cigarettes; for non-smokers, packets of condoms were an acceptable substitute. Roubles, as proffered by obvious tourists, were useless; they wanted US dollars.

Official buses, on which we relied for the students to be able to follow their quite punishing schedules, had often been given instructions to drive us somewhere miles away from where we needed to go. Such instructions could only be revoked by signed orders from the transport office, and on one occasion I did manage to get the driver to drop us off secretly at the School while he drove on to his office to get the necessary permission for having done that in the first place. Occasionally our bus would actually arrive at the hotel early, and then the driver would get out and wander about, or go and have a quiet smoke in some little-used corner of the building and wait for someone to recognise him, which as he wasn't in uniform and we'd never seen him before was perhaps a little unreasonable.

On the other hand the people, when they were being just people and not the representatives of some crumbling bureaucracy, were wonderful to us. Their selfless hospitality at this time of hardship and acute food shortages was extraordinary. There was a spirit of not perhaps wholly justified optimism abroad. Relief at now being able to speak reasonably freely and no longer needing to glance over the shoulder for KGB stalkers could be read clearly on faces in the food queues, school playgrounds and crowded trolleybuses.

We met the father of one of the MXAT students, whose job it was to unearth literary manuscripts that had been hidden away during the years of censorship, and another to whom Stalin had given the task of going through all the film libraries, retaining the Communist propaganda movies but throwing out everything else. Backing a hunch that no-one would ever have the patience to sit through the doctrinaire footage, he simply changed the labels on the cans, thereby preserving some of the world's great films for the Soviet audience.

Years later, Pru and I visited St Petersburg, and one day we went to the palace of Pavlovsk, just outside the city. This had been heavily shelled by the Germans during the war, and many of the nearby houses had been completely destroyed. Stalin decreed that repairs to the historic Palace were to take precedence over rehousing the roof-less residents. Was this due to a sentimental streak in the tyrant's make-up? Or might it have been clever policy publicly to demonstrate his respect for the history that in reality he worked to destroy? Perhaps. By contrast, we found that there is at the moment an acute shortage of public funds to maintain some of St Petersburg's most precious buildings which have fallen into gradual disrepair. Restoration is in many cases being carried out by an unpaid volunteer force in the evenings after their official jobs, for which most them are not getting properly paid either.

Chapter Thirty-Four

I had read *Scandal* by A.N. Wilson, a blackly funny novel whose central character, Derek Blore, is a self-important middle-aged Cabinet Minister given to slipping off every Wednesday to visit a young lady in West London, there dressing up as a schoolboy and being pleasurably disciplined by his hostess. His carefully-constructed world begins to fall apart when the girl recognises his picture in the paper, discovers his address and calls on him, genuinely to ask his advice about her National Insurance stamps. From that moment he becomes enmeshed in a web of international espionage and media exploitation.

Blore appealed to me irresistibly; pompous, cuckolded, not very bright, quoting repeatedly from the only book he has ever read right through, Somerset Maugham's *The Moon and Sixpence*, but nevertheless staunchly obedient to his political masters. I so badly wanted to play him that I bought the rights of the novel myself, engaged Robin Chapman to write the screenplay, and worked with the BBC producer Innes Lloyd to develop it for television.

Somehow in the transition from the novel to the screen, the story's individual flavour got slightly lost, and the final result, though well put together, had a slight air of *déjà vu*, intensified by recent accounts of real-life politicians indulging in similar personal enthusiasms. Devious, reprehensible characters are so much more rewarding to play than virtuous, admirable ones, and I think it may have been one of my best television performances. It wasn't a huge success though, and has never to my knowledge been repeated.

The whole process of purchasing the rights, commissioning the adaptation, assisting the director Robert Young with the casting and in general helping the project on to the TV screen was a fascinating and instructive exercise. I wanted to do it again if the right material came along. Oddly enough, almost immediately I received a letter from the West of England office of HTV, asking for my collaboration in the scripting and putting together of an entirely different sort of programme: four short films about the re-opening of the Kennet and Avon Canal, the basis of which would be my journey with Pru and a couple of friends in the narrow boat we owned, from Bath at one end of the canal to Reading, eighty-seven miles away at the other.

My involvement with this canal began when I was twenty years old. I went along with my friend Peter Davey to the inaugural meeting of the Society being formed to preserve it as a navigable waterway. The once valuable east-west link between the Thames and the Bristol Avon had fallen into disuse, the water had drained away, banks, lock gates and wooden bridges had collapsed; but a small group of enthusiasts supported by, among others, Chuter Ede M.P. and the Bishop of Bath and Wells were determined to put into gear a colossal restoration programme before a bill could be hurried through Parliament permitting the track-bed to be filled in and built upon.

This entertaining meeting had taken place in Bath on a Saturday afternoon, at the westernmost lock of the canal which lets boats down the last few feet to the level of the Avon just below Poultney Bridge. Up onto the lock gates clambered a farmer in a smart suit, and shouted his violent opposition to the scheme; apparently he had designs on some of the land concerned. He found little support, though, among the crowd, and presently a young zealot with a barge-pole toppled him backwards into the mud of the empty lock, drawing cheers from the hundred or so onlookers.

When the euphoria had died down, the enthusiastic band tried to look soberly at the task they'd undertaken. The whole canal bed would have to be re-lined, top and bottom pairs of gates be supplied for 106 broad locks, including the gargantuan 16-lock 'staircase' at Caen Hill; there were innumerable lift- and swing-bridges to restore, a huge reservoir to re-commission, and two historic pumping stations gradually to be brought back into use.

Back then in 1955 there was no promise, or indeed likelihood, of official funding, in fact the British Waterways Board thought the idea was crazy. Gradually though – very gradually – it started to happen. Groups of volunteers, including soldiers, boy scouts and even prisoners under the direction of unpaid experts reclaimed a stretch here, a few hundred yards there, and when the scheme began to be perceived as possible after all, money started to trickle in from various sources, a Trust was formed, and finally British Waterways came in with their full support, after which the project was guaranteed.

Little did I think as I stood on the side of that lock, listening to the idea being expounded for the first time, that when the canal reopened thirty-six years later ours would be the first boat to sail through from Bath to Reading in nearly forty years. Actually, I have to admit that on that first occasion we only accomplished eighty-six and a half miles of the 87-mile route; the Queen had officially to open the canal a few weeks later, so our 16-ton 60-foot narrow boat had to be craned out of the water just below the top lock of the Devizes flight, driven round the one-way streets of the town on a lorry, and deposited back in the water a little way above the same lock, so that Her Majesty could truthfully claim she had been there first.

Our own narrowboating days had begun some fifteen years earlier, when our friend Lynn Farleigh had lent us her boat for a fortnight, and my initial curiosity about the Kennet and Avon blossomed into a passionate love affair with the entire inland waterway system of this country.

I'd always loved messing about in boats, and as a child had gone with my family on holidays up the Thames. Since that time, though, the river seemed to have been taken over by a private navy of gleaming and rapidly-propelled gin palaces driven by successful-looking men in blazers and yachting caps and customarily adorned by a bikini-clad blonde on the foredeck.

We quickly discovered the canal scene to be very different. Size of craft is rigidly dictated by width of locks and depth of water. Speed is impossible. Blazers and caps are severely out, woolly hats and real-ale badges are in, though not compulsory. In place of the young lady on the foredeck, you are more likely to find an ancient bicycle.

On a canal, more often than not you're looking at England from the back. This is particularly true in built-up areas. In the nature of things, a town or village springs up around its local river; if in addition a canal has been built because the river is unnavigable, then it's probably been put round the back somewhere. The river is the natural thoroughfare, the canal the practical service road. This means that you are constantly coming across intriguing reminders of the canal's commercial past: warehouses, wharves, cranes that have probably remained there unremarked for upwards of two hundred years.

Out in the open country, too, canals have a way of retiring from public view. The original engineers, the Brindleys, Rennies and Telfords, had to find ways through the rising and falling contours of the land. Long cuttings, embankments, aqueducts and tunnels were expensive, and too many locks would slow up the traffic. If they met a hill, often their best solution would be just to go round it; and so the canal would go winding away for mile after mile, occasionally encountering a little brick-built hump bridge supporting an over-grown cart track, and finally edging discreetly back, once more to get in touch with the outside world.

This country, of course, once had a commercial canal network second to none. Many fell out of use in the latter part of the nineteenth century, the villains in most cases being the railway companies, who bought them up in order to let them fall into ruin, and then grabbed their traffic. A lot of our original canals have been built over, and anyone would have a hard time now tracing their track-bed. In the last twenty years or so, however, the waterways have seen a renaissance of which the Kennet and Avon rescue is the most dramatic example. There are apparently more boats around today than there were in the heyday of commercial traffic; consequently there is a continuing demand for canal restoration, now going on at an astonishing rate.

The summer of our initiation in 1976 is fixed in my mind as having been entirely cloudless; we chugged our leisurely way along the Grand Union and Oxford Canals, our two boys, burnt black by the sun, so blissfully exhausted by working the locks and swing bridges that they collapsed each evening straight after supper, leaving their parents to play Scrabble, make love or just sit on deck and watch the evening light fade from the sky while listening to the sleepy chatter of dabchicks, the plop of a water-vole or just the constant trickle of water from a nearby lock-gate.

Eventually we bought a half-share in Lynn's boat, and only sold it again when we had a slightly longer one built for ourselves. We named it after our accountant, through whose guidance and per-spicacity we had been able to afford it; so that although sadly she died a few years ago, her name lives on not only in the hearts of her many theatrical clients, but also on the register of the British Water-ways Board.

If there is a canal or river nearby when we're working away from home, we try to sail the boat down there (or, if that would take too long at a maximum speed of 4mph, bring it on the back of a lorry) and live on it, as I did while performing in Harold Pinter's production of *Twelve Angry Men*, which opened at Bristol.

Once the production had settled in, I invited the whole company aboard for a trip down the river. We were moored in the marina at Newbridge, just outside Bath, on a very pleasant stretch of the Bristol Avon. Nine of the other eleven Angry Men turned up, together with the understudies, stage management and wardrobe mistress. We were a full boat.

It was a fine day, but there had been a lot of rain, and the river was high and running quite fast. We were carried downstream comfortably with very little help from the engine.

We passed through the locks at Kelston and Saltford, but as we approached Swineford lock, the suddenly very strong current carried us away from the lock cut and towards the top of the adjoining weir. Quickly, I opened full throttle and brought the tiller round to try to steer back to the lock; but of course that was the worst thing to do, as it brought us broadside on to the weir, towards which we were being rapidly sucked. We were powerless to avoid being swept over and dashed to pieces.

In the next few microseconds, different images of the coming tragedy flashed through my mind: the dead and maimed actors in the water, the tangled wreckage of my boat, a very long pause from Harold Pinter . . .

THUMP! Not the noise I was expecting. The hull had fetched up against the wooden bar across the top of the weir. At each end, this beam was slotted into a groove in an upright post, and it had now risen with the water level right up to its highest limit. Our hull had just caught it. Kevin Whateley, who was standing beside me on the after-deck, had bravely not uttered a word, and now we both managed to force a smile to show there had never been any cause for alarm.

No, we were not going to tumble our deaths, but the trouble was now we were stuck. The force of the water rushing down the weir held us tightly against the wooden bar; nothing we could do with the engine or with the barge pole could budge us an inch. There was no one to turn to for help, the lock and the surrounding landscape were utterly deserted. Would someone swim against the strong current to the opposite bank, and go and seek help from somewhere? Nobody volunteered.

Suddenly, a boy appeared in a canoe. We hailed him, and he paddled over to us. I explained the situation, and he agreed to take the other end of our stern rope to the opposite bank, make it fast, and go and get a man he knew who owned a lorry.

We had lunch; that seemed the best thing to do. Everyone was very silent and pale to begin with, but a couple of glasses of wine and the assurance that we were no longer in immediate danger brought back a little colour and conversation. We heard the sound of a lorry approaching, the young canoeist tied the end of our rope on to its fender, and the lorry set off away across a field. The rope broke. Our young hero shouted that he would go to a nearby garage, and get a stronger rope. We uncorked another bottle or two and sat down to wait.

Paddling furiously against the stream, the boy got over to us with the new rope and went back with the other end. This time, with the lorry skidding on the wet field, we slowly began to edge away.

Everyone was in high spirits on the way back to Newbridge, but I could not help noticing some very new-looking plastic bags caught in the trees a good three feet above the present water level, indicating the height the river had reached the day before. Had we made our trip yesterday, and had a similar mishap befallen us, the protective bar, which had risen as far as it was able, could not have prevented us from going straight over the edge.

Chapter Thirty-Five

'Never assume' said George Bernard Shaw, 'that the philistine is indifferent to art. He hates it.'

At no time in my life did this seem so evidently true as in the latter days of the premiership of Our Lady of Grantham. Of course, we've always been a comparatively philistine nation, and rather than making good art popular it's easier for any Government to pretend that what is popular is necessarily good art. However, today it's not quite so usual to hear people protesting that theatres and orchestras ought to be self-supporting, and demanding why, as rate payers, they should have to shell out for something they don't like.

In the late 80's, when I had re-established contact with the Bristol Old Vic by joining their Board of Governors, these views were very prevalent. Indeed, we heard them expressed occasionally by one or two of the Governors themselves. Many regional theatre companies at that time found themselves supervised by what became known as Gamekeeper Boards, members of which were there simply to safeguard the interests of various funding bodies rather than possessing any real knowledge of, or fondness for, the theatre. There is no reason, of course, why these two areas of concern should not go hand-in-hand, and sometimes they did; but often we had to negotiate with people like the City Councillor who is reported to have replied thus to an official charge that not enough money was being spent locally on the arts:

'I would like categorically to refute, Chair, that accusation; and declare categorically that our Party has not only spent quite a lot of money on the arts, but also on plays, and music, and that.'

I won't tell you which Party he represented. He and a colleague were balanced on our Board by two Councillors of the opposite political persuasion, and this meant that the rest of us outside the Local Authority contingent came under continual fire from one side or the other. Our Chairman, Professor Ted Braun, together with

Vice-Chairman Tony Robinson and myself, were known Labour voters, which led to accusations that the theatre was being used to disseminate dangerous Communist propaganda; on the other side, there was a deep-rooted conviction that theatregoing was an intrinsically Tory occupation, and should be actively discouraged.

Once a month, I used to travel down to Bristol on the Wednesday afternoon, see the show at the theatre, go to the Board Meeting on Thursday morning, have lunch with the Artistic Director, and then take the train back to London. As I watched each show in the lovely Georgian auditorium I became more and more aware that a succession of cuts in both central and local government funding were gradually making it impossible to present, to an acceptable standard, the kind of costume plays that appealed to the bulk of our audience, who tended to be of late middle age. Younger patrons, who since it opened in 1972 had been drawn to our second theatre, the New Vic Studio – often for the perfectly good reason that their parents tended instead to go to the main house – had now been left out in the cold by the reluctant decision to close the smaller theatre until we had more money.

The Bristol Old Vic had traditionally been known, both by the public and the profession, as a regional centre of excellence for the production of Elizabethan and Jacobean classics, Restoration and Georgian comedy and Victorian and Edwardian drama. Actors happily came to work here for fairly derisory salaries, knowing that productions would be of the highest quality, the sets admirable, the costumes and wigs individually designed and made. Audiences knew they could rely on jealously maintained production standards, and so could the theatre company itself.

Actors' agents are normally unwilling to let their clients go away and perform in the regions when there might be a much better paid couple of days on a film in the offing, an episode of a TV Soap, or even a lucrative crop of voice-overs. The established actor, if he or she decides to ignore the agent and take the plunge, needs first of all to have confidence in the theatre's artistic director.

This pivotal appointment was causing problems for Theatre Boards generally throughout the eighties and nineties, because very few top-class people wanted to do the job. This had little to do with the salary or physical conditions; it was simply an unwillingness to spend the time in arguing with local politicians, lobbying the

Regional Arts representatives and lunching potential sponsors that ought to be given to reading plays, visiting other theatres, talent-spotting, and thinking about their own productions.

We had already made one unfortunate choice when selecting an Artistic Director, and so had to go through the disagreeable business of dismissal, compensation and re-advertising. But the next time we chose well. Paul Unwin, the successful candidate, was young, energetic and imaginative; he had previously directed plays at both our theatres, and was very popular with the staff. Within a few weeks, the sagging morale of the organisation was briskly revived, and exciting new plans were set afoot.

As soon as we had solved the question of the Artistic Director, we were faced with a problem of a different kind, to do with our other senior appointment, that of Administrator. Unlike most other theatre companies, the Bristol Old Vic had always fought shy of that title – what we had instead was a General Manager. Rodney West (no relation) had been doing the job admirably ever since the retirement of his predecessor Douglas Morris had promoted Rodney from being one of the country's best-known Front-of-House Managers.

Rodney West had been with the company for twenty-two years, and was as much a part of the theatre as the proscenium itself. When we were told, however, that his present job description failed to satisfy the Arts Council's new rules for subsidised theatre management, we were forced to explain to him that his job had legally ceased to exist, that we were required by law to advertise for the new post of Administrator, and that we wanted him to apply. But the atmosphere of Business Plans and computer-devised Projected Outcomes was not for him. Rodney's genius was for knowing the patrons, keeping them and the staff happy, supporting the artistic director and liaising with the Board, the City Fathers and the Theatregoers' Club. So we lost him, and his departure caused quite a lot of bad feeling among some of the old guard of the Bristol audience.

Meanwhile, I had been wanting to establish for myself a more hands-on relationship with the company. I had already played Ibsen's *Master Builder* for Paul, and now he asked me if I would like to join him as his Associate Director. I was unsure about this; after the London Old Vic saga, I had determined to take no further part in trying to run a theatre, and had completely lost the appetite to direct.

In the end I agreed just to assist with policy-making, be a sounding-board for Paul's ideas, help to build an acting company and perform a bit myself.

The new partnership kicked off with two very successful productions done back-to-back and sharing the same cast. The first was Garrick and Coleman's *The Clandestine Marriage*, which was first performed here in 1766, the year in which the theatre first opened its doors. We therefore decided to set the play in eighteenth-century Bristol, with Patrick Malahide giving a wonderful performance strikingly reminiscent of that well-known City Councillor to whom I referred earlier. I played Lord Ogleby and then the title role in the second play, *Uncle Vanya*. Malahide (an excellent Astrov, too), Carol Gillies, Saskia Wickham, Denys Hawthorne and Kate Lynn Evans led a strong company, and the box office response was very encouraging, in spite of a local notice for *Vanya* from a junior reporter which read: 'If I'd written this play, it wouldn't get a staging at St Werburghs Community Centre. But even if the disappointing script is Chekhov's equivalent of David Bowie's Laughing Gnome, at least there are some stirring contemporarily relevant speeches about saving trees.

Everyone does their best, but it's the play that holds them all back.'

I don't know why we thought that the encouraging upturn in the theatre's fortunes might be met by the restoration of the cut the City Council had made in our grant the previous year; instead, they announced they were going to cut us further. There had never been mandatory provision for arts funding by any Local Authority in the country, and just now the Council were finding that a combination of rate-capping and people's understandable refusal to pay Poll Tax was causing them considerable financial problems. Avon County, unlike the City, were staunchly behind us, and as helpful as they could be; but then Avon County was about to disappear under the new franchise. The Arts Council grant was frozen, and private sponsorship was – in Bristol at least – in its infancy. A mid-Georgian theatre is by definition costly to run, and our costs were spiralling ever upward.

Because the City were unwilling or unable to tell us the actual extent of the fiscal surgery we were about to undergo, future planning became virtually impossible. Any theatre that does not wish to be reduced simply to a hand-to-mouth diet of mediocrity must be able with confidence to commission work, buy rights and engage performers, directors and designers, well into the future. Our frustration led to acrimonious exchanges between certain Councillors and ourselves, and the local press had a field day. They decided that it was much more exciting to provide a lurid blow-by-blow account of this conflict than to continue their normal practice of describing the plays and interviewing the actors, so a casual reader of the *Bristol Evening Post* might have been excused for assuming that the country's oldest working theatre had now been given over to all-in wrestling.

Over the next year or so, Paul Unwin began to lose heart. Both he and I felt most keenly our inability to produce any new plays, new work always being a box-office risk and out of the question in our present circumstances. A theatre that is unable to present some amount of original work is not serving its audience, and is virtually moribund.

A cheering piece of news was that the National Theatre (I can't remember whether by that time it had decided to be Royal as well as national) wanted to do a co-production with us; the chosen play was to be produced and to open in Bristol, do a short tour and then play at the National's Lyttelton Theatre. Various plays were considered, and somehow it came to be agreed as a condition that both Pru and I should have leading parts in whatever play was chosen.

What emerged, rather surprisingly, was Eugene O'Neill's *Long Day's Journey into Night*. I say rather surprisingly, because the Good Fairy of Economy was not among the guests at Eugene O'Neill's christening, and a play lasting more than three and a half hours does not ordinarily recommend itself to regional audiences whose bus service may be unsympathetic to late-night excursion.

The production was physically all that could be wished for: a superb set by John Gunter, and wonderfully clever lighting by Mark Henderson. Howard Davies' direction was admirable, and we had fine performances by Stephen Dillane and Sean McGinley as the two sons. Somehow, though, Pru and I failed to deliver; at least that was the verdict of the national press.

We probably weren't in truth very good. The reviewers declared we were too English, though I have to say all our American friends were very enthusiastic. I suspect, however, that there may be an additional reason why we fell so foul of the critics on this occasion. When a reasonably well-known married couple are cast together in a play, there is an automatic assumption that they have personally selected the play as a vehicle for themselves, possibly with an eye to saving money on hotels and taxis. They are perceived as the proprietors of the play, rather than performers in it. The knowledge that the couple on stage are partners in real life also conditions the audience's response: if the story is of two individuals who may or may not come together, or whose relationship is torn with strife, people can nevertheless sit back happily and think, 'Well, they're all right *really*.' It takes away the danger. It's cosy. And *Long Day's Journey into Professional Suicide*, as I now prefer to call it, is not a very cosy play.

We determined that we would be very careful in future about what we appeared in together, and certainly must avoid doing so as a married couple.

I enjoyed working at the National, though, and a few years later was asked back to play Gloucester in *King Lear* for Richard Eyre. I had played Lear himself a couple of times, once for Prospect and a second time in Dublin, and I thought it would be interesting now to look at the play through the eyes (while he had them) of the other father who, like Lear, has misunderstood each one of his children.

Lear was played on this occasion by Ian Holm, an actor I admire almost more than any other in the business, and in the usual way of things Ian's, and Lear's, considerable box office appeal would have demanded that the play be produced in the capacious Olivier Theatre. Richard, however (and the fact that this was to be his farewell production after ten triumphant years as Artistic Director must have carried some weight), determined to do it in the small versatile space of the Cottesloe.

This gave the advantage of being able to start the play on a domestic level, so that what begins almost as a row over family lunch rapidly and alarmingly spins faster and further out of control, until Lear and his Fool are thrown, almost by centrifugal force, out on to the stormy heath.

Richard Eyre saw the play as the story not just of one old man who has tragically misplaced his affections, but of four. Shakespeare gives the Earl of Kent no wife, no children. David Burke suggested in his performance that he might carry with him to the grave an undeclared and quite unsuitable love for Cordelia. Michael Bryant's Fool, misanthropic, tired, ill, no longer funny, has devoted himself to one single person, and that person deserts him by going mad. Gloucester, catastrophically misjudging his two sons, makes up the quartet.

*

Shortly after *Long Day's Journey* opened at the National, Paul Unwin's contract at Bristol came to an end, and in spite of pleas from the Board to accept a further term of office, he opted instead for a speculative freelance career, principally in film. I resigned as Associate Director at the same time, but remained on the Board long enough to see Paul's successor Andy Hay in post, and then left. I had had six years as a Governor; six rewarding, frustrating, exciting, depressing, lively, debilitating, very instructive years.

I went on to be in a play of Hugh Whitemore's called *It's Ralph*, to be produced for the West End. A bad title, I thought, it sounded like a Ralph Lynn/Tom Walls farce, with people running about in white flannels. It wasn't like that at all, it was funny, certainly, but also quite painful, and was very nearly brilliant except that Hugh didn't quite know how to end it.

My chief memory of the play is of the opening night on our prior-to-London week at the Theatre Royal Brighton. The play began with Connie Booth and myself arriving at our country cottage for the weekend, and letting ourselves in through the front door. This was in fact the only door to the set, and it was fitted with a practical Yale lock, to which I had a key. Unfortunately, one of the resident stage crew, while doing something to the door shortly beforehand, had inadvertently pushed up the catch on the lock, so that, try as I might, I couldn't get in.

What could we do? The audience could see me through the glass panel of the door, but that ceased to be interesting after a while. I turned for advice to Brian Kirk, the Stage Manager. 'I'll have to bring the curtain down,' he decided, and went off to instruct the flyman. The flyman, however, having raised the curtain initially, had nothing else on his cue-sheet for the next fifty minutes, and was already next door in the Wheatsheaf. While Brian was fetching him, the very slim assistant stage manager, realising what was wrong,

275

managed to squeeze through the gap between the proscenium and the edge of the set, crossed the stage, and smiling reassuringly at the audience, released the catch and retired again to the prompt corner. So I turned the key, opened the door, and walked into the room.

It was at this moment that the flyman, having been hastily retrieved from the pub, brought the curtain down. Audience bemusement was now giving way to open laughter, and Brian announced that he was going in front of the curtain to make a speech. I was dubious about this, but bowed to his experience in these things, and Connie and I went back outside the door and waited while he sought his way through the central parting of the heavy velvet curtain.

When this was used at all, it was as a drop curtain, and probably nobody had attempted to use the gap in the middle for many years. Its murky folds were thick with dust and festooned with cobwebs, and when Brian finally battled his way through to confront the audience, the spectral pallor of his dinner jacket, face and hair caused actual alarm among the now unnerved patrons.

However, he managed to explain to them what had occurred; they gave him a round of applause, he fought his way back again, and came offstage, and after a moment the curtain rose once more. I opened the door, and Connie and I walked in.

Whether it was delayed panic that made the Chief Electrician hit the black-out button at this point, or whether it was just the next logical step in the nightmare, I cannot tell; the timing, however, was impeccable. The stage, on which I had not as yet been permitted to utter a word, was plunged into inky blackness; and our author, sitting at the back of the stalls and wishing that he were anywhere on earth other than where he was at this moment, got up to leave the theatre.

As he opened the door, the Exit sign fell on his head.

Chapter Thirty-Six

One year, Pru had a few inexplicably work-free days over Christmas, so I drugged her and took her to India. We visited a little boy we had adopted through the SOS Children's Village in Bangalore, and then pushed on further south, spending Christmas Day riding an elephant and eating curried turkey by lamplight beneath trees thoughtfully decorated with white cotton-wool, and listening to very old Pat Boone records.

We had got into the habit of spending every alternate Christmas away from home. The family was now rather large and far-flung. Joe, his French wife Hedwige and their two children lived first in Manchester and then in Cornwall. My daughter Juliet, her boyfriend and my other two grandchildren were in Winchester. My sister was in Sheffield, and Sam might be almost anywhere at Christmas time. The upheaval for them, and the accommodation difficulty for us, made it an exercise delightful every two years, but which repeated every single year might border on the irksome.

So as well as India, we have had Christmases in Egypt, in Australia, even in Leeds once, and in a house in the little village of Venasque in Provence belonging to our friends Henry and Jane Burke.

Henry Burke, who lives in Norwich, is an architect and designer, and had always wanted to run his own theatre and direct in it. Norwich already had a very good touring theatre, the Royal, and a very prestigious amateur company, the Maddermarket, with its own premises. What the city hadn't had, though, for many years was something in between: a professional producing theatre, a Rep.

Finding a disused small warehouse by the River Wensum at Gun Wharf, conveniently near to the Art College and a couple of decent restaurants, Henry and his partners did some very energetic fund-raising, and in due course there arose on the site the attractive little Norwich Playhouse.

I had worked at Norwich a number of times, at the Theatre Royal and for Anglia Television, and also at the University of East Anglia, at which I held an Honorary Doctorate. I thought the city might well be large enough to support one other theatre provided the work was good, so I helped a bit with the project, finally becoming its President, and appearing in the opening production.

Henry's assumption that we would be backed by grant-in-aid from at least some of the available sources was, I'm afraid, based on half-promises made in good faith. Eastern Arts had spent all their money on the theatres at Colchester and Ipswich. The City was only interested in their gigantic new 'Technopolis'. The County didn't consider it their problem. I felt that we had been here before.

As everyone was working for minimal salaries we could just about have got by with sufficient public support. There were some very good shows, including an excellent *Hamlet* by the entire Glover family – Julian directing and playing the Ghost, his wife Isla Blair playing Gertrude and their son Jamie having an admirable first stab at Hamlet. But audience figures remained disappointing, and eventually we had to cease production, wind up the company and hand the theatre over to the City authority, who weren't sure what to do with it.

There are probably a number of different reasons for the lack of support. Perhaps a theatre of that sort was not really needed, the Theatre Royal and the Maddermarket satisfying between them what appetite there was. Perhaps we had opened at a bad time; two of Norwich's major industries, Reckitt Colman and Nestlé, had relocated themselves, the Norwich Union had got rid of a lot of its staff, and Anglia TV, now amalgamated with Meridian, was a shadow of its former self. Also, I think we had counted too much on the support of the university students, who had their own extremely active Drama Department.

It was touch and go for a time whether the empty theatre would become a Theme Pub, a shoe shop, or just be pulled down. Ironically, public support now rallied sufficiently for the building to be allowed to remain as a theatrical space, to be used for one-night stands, small-scale tours etcetera. So, fortunately, it's still there, and being very well run as such. I decided, though, that this really was the last time I would ever have anything to do with trying to run a theatre.

After the Glovers' *Hamlet*, journalists had reached into their bottom drawers for that tired old cognomen The Theatrical Dynasty –

were we about to experience an epidemic, they asked? The Redgraves were cited, the Cusacks, the Stephenses. Eventually it would be our turn, and Sam and I partially satisfied them by appearing together in a production of *Henry IV*, for English Touring Theatre – Sam as Hal and myself as Falstaff.

Michael Billington came to rehearsal to interview us both on tape for the BBC. He wanted to know how we would describe the different ways in which the two of us worked. We looked blank. Then I happened to notice that we both had our scripts open in front of us at the same page. In his margin Sam had written *Ambivalent attitude to Poins – excitement about robbery – do I dare? – how will F. react to trick? – any excuse to stave off responsibility.*

On mine was written *Pick up bool.*

Sam and I enjoyed our scenes together, and we had a happy tour, staying part of the time in Landmark Trust properties: the Old Parsonage in Oxford, the Georgian Music Room in Lancaster (commuting to and from Matcham's superb Grand Theatre in Blackpool) and best of all Roslin Castle in Midlothian, home of the St Clair family, where we sat before the fire listening to the wind and reciting Sir Walter Scott's *Rosabelle.*

English Touring Theatre, for whom we were performing, was the natural descendant of the old Prospect Theatre Company. The immediate gap left by Prospect/Old Vic was filled by Michael Bogdanov and Michael Pennington with their English Shakespeare Company, and in turn the baton was passed to Compass Theatre, under the direction of Tim Pigott-Smith. Then they, too, folded, and there was a classical touring vacuum until the ETT, under the direction of Paul Unwin's brother Stephen, and based in the offices of the old Century Theatre Company adjoining the Lyceum in Crewe, began operations in 1993. Crewe is not the most attractive place in the world, but its townsfolk are kind, and audiences appreciative. We opened there, and then toured to Oxford, Cambridge, Dartford, Darlington, Warwick, Richmond, Blackpool, Edinburgh and Bath – a wide variety of audiences – and finished up with a few weeks at the Old Vic. It felt good to be back on the road again, selling good plays to a variety of people, and when a couple of years later Stephen Unwin asked me back to the company to play Solness in Ibsen's *The Master Builder*, I accepted happily.

I'd done the play years ago at Bristol, for Stephen's brother, and it now struck me as being full of difficulties of which I hadn't been aware when we did it before. This could mean (a) that I wasn't intelligent enough to see the difficulties then, (b) that I had understood it perfectly well before, and was now making difficulties, or (c) that it was high time I stopped trying to do difficult plays.

In the end I think I did more or less get on top of it, and it was a pleasure to play the very long second-act duologue with the brilliant young actress who played Hilde, Emma Cunniffe. I still have problems with the soul-baring that goes on in the last act, when it becomes clear that the guy's only doing it for some troll, but it's one of the few plays I wouldn't mind attacking for a third time, just out of bloody-mindedness.

During her preparations for the production, our designer Pamela Howard was visited by a design student (not one of her own) who had just graduated, was starting to work professionally, and wanted to consult Pamela about something. She took him to her studio at the top of the house.

'What's that?' enquired the young man curiously, looking at her large drawing-board. She told him.

'And what do you do with it?'

'Do with it? Well – I design. You know. Sets, costumes. I'm a designer.'

'You mean, you *paint . . . draw* costumes?'

'What? Well yes.'

'Oh, you don't need to do that,' he said kindly. 'When I design costumes, I get the special software – let's see, what are you doing, *The Master Builder*, that's Norwegian, isn't it; I just punch up Scandinavia, Late 19th Century, Professional Man, and up comes a picture. I put the mouse on his coat, longer, shorter; then trousers – I've got an option, click on striped, checked or plain. Lighter? Darker? Bow tie or cravat, boots or shoes, and there you are. I can do three shows in an afternoon.'

I suggested to Pamela that perhaps all of us involved in the production should go and occupy a closed booth at the Theatre Museum, with a peephole through which families could peer in wonderment. 'See, child, this is how they were, the theatre folk of old, before they were swept away by computer graphics and digital engineering and virtual reality . . . '

Some indication of what no doubt is to come was shown me

several years ago, when I was transformed into what is called an Animatron, for the permanent exhibition about to be installed at Tower Bridge to mark its centenary. Every dimension of my body (with a few permissible exceptions) was minutely measured, I had a face-cast, a sample was taken of my hair, my voice was recorded and the movements of my mouth were filmed as I spoke. What emerged, so I understand, is a life-sized moving, talking replica of me in the character, costume and facial hair of the Chairman of the consortium which financed the construction of the bridge. I find the idea so creepy that I haven't dared to go and see it.

Genuine concern is voiced nowadays as to where the live theatre fits into a world where new and exciting modes of electronic entertainment are being developed all the time. I think it's essential to remember that theatre, even from its earliest days, has probably only ever appealed to a minority. Democracy, education and modern marketing find minorities a nuisance, but the world is after all made up of a confederation of different minorities; they deserve some consideration, and in particular the right not to be labelled with that emotive and dangerous word 'elitist'. In the 1970s, the theatrical producer Donald Albery maintained that there were only 100,000 people in London who habitually went to see a straight play, and I think that figure has probably not altered very much over the years, though obviously the floating tourist population can boost it considerably in a good year.

People also worry unduly, I think, about the average age of audiences. Sometimes, as we look across the stalls, we are lucky to pick out anyone who appears to be under the age of fifty. But remember that we used to say the same thing twenty-five years ago: the people who are coming now are the very same people who weren't coming then. Theatregoing has never been high on the list of youthful pursuits.

For one thing, it's the cost. Richard Eyre has remarked that at present a seat in the West End costs about the same as a pair of shoes, with the difference that the shoes are a reliable purchase; they do what they're meant to do, you can walk in them and keep your feet dry. The theatre visit cannot, by its very nature, be *reliable* – different people like different things, and you might find your initial visit personally disappointing. Risking a second try will largely depend on how much you paid for your ticket.

A great deal of what is going on in the theatre today can be of little interest to the young. On the other hand, on many evenings recently – at the two Racine plays at the Albery for instance, and at Theatre de Complicité's *The Chairs*, not to mention countless evenings at the National and the Barbican – I have seen the auditorium packed with a predominantly youthful audience.

Here I'm trying to make the point that the *age* of a play is irrelevant if it's done well and excitingly. Some of our cultural pundits, having assumed that a violent explosion of enthusiasm for the performing arts was bound to follow hot upon the election of a more sympathetic Government, are now baffled by its apparent failure to have done so, and are running around looking for scape-goats and prescribing remedies, the universal panacea being their favourite word *innovation*.

'Nurse! 20cc of Innovation, quickly!' The syringe is plunged into the flaccid carcase of the dying Theatre; there is a violent spasm, and then, magically, the creature rises from the table, erect, potent, fizzing, indomitable . . .

What do they really mean, what *should* they really mean, by such 'innovation'? First and foremost, finding good new plays. Nurturing new writers. Tempting black and Asian playwrights away from tele-vision to write for the stage. Looking at new theatrical forms, cross cultural, multi-disciplinary work. More use of music. Exploring tech-nology: holograms, special effects, ways of using light and sound. But it also means, and this is something the pundits in their sweep-ing evangelism tend to forget, the continual shedding of new light on what are termed classical texts, so-called because people have been enjoying them for hundreds of years. The implication that every decent theatre director is not continually trying to think of new ways of ex-pressing ideas that have been around for a long time is just insulting.

Get rid of the classics, cry the seekers after Innovation, and we'll soon see the people flocking in. The increasingly voiced argument that if every play written before the last decade were banned for five years we should see an immediate incursion of new young audi-ences, is as battily implausible as to suggest that if Mozart, Haydn and Beethoven were banished from the repertoire of the concert hall, the same thing would happen there.

We tend to forget that our dramatic literature is studied and revered the world over. We ourselves don't set a very high store by it, because we have always taken it for granted, and not since the Civil War has our cultural heritage ever been politically threatened.

An acquaintance of mine was in Sarajevo at the time when the city was being shelled by the Serbian forces. As they moved in near enough to be able to use mortars on specific targets, my friend turned to a local official who stood helplessly watching the devastation, and asked why they appeared to be ignoring banks, factories and business premises, and instead concentrating their fire on the university buildings, the theatres, art galleries and concert halls.

'Well, of course,' his companion answered. 'If you want to destroy a nation, the first thing you have to do is to destroy its culture.'

Chapter Thirty-Seven

I am now sixty-five, and can travel all over London for nothing, which is delightful. This is the point at which serious people retire, but then I'm not sufficiently serious. To say that I intend to keep on going doesn't mean that I have any specific ambitions left to fulfil, merely that I enjoy the work I do and many of the things associated with it.

When exasperated colleagues eventually call loudly upon me to stop, it will be a comfort to know I'm leaving the family business in capable hands. Sam shares his parents' love of language, which is something that has stood him, and those who employ him, in pretty good stead.

His mother and I joined the profession at a time when theatrical progeny were rather frowned on; directors wanted 'real' people from severely non-theatrical backgrounds. Nowadays, nearly every second person we meet in the business turns out to be the son or daughter – or grandchild – of someone with whom we've worked in the past. Perhaps this is an indication of a growth toward a global family feeling within the profession. As we travel more, work more with each other, and allow common aims to break down cultural barriers, actors are beginning to consider themselves part of a world-wide family of beings who, in different forms and in different languages, have devoted their lives to the centuries-old pursuit of telling a story to a group of listeners.

*

Reader, I think you had a right to expect, in a book of this kind, an account of the sayings and doings of a host of exciting celebrities, and I am conscious of having let you down. I have landed no big fish for your table, I have hunted you no lions and feasted you with no panthers. This is because I have never known such people suffi-ciently well to anatomize them here. I am not, I'm afraid, in that league.

Richard Strauss said of himself, 'I may not be a first rank composer, but I think I might be a first-rate composer of the second rank.' Hardly any of the more important parts I have played in the theatre have been for either of the two national companies, and that, I suppose, places me at best in the second rank of actors. But that is how I've wanted it. It's been a privilege to be allowed to play Falstaff, King Lear, Prospero, Halvard Solness, Willie Loman, Uncle Vanya; parts that would probably never have come my way if I'd turned my back on regional and touring theatre. Anyway, I'm not too proud to share a sentiment with Richard Strauss . . .

Recently I was interviewed at home, on a tape-recorder, by someone from the BBC, I can't remember what about. The inter-viewer asked me a few standard questions, then her face got very serious and her voice dropped a perfect fifth, and she said, 'I'm so sorry to hear about you and Prunella.'

'What?' I asked anxiously. Clearly she knew something I didn't.

'Well, that you're no longer together,' she explained sympa-thetically.

'Oh,' I said. 'I didn't know. She's upstairs having a bath – maybe I should go and talk to her about this – '

The poor woman was deeply embarrassed. 'I'm so sorry,' she said. 'Obviously I've got it quite wrong; I'm simply reading what it says here on your C.V.: '*was* married to Prunella Sc . . . ' Oh dear. Sorry. They've given me your obituary.'

I thought it a little premature, but I've certainly found that about this time journalists start sending you questionnaires asking what you've done with your life. I generally have no idea what to say, and feel deeply depressed about it. They often ask about our marriage; how extraordinary, they say, that you and Prunella have been mar-ried for thirty-seven years, show-biz marriages are just not *like* that.

Aren't they? I can think of a dozen couples in our business who have been together as long as we have, or longer; there are also estate agents, footballers, dentists and haulage contractors of our acquaintance whose marriages have fallen apart after a few months. Actors are no different from anybody else in that respect; what perhaps tends to hold us together more than some people is a shared commitment to something else, and a respect for each other's commitment to that something.

In the questionnaire there is sometimes the enquiry, *What is the individual thing you are most proud of?* I once heard an American film director – I can't remember who – answering the same question with 'The fact that my children still talk to me.' I'd go along with that.

After that the questions usually get sillier:

How would you like to die?

Not much.

And written on your tombstone?

'Is he – ?'

'I'm afraid so.'

(*A moment towards the end of the play.*)